Cent
Doug
St M

Irish Music in the Twentieth Century

IRISH MUSICAL STUDIES
General editors: Gerard Gillen and Harry White

1 *Musicology in Ireland* (1990)

2 *Music and the Church* (1993)

3 *Music and Irish Cultural History* (1995)

4 *The Maynooth International Musicological Conference 1995
   Selected Proceedings: Part One* (1996)

5 *The Maynooth International Musicological Conference 1995
   Selected Proceedings: Part Two* (1996)

6 *A Historical Anthology of Irish Church Music* (2001)

7 *Irish Music in the Twentieth Century* (2002)

Irish Musical Studies

7: IRISH MUSIC IN THE TWENTIETH CENTURY

Edited by

Gareth Cox & Axel Klein

FOUR COURTS PRESS

Published by
FOUR COURTS PRESS LTD
7 Malpas St, Dublin 8, Ireland
email: info@four-courts-press.ie
http://www.four-courts-press.ie
and in North America by
FOUR COURTS PRESS
c/o ISBS, 5824 N.E. Hassalo Street, Portland, OR 97213.

ISBN 1-85182-647-5

A catalogue record for this title
is available from the British Library.

Printed in Great Britain
by MPG Books, Bodmin, Cornwall

Contents

Contributors

GARETH COX is Senior Lecturer and Head of the Department of Music at Mary Immaculate College, University of Limerick. He graduated from Trinity College Dublin and the University of Freiburg. He is the author of *Anton Weberns Studienzeit* (Frankfurt, 1991), is a contributor to *The New Grove* and *Die Musik in Geschichte und Gegenwart*, and is co-editing a book on the music of Brian Boydell (Dublin, 2003).

PASCHALL DE PAOR was originally a master glass-blower at Waterford Crystal before studying both music and technology in Ireland and the UK. He currently directs the MA/MSc in Music Technology programme at the University of Limerick. His primary research areas are the phenomenology and ontology of electroacoustic music, composition, and music production.

ROBIN ELLIOTT studied music in his native Canada and in Vienna. He joined the Department of Music at University College Dublin as a lecturer in 1996. He recently co-edited and wrote three chapters for the book *Istvan Anhalt: Pathways and Memory* (Montreal and Kingston, 2001). In 2002 he was appointed to the Jean A. Chalmers Chair in Canadian Music at the University of Toronto.

PHILIP GRAYDON graduated from NUI Maynooth in 1999 and is currently pursuing doctoral studies at Queen's University, Belfast, on the music of Richard Strauss in the 1920s. He has published on the music of Aloys Fleischmann and contributed numerous articles on Irish art music to *The Encyclopaedia of Ireland* (forthcoming).

AXEL KLEIN studied at the universities of Hildesheim and Trinity College Dublin taking his PhD with the first major study on twentieth-century Irish music, *Die Musik Irlands im 20. Jahrhundert* (Hildesheim, 1996). He has published *Irish Classical Recordings: A Discography of Irish Art Music* (Westport, CT, 2001), is co-editing a book on the life and music of Brian Boydell (Dublin, 2003), and has contributed to *The New Grove* and *Die Musik in Geschichte und Gegenwart*.

JOHN PAGE was born in Derry, Northern Ireland and has studied at King's College London, University College Dublin and Harvard University. He is currently completing doctoral research into Mahler's middle symphonies at Trinity College Dublin. He now lives in the South of England and as well as pursuing his academic interests, works as a freelance conductor.

MICHAEL RUSS is Head of Music at the University of Huddersfield. He has published analytical work on Musorgsky, Bartok, Webern and Ravel and a monograph on Musorgsky's *Pictures at an Exhibition*. (Cambridge, 1992). His interests have also taken him into Schenkerian analysis and pitch-class set genera. He won a Westrup prize for musicology in 1994 and is also a clarinettist and conductor. He has a strong interest in teaching and learning issues in higher education and won a distinguished teaching award from the University of Ulster in 1995.

JOSEPH J. RYAN has broadcast and published extensively in the area of music in Ireland and is a contributor to *The New Grove*. He is current chair of the Contemporary Music Centre and also of the representative body, The Forum for Music in Ireland. A former executive officer of the Defence Forces School of Music and principal conductor of the Army No.1 Band, he is now Registrar of Athlone Institute of Technology.

ROBERT W. WASON is Professor of Music Theory, Chair of the Department of Music Theory, and Affiliate Faculty in the Department of Jazz Studies and Contemporary Media at the Eastman School of Music, University of Rochester (NY). A recipient of grants from the Guggenheim Foundation, National Endowment for the Humanities, Paul Sacher Foundation, and the German Academic Exchange (DAAD), he is a winner of an ASCAP Deems Taylor Award for 2001.

HARRY WHITE is Professor of Music at University College Dublin and general editor of *Irish Musical Studies*. Recent publications include *The Keeper's Recital: Music and Cultural History in Ireland, 1770–1970* (Cork, 1998) and *Musical Constructions of Nationalism* (co-edited with Michael Murphy, Cork, 2001). His *The History of a Baroque Oratorio* will be published by Ashgate in 2002.

Preface

This seventh volume of *Irish Musical Studies* is devoted to aspects of Irish art music in the twentieth century and was stimulated by the recent expansion in scholarly interest in this area. The publication in the 1990s of many scholarly articles and books on Irish music (including this now well-established series of studies), the appearance of many academic theses on Irish composition, the numerous entries on Irish composers in the latest editions of *The New Grove* and *Die Musik in Geschichte und Gegenwart*, and the extensive bibliography in this present book, all clearly demonstrate that Irish music can and does provide fertile and rewarding ground for musicological study. The recent flood of CD recordings of works by Irish composers into the market place also testifes to an emerging interest in Irish music as we begin the third millennium.

Although this collection of articles can not aim to be representative of the many diverse paths trodden by over one hundred Irish composers, it does however purport to give a broad taste of certain notable developments in twentieth-century composition in Ireland. Perhaps the most salient characteristic of Irish music in the twentieth century has been its ability to mirror and absorb international trends without losing its originality or 'Irishness' and several articles reflect on the idea of Irish music within a European art-music context. The emergence of musical modernism in Ireland is examined in two analytical studies of landmark string quartets by Frederick May (1936) and Seóirse Bodley (1968) and also within its cultural context in an essay considering mid-century works by May, Aloys Fleischmann and Brian Boydell. This volume also includes essays on Irish opera in the first quarter of the century and the post-war 'Irish' symphony, and considers various directions taken by Irish composers in the last hundred years. Much of the content resulted from the freedom allowed to the contributors in their choice of topic and it emerged that two authors decided to focus on compositions by Ian Wilson written during the last decade of the century.

It is appropriate here to pay warm tribute to the sterling work over the last ten years of the Contemporary Music Centre, Ireland and its director, Eve O'Kelly. It is inconceivable that the recent boom in interest in Irish music nationally and internationally could have been achieved without the presence of such a Centre and the editors wish to use this opportunity to encourage scholars and performers interested in Irish music to contact the CMC where a wealth of music and research material lies waiting to be performed and studied.

Acknowledgements

The editors wish to thank the following for their kind permission to reproduce copyright material in this volume: Universal Edition (London) Ltd. (chapter 7 and pages 84 & 154), Woodtown Publishers (pages 59-61 and chapter five), the Contemporary Music Centre, Ireland (chapters 4, 5, 6, and 8), and the Design and Artists Copyright Society (page 156). They also wish to thank Mary Immaculate College, University of Limerick for a generous grant and Michael Adams and his colleagues at Four Courts Press for their invaluable assistance in the preparation of this volume for publication.

1

The divided imagination:
music in Ireland after Ó Riada

HARRY WHITE

I

In Wallace Stevens' poem, *Anecdote of the Jar*, the line that always strikes at my heart is: 'It took dominion everywhere.' Stevens is describing how his perception of an object has become more important, more real, than the object itself; or in any case, he is trying to register how the perception of an object, in this case an ordinary jar, can transcend the commonplace understanding of that object and attain a kind of terrifying ubiquity. The poem is about perception, but it shades into obsession: it recognizes ways in which an object, or a person, or one's perception of these, can somehow spread like a contagion to the point where everything else is subordinated to the paralysing beauty of its presence. Or to the desolation of its absence, as the case may be.

In this essay, I would like to countenance ways in which this kind of extreme perception, this profound awareness of presence and absence, has conditioned the state of music in Ireland since the death of Seán Ó Riada in 1971. But before we say goodbye to the Stevens poem, let me press home its metaphorical relevance to what follows here. If Stevens is writing about the difference between an object and the sometimes unbearable presence or absence which its perception can induce, I am also writing about an object. In my case, the object is 'Irish music', and more precisely the *idea* of Irish music which the traditional repertory of folk melodies both embodies and symbolises. I am talking about an idea which dominates the musical imagination, and expressly the Irish musical imagination.

As an idea, the traditional repertory – what people ordinarily call Irish Folk music – has had a long and accumulative career in Irish cultural history. Among the things which it has accumulated, notably since its dramatic and redemptive retrieval in the late eighteenth-century – are a symbolic resonance and power unequalled by any other marker of Irish identity, with the possible exception of the Irish language itself. And in a country whose cultural growth after the Flight of the Earls was largely determined by the loss of Irish as a *modus vivendi*, a loss enforced by British misrule and then encouraged even by those avatars of Catholic emancipation (strikingly by O'Connell himself), music assumed many of the burdens which language would otherwise have more easily and naturally absorbed. One of these burdens was an awareness of national identity. It is not too much to say that during the nineteenth century, when Irish lapsed into near silence, music became a conduit for this growing sense of identity, to the extent that ideologues of Irish culture, eager to join the gap between cultural and political autonomy, fastened upon the music not only as a source of cultural regeneration but as a means of nourishing that impulse towards autonomy which is the distinctive feature of any nation oppressed by long centuries of colonial mismanagement. 'Music is the first faculty of the Irish,' Thomas Davis wrote in 1841, a declaration which implies, correctly, as it turned out, that language, and specifically the Irish language, was no longer a faculty that was widely available as a definitive marker of national integrity. Indeed it was the absence of the Irish language from the cultural and political enterprises of Young Ireland which excluded the movement from membership in those European associations which espoused similar ideals of political nationalism, notably in Italy and Germany.[1]

But with Irish music, the case was different, and with fateful consequences. As the nineteenth century wore on, music itself became ever more characterised by two conditions of reception: one was that the native repertory was pressed into service of textual expression, almost to the exclusion of everything else it might have done (a process initiated with vital success in the *Irish Melodies* of Thomas Moore); the other condition was that the repertory itself then became the absolute icon of nationalism in Ireland. This was true in literal terms even by the end of the eighteenth century: the United Irishmen bore as their emblem the harp, with the motto 'it is new strung, and shall be heard'. But in symbolic terms, the use of the folk melodies to incorporate an idea of cultural and political autonomy for Ireland was even more powerful.

This two-fold process of textual support and symbolic intelligence was to entail the most severe difficulties for the rehabilitation and development of music itself in Ireland. As cultural autonomy metamorphosed into the demand for political autonomy, as the Gaelic League was overtaken by Sinn Féin, the condition of music in Ireland, at once powerfully symbolic and artistically inert, could not free itself from its obligations to nationalist propaganda. These obligations took dominion everywhere.

It was against this background of musical atrophy *vís-à-vís* an unbridled surge of cultural nationalism that Seán Ó Riada finally emerged as a radical

---

1 I have developed this reading in much greater detail in White, *The Keeper's Recital: Music and Cultural History in Ireland, 1770–1970* (Cork: Cork University Press, 1998).

voice for Irish music in the late 1950s. Of course his achievement did not orig-
inate from nothing: as the new Free State confirmed the official status, as it
were, of the traditional repertory it also gave new impetus to the uncertain
efforts to establish art music as a mode of creative expression in Ireland. Before
the founding of the State, such efforts had foundered repeatedly in Ireland since
the Act of Union, partly because the European musical aesthetic was regarded
as an expression of colonial ideology, and partly because the traditional corpus
assumed ever more powerful images of integrity in the Irish mind.

Those composers who form the immediate context from which Ó Riada
emerged – and they include his teacher, Aloys Fleischmann, Frederick May,
Brian Boydell and Éamonn Ó Gallchobháir – were, in the main, preoccupied
by the viability of composition in one of two ways: either they repudiated the
traditional repertory because it represented a cul-de-sac, an inhibition to free
composition and the absorption of European forms and techniques; or, like Ó
Gallchobháir, they were drawn towards the self-standing integrity of this
repertory, not as a shibboleth of nationalism, but as a definitive musical statement of what it meant to be Irish. The defensive tone of Ó Gallchobháir's writings on this subject in particular tends to prefigure the more strident claims of
Ó Riada which attended the latter's Pauline conversion to Irish music. But Ó
Gallchobháir notwithstanding, many Irish composers of the pre-Ó Riada generation sought emancipation by studying elsewhere: in London, Heidelberg,
Vienna, Munich. Ó Riada, as it happens, did likewise.

Ó Riada's commitment, in fact, to the European aesthetic was unaccom-
modating at the beginning of his career. Educated by Fleischmann, appointed
in succession to May as Music Director at the Abbey Theatre, and then in succession to Ó Gallchobháir as Assistant Director of Music at Radio Éireann, he
produced a small body of works which in hindsight we might judge to be of
greater promise than actual achievement. But my purpose here is not to judge
Ó Riada's considerable talents as a composer. Rather it is to suggest that the
most interesting voice by far in Irish music, and certainly the most imaginative, was drawn away from the European aesthetic in a crisis of such magni-
tude (personal, aesthetic, musical and perhaps even psychological), that it
forced a crisis in turn that was to affect music in Ireland for long after his death.

I don't propose to trace the curve of that crisis here, having done so elsewhere.[2] My purpose rather is to offer some thoughts about the Ó Riada legacy,
as it were, insofar as this has continued to affect the composition and reception of music in Ireland. There are perhaps four elements of this legacy which
we might briefly inspect in order to contemplate the anxiety of his influence
in Irish musical affairs. These are (1) the original compositions (2) the radio

---

2 Ibid., 'Seán Ó Riada and the Crisis of Modernism in Irish Music', 125–50.

lecture series *Our Musical Heritage* (3) the music for film and (4) Ceoltóirí Cualann.

Each of these elements entered a vital claim on the Irish musical imagination and in notably different ways. The original compositions, especially in their limited engagement with serialism, their striking continuity with techniques of modernism already espoused by May and Boydell in particular, and above all, perhaps, in their engagement with European (German) texts, prefigure with uncanny exactitude that search for voice, aesthetic belonging and contemporaneity which characterises a whole seam of Irish music from the mid-1970s onwards. By contrast, *Our Musical Heritage* (1962) represents a vehement ideology of disavowal by which Ó Riada repudiated not only the enterprise of his own engagement with modernism, but the very relevance of art music to the Irish mind. In his own restless search for an authentic voice, he realized – however impatiently, however stridently – that the enterprise of modernism in Irish music, indeed the concept of composition itself, was radically undermined by the absence of a firmly-established European aesthetic from the Irish mind. Of course Ó Riada versed this absence in terms of a redefinition of the traditional repertory, which in the early 1960s began to assume in his mind something more than a symbolic presence; he then began to regard it as the essential and exclusive expression of Irish musical thought. He felt the need to justify this exclusivity and although he avoided the pitfalls and clichés of nationalist dogma, he invented fresh pitfalls of his own. Chief among these was the notion that the Irish mind could have no part in European art music because the essence of Irish music was historically antithetical to the tonal grammar of Western Europe.[3] And however wrongheaded, this was an idea powerful enough to direct Ó Riada himself ever more imaginatively towards a recreation of the traditional repertory, not as a dutiful and lifeless importation of one tradition into another, but as a synthesis of virtuoso technique, ensemble texture and melodic variation.

This synthesis expressed itself with magisterial success in Ceoltóirí Cualann. When Ó Riada announced in 1970 with characteristic abruptness that he was disbanding the ensemble, he surprised and dismayed everyone with an interest in the matter, not least the members of the ensemble themselves. But by then it was too late for everyone except Ó Riada himself. He had released into the Irish cultural stratosphere an arresting and persuasive model of musical discourse which survived his own steep descent into silence.

---

3 See Seán Ó Riada, *Our Musical Heritage* [ed. Thomas Kinsella] (Portlaoise, 1982), 20: 'Irish music is not merely not European, it is quite remote from it. It is, indeed, closer to some forms of Oriental music. The first thing we must do, if we are to understand it, is to forget about European music. Its standards are not Irish standards; its style is not Irish style; its forms are not Irish forms.'

Without Ó Riada, there would have been no Ceoltóirí Cualann, and without Ceoltóirí Cualann, there would almost certainly have been no Chieftains.

Fourthly, and finally, there are the film scores, 'written in the idiom of a symphonic tradition that never existed', as Louis Marcus observed. These scores interpose themselves between Ó Riada's adventures in modernism and his final commitment to the traditional repertory. As with Ceoltóirí Cualann, the film scores too have exercised profound influence. It is true that Ó Riada himself was increasingly uncomfortable about their uneasy marriage of folk melody and orchestral idiom (if only because they sustained that dreary tradition of folk song arrangments which he incisively dismissed), but they earned for Ó Riada an acclaim, a reception into the Irish cultural matrix, scarcely enjoyed by any other musician hitherto. Here too, his legacy remains and endures.

When we begin to survey the state of music in Ireland after Ó Riada, it is not hard to discover that his influence remains to be countenanced. Having forced the issue of modern Irish composition so stringently, Ó Riada left behind him a divided imagination. We have no need of rhetoric or histrionics in this regard: better by far to consider calmly the claims and counterclaims of the traditional repertory as these have been received and understood not only in Ireland but throughout Europe and North America in the generation which has elapsed since Ó Riada's death in 1971.

We have, in the main, two traditions of art music in the wake of Ó Riada's achievements. One of these has been widely understood at a multiplicity of levels as an authentic voice for music in Ireland. The other, for all its enterprise and plurality of technique, has not. In making this observation, I am not espousing a preference for one over the other. But I am interested in responding to the recent history of contemporary Irish music against the wider background of Irish cultural history and the more narrowly defined consequences of Ó Riada's achievement as I have outlined these here.

If there are two traditions of contemporary Irish music, how might they be distinguished one from the other? Might it be safer, more prudent, to suggest that there are no traditions, only conventions, or some kind of plural, value-free multiculturalism of musical discourse? This might be more prudent, but it wouldn't say much for the enterprise of writing about music in Ireland that it would shelve its responsibilities to history in this way. And so instead, let me concede that the main distinction between the two traditions which I am trying to identify is vested in the traditional repertory itself. It continues to take dominion everywhere, by its presence, and sometimes by its absence.

The tradition of contemporary music, which espouses and centralises the ethnic repertory is explicit in its address to the Irish mind and in its appeal to the Irish expatriate mind, for that matter. And not only in America, but

throughout Europe. Of whom do I write? Of composers like Mícheál Ó
Súilleabháin, Shaun Davey, and Bill Whelan, whose range of techniques bril-
liantly sustain and develop the intensity of Ó Riada's preoccupation with the
traditional air, either as a means of narrative – as in Davey's *The Brendan
Voyage* – or as a means of cross-fertilized variation – as in much of Ó Súilleabháin's music. In such work, the Irish mind represents itself not as a strug-
gling symbol of nationalist culture, but as a distinctive voice which is clear,
articulate, polished, *engagé*, imaginative and unmistakably Celtic. Nevertheless, this voice is one which remains aloof from the enterprise of musical modernism, which eschews the European aesthetic except in the most popular and
derivative terms, which nimbly sidesteps the whole confused century of art
music which has just recently ended. As a voice, it intimately neighbours the
folk music revival itself. It therefore comes as a surprise to discover that those
who maintain this tradition, those who actually sit down and compose, are so
few in number. Few they may be, but they are no less influential for that.

The other tradition is much more numerous and fantastically more plural
in its espousal of European modes of musical modernism. And herein lies the
prevailing irony of contemporary music in Ireland. We are arrived, insofar as
I can tell, at a moment in our cultural history when the sheer plenitude of those
who participate in the traditions of European modernism – a glance at the
Contemporary Music Centre's catalogue of composers would confirm this[4] –
is out of all proportion to the silence in which this second tradition has been
received by the cultural mileau which is (post)modern Ireland. Raymond
Deane has famously called this disproportion 'the honour of non-existence',
but I am not sure I would want to go that far.[5] Nevertheless, in the argument
developed in this paper, I will venture to suggest that the prestige of the first
tradition has so widely eclipsed the second one that another, less polarized
reading is required if we want to understand the condition of music in Ireland
within the past thirty years.

Consider for a moment how the modernist tradition engages with Ireland:
it largely avoids the traditional repertory, but it is in part unmistakably Irish in
other forms of engagement, notably with the literary tradition. This tradition
is a subtle but vital presence in the work of John Buckley, for example, whose
piano music re-reads the poetry of Yeats in a context far removed from the
cultural hostilities of Ireland's literary afterlife. And more generally, the work
of Buckley and many of his likeminded contemporaries is a vital marker of
Ireland's coming-off-age not as a nation state, but as a European country. If

---

4 The Contemporary Music Centre's *Index of Irish Composers* (8th edition, 2000), lists about 100 living
composers, including extensive worklists.   5 Raymond Deane, 'The Honour of Non-Existence: Classical
Composers in Irish Society', in: Gerard Gillen and Harry White (eds.), *Music and Irish Cultural History
(Irish Musical Studies 3)* (Dublin: Irish Academic Press, 1995), 199–211.

the latter is more than an economic arrangement in Irish affairs, then it seems reasonable to expect that in some measure music in Ireland should be European first and Irish second. I don't suggest that this reading is a collective or even individual gesture of self-consciousness on the part of those composers who list their work for inspection in the Contemporary Music Centre, but I do suggest that their imaginative space derives from Europe and not only from Ireland.

It is all too tempting to think in divisive terms when we examine the cultural history of almost anything in Ireland. As Joseph Ryan remarked several years ago, the first meeting of the Feis Ceoil committee was a typical instance of this, because the split between those who favoured the encouragement of traditional music and those who did not was the first thing on the agenda. And yet, I am wary of watering down the perception of two traditions in what follows here in favour of a value-free discourse which ignores the whole-hearted endorsement of one and the polite tolerance of the other. 'The island is full of noises': that much is clear. But something else is also clear, and that is the emergence of two distinctive aesthetics for art music in Ireland.

II

> *The Brendan Voyage* is an emotive, symbolic work, seeming to answer a need in the Irish people to recognize and prove that a soloist representing an aural tradition can hold the stage on equal footing with members of a symphony orchestra.[6]

Shaun Davey's comment on *The Brendan Voyage* (1982) is an aesthetic observation, if ever there was one. It speaks clearly enough of an awareness of two traditions (in the sense that these have been identified here), but it also overrides the potentially defensive condition of this awareness in favour of a *fait accompli*, which is the work itself and the success which it has enjoyed in Ireland, in Europe and in North America within the past two decades. *The Brendan Voyage*, and those works which we might generically or stylistically associate with it, demand evaluation, not only in terms of a distinctive voice for art music in Ireland, but also in relation to other kinds of Irish music, including an art music which radically disdains the 'aural tradition' in favour of a European mode of discourse.

The benefits of trying to locate this discussion within the parameters of Irish cultural history are considerable: Although Davey's own music is strongly suggestive not of Ó Riada, but of Carolan, there can be little doubt

6 Shaun Davey Website (www.shaundavey.com)

that it embodies what I shall describe here as narrative modes of cultural kinship with the wider community of Irish ideas which have taken dominion in this country since the early 1970s. There are multiple levels (at least two) of address in Davey's music which need to be countenanced in order to understand not only its success but its aesthetic function as an expression of Irish ideas. In strictly musical terms, Davey revisits and re-invigorates that model of intra-cultural, mutual discourse which Carolan originated in the mid-eighteenth century, notably in his concerto. Despite the sheer presence of the aural tradition in Irish music between Carolan and Davey – notably in the long history of failure which attended its integration into the orchestral repertory, a failure represented by the 'variation on an Irish air' – it was Davey who reformulated the equation of two traditions by borrowing the generic prototype of the solo concerto and imbuing it, as Carolan had done, with the texture, expressive technique and formal strategies of traditional music. By wedding the uilleann pipes with an orchestral ensemble, Davey did not solve at a stroke two centuries of musical dislocation in Ireland, but he vividly refreshed and renewed the currency of this problem. Moreover, he did so by drawing upon the natural affinity between the concerto as a musical genre dominated by paradigms of discourse and dialogue and the narrative (and frequently lyric) function of Irish traditional music. In fact the narrative drive of *The Brendan Voyage* explicitly attests not only its aesthetic and structural reliance on the idea of programme music (an idea sufficiently flexible to mediate between almost any two traditions), but also its expressive kinship with language. This kinship is worth a moment's further deliberation.

It does not require a theory of deconstruction to read *The Brendan Voyage* for what it is: the link between Tim Severin's travel writing and Davey's music is expressly forged by the very title of the work, even if Davey's composition is self-evidently more than a naïve transposition of Severin's narrative. Although the parallels between Severin and Davey are close enough to interpret the music as a recreation of Severin's journey (rather than his account of it), the point at issue is that Davey's music both narrates and meditates upon an extra-musical event. It communicates musical structure as a model of narrative discourse, in ways which invite comparison with Mendelssohn and Berlioz to be sure, but also with Chopin, Liszt and even Richard Strauss. The programme symphony, the orchestral tone poem, the piano *ballade* are genres which establish precedents for Davey's work within the European repertory, and all of them depend on a relationship between structure, mimesis and gestural configuration which is extra-musical at almost every turn. This relationship is fundamentally a linguistic one. In strictest terms, it is a metalinguistic relationship, but in any case the narrative energies of the music derive from something other than music itself. This can be anything from the claims of

Polish independence (Chopin) to the love of a difficult Irishwoman (Berlioz), but in each case the relationship between music and narrative is clear.

When we turn back to *The Brendan Voyage*, however, the precedent of European progamme music is insufficient to account for the dominating presence of the uilleann pipes, to say nothing of its rapt integration into the texture of the work as a whole. But here, too, the question of narrative is pertinent. If the structures of the traditional repertory are now generally regarded as a formulaic matter of variation (insofar as variation technique dominates the creative process in Irish music and the forms which arise therefrom are brief in length and luminously clear in pattern), it is nevertheless equally clear that the traditional repertory survived the language crisis in Ireland partly and unmistakably as an adjunct to verbal communication. I have already argued as much in this essay (and elsewhere), but the point becomes sharply relevant with regard to the narrative function of the uilleann pipes in *The Brendan Voyage*. Davey's music relies for its intelligibility on a verbal programme, but that programme only matters insofar as it enjoys a persuasive advocate in the music itself. In the case of *The Brendan Voyage*, the thematic transformations and gestural intensity of the uilleann pipes conjoin both narrative function and instrumental virtuosity in a synthesis which allows the aesthetic of the 'aural tradition' to arise without prejudice to the orchestral conventions on which it so productively depends. The music *is* a synthesis, but not, in my view, a debilitating compromise. And this is because the question of 'dominance' is obviated by the implications of the genre itself.

In any solo concerto worth the name, virtuosity encodes a primary transformation of thematic material (the case is magisterially if magically determined by Mozart) which ensures an expressive continuity of discourse between soloist and ensemble. Davey has in fact described his work as a 'suite', but the precedent, the instructive and accommodating model of the concerto is in fact far closer to the terms of his argument. And if the gesture of reconciliation is unmistakable in this work, as between the narrative-formulaic condition of the soloist's writing and the generic interdependence of the concerto dialogue which the score proposes, then so too is the reconciliation between European modes of programme music and the singular intervention of an Irish traditional instrument.

The lines out from Davey's work to certain other forms of contemporary Irish music (including, of course, traditional music) are not hard to discover. The context which this music almost automatically provides for Davey is, however, problematic. In a wider, European context, there *is* no problem, save for the fact that the perception of Davey's score as inherently Irish can inhibit the work's progression into the common repertory of European masterworks. By comparison, a work like H. K. Gruber's *Ariel* (1999), a trumpet concerto which traverses a similar musical admixture of virtuosity and descriptive-narrative impressionism, enters the repertory unencumbered by any cultural dogmatism whatsoever. It is not just the trumpet which makes Gruber's work 'accessible' in this way[7], but the work's freedom from any categorical expectations of what an Austrian work ought to be.

In Davey's case, however, expectations are rife. It is, for example, a matter of some debate as to whether a work like *The Brendan Voyage* belongs at all to the canon of Irish art music: certain commentators, notably Raymond Deane and Axel Klein, tend to take a notably stringent view of such matters.[8] Rather than rehearse these (occasionally) sour polemics here, however, it is more pertinent to recognise the almost dysfunctional imbalance between the prestige which work such as Davey's enjoys in the wider arena of Irish cultural life and the silence which greets it among those who espouse the European aesthetic of art music. There is also the converse problem by which the greater part of contemporary Irish music is received in silence, especially in the Republic of Ireland, where the Davey model, as it were, enjoys a cultural ascendancy out of all proportion to its size and significance in purely musical terms. I shall return to these problems at the close of this paper, but the question of context is immediately relevant. Here, also, the precedent and influence of Seán Ó Riada are never very far away.

The pervasive presence of the ethnic tradition in Irish popular music of the last thirty years is strong evidence of that 'terrifying ubiquity' to which I referred at the outset of this discussion. Except, of course, that this presence is anything but terrifying. The astonishing gamut of Irish music – most of it popular – which has refracted the aural tradition in the last thirty years reflects two things in particular. One is that the model which Ó Riada devised for the representation of the ethnic repertory is one capable of protean development and revision. The other is that the repertory itself has finally been disabused of its nationalist burdens in favour of a more domesticated and indeed marketable celticism. This is not to suggest that the tradition is not 'authentically' perpetuated by musicians wholly unconcerned with *Riverdance* and the commercial development of Irish music as a striking and highly professional model of international entertainment. But I do mean to observe that anyone with even a passing interest in Irish music since Ó Riada cannot mistake the central presence of the repertory in a host of otherwise diverse modes of representation. Clannad, Planxty, Anúna: the international reach of such ensem-

---

7 Gruber and Davey both wrote with specific soloists in mind, even if Gruber's trumpet part by its nature does not address the integration of traditions explicitly proposed by Davey's composition.   8 See Deane (as n. 5), 209–10 and the essay by Axel Klein in this volume, 'Roots and Directions of Twentieth-Century Irish Art Music', and the end of his 'The Composer in the Academy (2) 1940–1990', in: Richard Pine and Charles Acton (eds.), *To Talent Alone – The Royal Irish Academy of Music, 1848–1998* (Dublin: Gill and Macmillan, 1998), 419–28.

bles vitally depends on the aural tradition, however radically different and plural the result is in each individual case. The Chieftains have been pre-eminent in this regard, but I would argue that this all-important and elusive question of 'voice' in Irish music (no less in The Corrs than in The Chieftains) is frankly derived from the timbre and profile of the traditional repertory.

If this is the case, if Irish popular music in particular has achieved its voice through the ethnic tradition, then it is not unreasonable to press home this argument by suggesting that one of the two art music traditions which I have identified here does likewise. It neighbours popular music, it enjoys a continuity with the tradition itself and it profits from those modes of cultural kinship which the tradition bestows. And, of course, it takes its cue from the precedent of Seán Ó Riada. The public perception of contemporary Irish art music is largely determined by this tradition, however small the number of its exponents. Alongside Shaun Davey, one can nominate Mícheál Ó Súilleabháin, Michael McGlynn and Bill Whelan. These are not many, but their prestige has been immense. Each of them has revisited the aural tradition – however differently one from the other – and each has re-contextualized that repertory, to the extent that original composition has become a matter of re-composition, to which the canonic ordinances of the European repertory and the language and aesthetic of modernism remain largely irrelevant. In this tradition, it is sound and voice which matter rather than structure and technique. And where structure *does* count, as in Davey's music, the narrative feedback into verbal analogues tends to eclipse any preoccupation with musical structure itself. This is music which accommodates itself to linguistic comprehension (is there any other kind?), and in that respect, too, it neighbours the aural tradition. Whether or not this represents a form of 'cultural imperialism' (Raymond Deane) I cannot say. But I can say that it is *there* and that it radically differs in almost every respect from the canons which prevail in contemporary Irish music as these are understood by the greater number by far of Irish composers. This discrepancy is at the heart of the matter.

III

In view of what has happened in Europe and what further threatens the world, it will appear cynical to squander time and creative energy on the solution to esoteric questions of modern compositional techniques [...] These impotent late heirs to a traditional hostility towards true originality resemble one another everywhere in their feeble mixture of compositional facility and helplessness. Shostakovich, unjustly reprimanded as a cultural Bolshevist by the authority of his home country; the facile pupils of Stravinsky's pedagogical supervision; the triumphant meagerness of Benjamin Britten – all these have in common a taste for tastelessness, a

simplicity resulting from ignorance, an immaturity which masks as enlight-
enment, and a dearth of technical means. In Germany the National Socialist
Chamber of Music (Reichsmusikkammer) has left behind a total rubbish
heap. The commonplace, everyday style following the Second World War
has become the eclecticism of a destroyed and shattered nation.[9]

Nothing if not comprehensive in its sweeping disdain, Adorno's notorious
indictment of almost every manifestation of 'new music' after the Second
World War gives some indication of the confused aesthetic which dominated
music in Europe just at the point when it began to attract the serious attention
of Irish composers. In a very practical sense, Ó Riada's repudiation of European modernism stems partly from this confusion, if also from the corresponding clarity with which he began to regard the aural tradition after his
return from Paris in 1955. It was in the years immediately following his year
in France that Ó Riada embarked on his own absorption of modernist techniques, in which respect he followed Frederick May, whose *Songs from Prison*
provided an important precedent for Ó Riada's own essays in extended forms,
above all in his *Nomos No. 2.* It is a matter of simple historical record that these
compositions failed to satisfy Ó Riada's restless (and ultimately tragic) quest
for authenticity in his own music, a determination which extended to pre-
scriptive and often histrionic readings of the aural tradition, readings which
are loudly delivered in *Our Musical Heritage.* By the mid-1960s at latest, Ó
Riada's encounter with the crisis of modernism had engulfed him to the point
that original composition became thereafter a peripheral activity.

The solution to the Ó Riada crisis which most Irish composers preferred
was to pretend that it didn't happen. As Axel Klein has shown, many of them
in any case had sought tutelage in Austria, Germany and Britain long before
Ó Riada.[10] We have already mentioned May, who studied with Wellesz in
Vienna; Brian Boydell's musical education took him to Heidelberg and to
London; Seóirse Bodley studied in Stuttgart, and like Gerard Victory, was also
a regular visitor to Darmstadt. Frank Corcoran, whose career as a composer
has been largely made in Germany, was a student in Berlin in 1969–71. In the
1970s, we find Gerald Barry in Cologne and Vienna, Raymond Deane in
Basel, Cologne and Berlin, and so on. What is sufficiently clear from these
examples is that composers found refuge from 'the shocking state' of music
in Ireland by encountering the European aesthetic at first-hand.[11] The result of
this enterprise was compelling and problematic.

9 Theodor W. Adorno, *Philosophy of Modern Music,* trans. by Anne G. Mitchell and Wesley V. Bloomster
(London: Sheed and Ward, 1973), 7.   **10** See Axel Klein, 'Irish Composers and Foreign Education: A
Study of Influences', in: Patrick F. Devine and Harry White (eds.), *The Maynooth International
Musicological Conference 1995, Selected Proceedings, Part One (Irish Musical Studies 4),* (Dublin: Four
Courts Press, 1996), 271–84.   **11** The phrase is Brian Boydell's.

If Ó Riada discovered for himself that the verbally-dominated matrix of Irish culture was inclined to favour even those works which he himself disdained (the film scores in particular), provided that they corresponded to a musical image of Ireland determined by the ethnic repertory, those who succeeded him radically altered the complexion of contemporary music in Ireland. In the 1970s and early 1980s especially, the terms of cultural kinship shifted away from this repertory towards Europe, and to a lesser extent towards North America. The unmistakable evidence for this was the Dublin Festival of Twentieth Century Music, an event which at once internationalised the whole question of Irish art music and which showcased it alongside (often in the presence of) leading European and American exponents, including Carter, Messiaen and Stockhausen. The problem with the Festival (which lapsed in 1984) was not that it sealed off contemporary music from Irish culture (if anything it increased the perception of music in Ireland as a living force rather than as an adjunct to verbal art forms), but rather that it co-existed with other forms of musical endeavour which were doomed to remain tentative and insecure because of Ireland's strikingly underdeveloped musical infrastructures.

In a country then preoccupied with the disintegration of Northern Ireland as a viable political entity, it was scarcely surprising that the plural condition of contemporary Irish music, especially in its committed espousal of what Alfred Schnittke famously described as 'polystylism', should not find much support among the wider community of the arts in Ireland.

The question of Northern Ireland requires particular care. The Northern Irish crisis found an immediate address in drama and poetry (consider its transformative presence in Friel and Heaney), but it scarcely registered as an issue in contemporary Irish art music until very recently. If Friel could write *The Freedom of the City* (1973) less than a year after the events on which it was based took place, an opera on the same subject would have seemed preposterous, if not ludicrously offensive. Other forms of music were quickly harnessed in favour of both sides of the divide, to such an extent that The Wolfe Tones, memorably described to me some years later as 'the musical wing of the Provisional IRA' found their music prohibited on the national broadasting service. Verdi's 'Va, pensiero' re-worked as 'Stand beside me [and fight for old Ireland]' provoked not only an aesthetic but also an ideological vehemence which would have seemed entirely inconceivable within the parameters of art music. The greatest enemy which this new-found tradition of art music faced was indifference. It just wasn't sufficiently important enough to stimulate much beyond the polite tolerance expected of any nation with serious aspirations to full membership of the European Community (as it then was).

If this reading seems unduly harsh (however much it echoes the disenchantment expressed by some composers with regard to the reception of music in Ireland), it is one which is nevertheless redeemed by the scale and complexity of the problem. In Northern Ireland itself, for example, where the provisions for music were substantially better than in the Republic (I am thinking especially of music education, of opportunities for performance and of the presence of specific infrastructures for contemporary art music), we find a commentator observing in 1995 that 'at first glance, these composers [born in Northern Ireland] seem to be only superficially interested in their Irishness, if at all, uninterested in the troubles they have lived through.'[12] Although I shall want to return to that observation and its subsequent modification at the close of this essay, it is useful here to recognize that in the North as in the South, the immediacy of 'Irishness' gives way before the stronger claims of the European aesthetic. These claims require further scrutiny.

With the sovereign exception of Seóirse Bodley (whose *The Narrow Road to the Deep North* [1972] Axel Klein regards as a milestone in contemporary Irish keyboard music), the surge of composition which followed Ó Riada's death in 1971 largely eschewed both the Northern crisis in particular and that confrontation between European modes of musical discourse and the traditional repertory which preoccupied Bodley in the early 1970s.[13] Instead, it was Europe itself which drew the attention of Irish composers: as a source of literary inspiration, in the rehabilitation of genres (notably the symphony and chamber music) and in the development of an oeuvre which in many cases remained modest in scope.

As Axel Klein has shown, it was in the 1930s and 40s that composers like May began to absorb the processes and aesthetic *mentalité* of European modernism, but the period immediately following Ó Riada's death produced a substantial body of work which allowed this process to define itself against the commonplace perceptions of music in Ireland. The substantial increase in orchestral works is a case in point: Wilson, Kinsella, Victory and Bodley all made important contributions to the symphonic genre, and all except Bodley did so without much (if any) recourse to the aural tradition. But of even greater moment, perhaps, was the consolidation of European modernism as the prevailing intelligencer of contemporary music in Ireland which the next generation achieved in the 1980s. Writing of Gerald Barry in the second edition of *The New Grove*, Gareth Cox offers the following summary of the composer's technique as follows:

Barry's pitch material is often derived by means of aleatory processes from such abstract sources as a chart showing the locations of John Jenkins'

12 Hilary Bracefield, 'The Northern Composer: Irish or European?', in: Devine and White (as n. 10), 257.
13 See Axel Klein, *Die Musik Irlands im 20. Jahrhundert* (Hildesheim: Georg Olms Verlag, 1996), 269–70. I am indebted to this seminal study for much of the information upon which this essay relies.

manuscripts ... the words of the BBC Radio 4 shipping forecast and dissonant harmonies formed by selective use of the passing notes in Bach's
chorales ... [or], ... the addition and use of inessential contiguous pitches in
the Irish melody *Bonny Kate.* Structurally, his pieces appear to start suddenly in mid-flow and end just as abruptly; elaboration of material is more
important than any developmental progression and prolonged pauses can
punctuate the course of the music unexpectedly.[14]

The music produced by this kind of compositional technique may be of
undoubted interest (Barry is by far the most widely-performed and publicised
of contemporary Irish composers), but it stands deliberately aloof from any
engagement with 'Ireland' as a received idea. In fact, Barry's music apostrophises not only that impatience with the tyranny of Irish musical ideas (and
the educational conservatism with which they were perpetuated), but also that
modernist sensibility which tends to repudiate any bridge back from music to
linguistic comprehension. It is the music of structural intelligence, but it does
not admit of an easy transliteration to linguistic intelligence. As so often with
the music of his mentor Stockhausen, Barry invents a sound-world which is
defiant of narrative contiguity and which prefers instead a holistic preoccupation with generative clusters of sound. Because his reliance on generic pro-
totypes is much less than that of his predecessors, Barry's music is much more
resolutely (and often elegantly) disdainful of continuity. Stockhausen may be
an electronic *Kapellmeister,* seated at the manuals of his computer (so that
much of his music depends, in a time-honoured, German way on the presence
of the composer himself), but Barry's music depends on nothing except itself.
Least of all does it depend on Ireland.

This freedom from 'Ireland' is, one can presume, not a difficulty for Barry
(if anything, the reverse), but it is problematic in terms of how his music is
understood. Barry works at large in the world: his music stands apart from any
consensus on what constitutes a fundamentally 'Irish' aesthetic in music or
anything else (except perhaps in its ironic condescension to parody). But again
the parallel with Stockhausen – whose didactic influence on a younger generation of Irish composers has been considerable – is instructive. Stockhausen's *Licht,* for example, has the exhaustive pretensions which are so characteristic of German music not only in the music dramas of Richard Wagner
(the cycle's obvious precedent), but even in the cantata cycles of J.S. Bach (if
the helicopters in *Licht* are not Wagnerian, it is difficult to say what is). The
drive to complete such a project, to say nothing of the bond of discipleship
which Stockhausen's musicians proclaim, speaks unmistakably of an impulse

14 Gareth Cox, 'Barry, Gerald', in: Stanley Sadie (ed.), *The New Grove Dictionary of Music and Musicians,* revised edition (London: Macmillan, 2001), vol. 2, 773.

which transcends and characterises German musical culture, whatever the apparent anarchy of Stockhausen's own discourse. Which is to say that in the scale and tenacity of his musical vision, Stockhausen visibly, audibly and aesthetically enjoys a strong continuity with the German music that precedes him. And in such terms he is received, performed and understood.

No such continuity is available to Barry: he stands in constant danger of seeming wilfully eclectic, because Ireland, meanwhile, continues to develop a strong cultural continuity which all but ignores the European aesthetic in music. I have already suggested, indeed, that it endorses another tradition.

This sense of place or tradition is not unique to Germany: despite Adorno's withering disdain, it is also a strong feature of postwar British music. Britten's Aldeburgh and Maxwell Davies' Orkney are prominent examples, and the relationship either composer established between place, performance and composition is one which has largely defined whole areas of British music, notably opera. In England, this sense of place is in the first instance a literal one. But it is also expressive of continuity, and in Britten's music, of stylistic identification. His music is rooted in the particularity of Aldeburgh (and the performers who worked there) but it travels outwards without losing anything of this sharply-profiled individualism. It is a marker of identity of the kind which we associate with contemporary Irish poetry, but not especially with music, except, of course, traditional music. And therein lies the problem.

Within Ireland, two solutions to this problem of reception seem to have gained ground among composers who are intensely interested in the history of Irish ideas and who yet remain firmly committed to the European aesthetic. The first solution is to revisit the preoccupations of Irish cultural and indeed social history without recourse to the aural tradition, and it is one which is voiced, as I indicated earlier, in the piano music of John Buckley. Buckley's *Oileáin*, for example, does afford a bridge back to the narrative past, based as it is on an Irish saga. But as with other of his works, the discourse is resolutely independent of folk music, to such an extent that a useful comparison could be tentatively advanced between Buckley's technique in this suite and Mícheál Ó Súilleabháin's similarly titled *Oileán*. A one-to-one likening would be trite, but there can be little doubt that whereas Ó Súilleabháin explicitly and creatively depends on the idiom and discourse of the aural tradition, Buckley never does. Instead, he adopts a relationship with Ireland that is crucially at one remove. This strategy, I would submit, enjoys a precedent in the music of Arnold Bax.

Bax is problematic in the history of Irish music, not because he himself was *not* Irish, but because his early compositions were so deeply imbued with the spirit and influence of the Celtic Revival. Yeats in particular was a vital source of inspiration to Bax, and without stretching the comparison to breaking point, so is he also to Buckley. But as with Buckley, Bax avoided any kind of reliance on the music of the ethnic repertory to 'hibernicize' his music. Indeed he castigated Stanford for doing so, and repulsed any naïve correspondence between folk music and his own enterprises as a composer.[15] We find the same distance between the tradition and a music which is nevertheless directly concerned with Ireland not only in Buckley but also in composers as diverse as Brian Boydell, Eibhlis Farrell and Kevin O'Connell.

O'Connell's *From the Besieged City*, orchestrated in 1989, is a work which responds to the Northern crisis in particular terms that are stringently unconnected with Ireland but which nevertheless address Derry and its history by allusion to a Polish text which O'Connell sets as the main focus of the piece. It is this indirection which at once preserves O'Connell's freedom from that fatal cul-de-sac of melodic citation and yet draws the Siege itself into the socio-cultural métier of European history. And O'Connell's work in chamber opera (to texts by Gerard Stembridge and James Conway [from John Mc-Gahern]) suggest that the incisive intelligence of his musical discourse, which remains resolutely European, can nevertheless attain to a voice which speaks of a more immediate sense of place. This second solution to the problem of obviating the dominant forms of musical perception in Ireland is much more difficult to develop than the first. It does, however, allow for the integration of 'Ireland' as an idea in terms of a European musical discourse which has often hitherto been characterised by the absence of this idea.

Presence and absence have been prominent themes in this essay: the presence and absence of the aural tradition from certain forms of contemporary Irish music. As the bibliography attached to this volume indicates, the greater part of this music awaits extensive scrutiny, notwithstanding the exemplary attention it has received from Axel Klein, among others.[16] But the literature that is beginning to grow around the subject does at least allow us to identify an anxiety of influence (of a kind which Stevens so memorably apostrophises in his poem) which has resulted in an Irish musical imagination that is divided, and to good purpose. Very tentatively, I would conclude that the Ó Riada crisis produced an 'either/or' condition in Irish art music which has yet to be resolved. That many of those composers concerned with the development of a European aesthetic achieved a degree of success independently of Ó Riada is beside the point: in the aftermath of his failure, the situation that has emerged is strikingly clear, even if the reasons for it are complex. The environment of Irish culture is one which is still dominated by the aural tradition, even if the music no longer functions as an agent of nationalist ideology.

---

15 See White, 1998 (as n. 1), 117–24, for a consideration of Bax's development as a composer in the light of the Literary Revival.   16 An exemplary instance is Gareth Cox's essay 'Octatonicism in the String Quartets of Brian Boydell' in: Devine and White (as n. 10), 263–70.

The emancipation and rehabilitation of this repertory, in addition to its immensely fertile re-deployment in popular and commercial forms of music have nevertheless confirmed its central status in Irish cultural discourse. At the same time, the greater number by far of Irish composers disdain any direct engagement with traditional music. And since we have arrived in Europe at a moment when the aesthetics of art music tend to favour a radically simplified and accessible mode of address (Gorécki in preference to Stockhausen, for example), the claims of modernism in Irish music can seem attenuated or simply outdated.[17] It is not always easy to be Irish and European at the same time.

---

17 In a conversation with John Buckley which followed the presentation of a first draft of this essay in March 2000, I suggested to him that the appeal of composers such as Gorécki, Adams and Pärt endangered to an extent the reception of more stringent avatars of musical modernism. Buckley suggested in turn that this was not necessarily the case, and that the level of exposure which such music enjoyed, rather than any inherent 'simplicity' accounted for its prominent reception and appeal.

2

The development of electroacoustic music in Ireland

PASCHALL DE PAOR

INTRODUCTION

This chapter examines the early development of electroacoustic music in Ireland. It provides a timeline of compositions, with a brief discussion of several indicative pieces, and an educational perspective. It concludes with a summary of key developments.

There were several key musical developments in the twentieth-century. It has been argued that one such development, electroacoustic music, was so innovative, that it constituted the singular most radical break with musical tradition[1]. Many of the key elements can be traced to the research initiated at two centres – Paris (in 1948), with Pierre Schaeffer; and later Cologne, with Werner Meyer-Eppler.[2] Some of the key issues raised by this genre include sonic typology, spectromorphology, gesture, soundscape, technology, and listening.[3] At a more basic level these were the inclusion of all sound as legitimate musical material (and the problems of association and surrogacy), the absence of visual performers, the fixed medium of tape, and the limitations of technology. This technology, in its early primitive state, was expensive and rare in its availability. Access was a major problem, and this contributed to its delayed development in many European countries, including Ireland.

Dealing with the above issues required considerable musical openness, experimentation, and resourcing. The musical genre faced considerable barriers both conceptually and technologically, and many of these difficulties continue today.

---

1 Simon Emmerson (ed.), *The Language of Electroacoustic Music* (London: Macmillan, 1986). 2 Peter Manning, *Electronic and Computer Music* (Oxford: Clarendon , 1993, 2nd ed.). Earlier work is excluded here. For instance, Thaddeus Cahill's Dynamophone of 1897, Busoni's *Entwurf einer Ästhetik der Tonkunst* (Trieste: 1907, Eng. trans. as *Sketch of a New Aesthetic of Music,* 1911*)*, Luigi Russolo's *Art of Noises* (1912, trans. Barclay Brown, New York: Pendragon: 1986), and Varèse' visionary comments in the *New York Telegraph* in 1916. 3 Denis Smalley, 'Spectro-Morphology and Structuring

From 1948 onwards, developments in Europe gathered momentum. Pierre Schaeffer and Pierre Henry co-composed their *Symphonie pour un homme seul* in 1948, Stockhausen finished his *Gesang der Jünglinge* in 1956, Varèse' *Poème électronique*, and Xenakis' *Concret PH* both completed in 1958.[4] In general, many Irish composers tried to keep abreast of European musical developments. However, electroacoustic musical developments were not as quick to travel as others. Nevertheless, within a decade of Schaeffer's efforts, the first Irish exploration began.

Brian Boydell (1917–2000), in *c.*1950, experimented with one of the first tape recorders in Ireland. Later, he employed a tape machine for sound effects in *Errigal* (1968, film), and although aware of the potential for music, regarded the medium only as a 'fascinating game'.[5] This was unfortunate, given his influential position as Professor of Music at Trinity College Dublin for twenty years (1962–82), and could be regarded as a missed opportunity for the development of this genre.

In 1955, Gerard Victory (1921–95), through his work as a 'Talks & Interviews' producer at the national broadcasting station (Radio Éireann, now RTÉ), became aware of the use of sound effects (through technology) in radio drama. The previous year the Dutch composer Henk Badings was awarded the Prix Italia for his radiophonic opera *Orestes*, which had a substantial electronics element. This ignited an interest in this area, and in 1957 Victory wrote *The Orphans*, a commissioned piece for the drama section of the Prix Italia. He employed sound as a contextual design feature, and it marked the first Irish venture into the genre of electroacoustic music.

THE REAL BEGINNING

Roger Doyle (b. 1949) composed the first Irish electroacoustic piece in 1971. He had studied harmony and piano for three years at the Royal Irish Academy of Music in Dublin, where he was awarded numerous composition prizes.[6] His interest in electroacoustic music, however, was aroused

processes', in: Emmerson (as n. 1), 61–96; Denis Smalley, 'The Listening Imagination: Listening in the Electroacoustic Era', *Companion to Contemporary Musical Thought*, vol. 2, ed. John Paynter et al. (London: Routledge, 1992), 514–54; Trevor Wishart: *On Sonic Art* (New York: Imagineering Press, 1985); Paschall de Paor: 'Defining a Music', *Occasional Research Papers*, ed. Timothy Stephenson (NAEA, 2000), 51–64. **4** See Manning (as n. 2). **5** Boydell in personal correspondence with the author, 24 October 1990. **6** Doyle also retained an interest in rock music, and a curious mixture of the two has remained with him. He played drums in the rock bands 'The Malabeats', 'Jazz Therapy' and 'Supply, Demand and Curve', touring Canada with the latter in 1973.

after hearing a piece by the French *musique concrète* composer, Pierre Henry in 1969. Although technically studies, the 1971 pieces *Obstinato* and *Why is Kilkenny so Good?* are both tape pieces in the style of Henry. These are not sound design, but a genuine exploration of the medium of tape as a means of musical expression. Both are only possible on tape, and take advantage of its innate potential. *Obstinato* is a simple first study, consisting of spoken text and organ-like chords *obstinately* repeating for nearly two minutes (and composed in the back room of his parent's house). *Why is Kilkenny so Good?* is slightly more adventurous in its technology (tape recorder, microphones, and echo units). A mixture of radio-culling (voices and sounds) and interviews (in Kilkenny), it is a narrative of self-doubt, alienation, and drug-addiction, which is manifest structurally and teleologically as a drug-induced 'trip.' The vocal semantic and meaning are key elements, with strong associativity and narrative. In 1974 he was awarded a Dutch government scholarship to study electronic music at the University of Utrecht's Institute of Sonology, and it was here that he produced his first LP *OIZZO NO* (1974).[7]

Fin-estra (1977) is basically a transformation of Doyle's *All the Rage* (1974, orchestra), and is accompanied by the sound of children playing outside the recording studio window. These sounds are a key element in the piece – the dialectic of the finished piece with the process and location of composition. The listener is regularly switched between the final realisation, and the place and process of compositional performance. This is achieved in places by the sudden reduction of music, allowing the children's voices, microphone moving, and so on, to be heard as solo items, thus (re)focussing attention. It is a good example of Doyle's early developmental period, exploring the continuum of aural discourse and association. Other large-scale tape pieces from this time include *Solar Eyes* (1975) and *Thalia* (1976)

Rapid Eye Movements (1980) is, in many respects, similar to *Fin-estra*. Here there is a clear dualism at work, between an abstract soundscape and locational association. The title indicates the key to the piece – the dream state exemplified by rapid eye movement, in which multiple imagery, sound, and experience exist within a (mostly) non-rational domain. This is achieved through the interspersion of studio personnel voices (including the composer's voice), with each of the eleven sections starting with a new 'take', spoken by the engineer. Furthermore, piano is used as a structural component, providing cohesion through its return at various points. The

---

7 Other scholarships followed, and subsequent studies ensued at Salzburg, The Hague (Royal University of Music) and Helsinki (Finnish Radio Experimental Music Centre).

use of such sonic objects as radio broadcasts, footsteps, and public address systems lends it its dreamlike status. Here Doyle further explores the innate artistic potential of tape music, where such abstract and concrete experiences can exist.

Charlotte Corday and the Lament of Louis XVI (1989) was commissioned by the Group de Musique Experimentale de Bourges (GMEB) to commemorate the bicentenary of the French Revolution. The text is based on Corday's letters and two eighteenth-century songs, one of which (The Death of Marat) is spoken by the singer and longtime collaborator with Doyle, Olwen Fouere.[8] The piece is full of evoked images and associations, and has a strong syntactic and timbral mimesis. It is one of Doyle's more successful early narrative pieces.

Doyle's mode of composition is quite eclectic and idiosyncratic. He is, in many respects, a self-taught composer. His compositional strategy is very intuitive and improvisational, and the compositional methodology he employs is intertwined with technological developments. It seems his style follows a ten-year cycle, going from note-based music to sound composition to note music and back again to his present preoccupation with sound. One of the many reasons for this cycle is the changing technology. He purchased a tape recorder in 1970, which lends itself to a style that resulted in *Obstinato* and culminated in *Rapid Eye Movements*. In 1982, STS studios in Dublin acquired a Fairlight Computer Music Instrument, and Doyle enjoyed considerable access to it. This instrument is keyboard based, and thus Doyle fell back into tonal, note-based music. He bought a digital sound sampler in late 1989 and the resultant works were sound-based.

Michael Alcorn (b. 1962) took his primary degree at the University of Ulster and it was during his studies there that he developed an interest in electroacoustic music. He assembled a primitive but functional studio there and produced *Electronic Studies I & II* (1984 & 1985) followed by his first major piece *Hanging Stones* (1985), composed as part of his final undergraduate dissertation. It is a combination of recorded voices, natural and synthesised sounds. The voice functions as a ritornello, and is a strong mimetic presence. Against the backdrop of the soundscape, one is continuously drawn to this element, and in conjunction with the slides, makes for an interesting oscillation between sonic abstraction, visual passivity, and direct meaning carried by the voice.

Paul Hayes (b. 1951) studied at the Leinster School of Music, the Royal Academy of Music and later read music at UCD. Hayes began composing in the electroacoustic medium after hearing Doyle's *Why is Kilkenny so good?* at a Young Composers concert in July 1973 (Dublin). *Players 2*

---

8 In 1981, he formed the music-theatre company 'Operating Theatre' with Fouere.

(1974) is his first electroacoustic work, written while in his third year at
university. Based on the 'found' sounds of a prepared piano, it was composed prior to the film recording, with Hayes himself featuring in the subsequent improvised filming. It is the first mixed-media electroacoustic
work by an Irish composer, and was premiered at the Young Composers
Concert in Dublin, 1974. In 1988, Hayes composed *Pieces of Yeats*. Essentially a collage, it is based on recorded material from other compositions.
Key elements are the musical interaction between the voices – in their original state and subsequent transformations, and their semantic characteristics. *Alla Soliloquy* (1987) is a collaborative effort between Hayes and the
composer Donal Hurley. It is a music theatre piece, inspired by the performance art of Jochen Gerz. The piece references many differing musics,
such as the *Lamentations* of Thomas Tallis, with an interwoven spoken
voice as a key textural component. The text predates the composition by
ten years, with construction based on the Tristan Tzara instructions for writing a Dadaist poem.[9] The electroacoustic music of Paul Hayes is primarily
based around collage techniques (especially voices), with a significant element of pantonality when notes are introduced. His thinking on electroacoustic music (brush strokes in sound) led to his collision of styles, not rec-
onciled in his earlier work.

Moonsplinters (1988) by Michael Holohan (b. 1956)[10] is based on an
expressionist poem by Susan Connelly, the composer's wife. It is a programmatic work, which opens with a reading of the poem, with the music
subsequently expanding on the sentiments expressed. Containing a mixture of synthesised and recorded natural sounds, the evocative imagery is
the tension bearer between the musical relationships of the images and the
sonic poetry. *Skull Boxes* (1989) is a collaboration between Holohan, sculptor Ronan Halpin, and painter Paki Smith. It is the first installation piece
by an Irish composer. The Halpin construction consisted of eight pillar
boxes, four placed on either side of a temple entrance, with a skull atop and
a loudspeaker inside each unit. The tape was looped and run continuously
for the duration of the event. The sonic material is derived from voices
(recorded and synthesised) and prepared piano. Most of Holohan's electroacoustic music is note-based and rhythmic, and his sound world is dominated by preset synthesizer sounds. Unfortunately, this synthesizer syn-
drome is shared by almost every Irish electroacoustic composer. He does,
however, incorporate a lot of 'found' sounds (especially unusual piano

9 Cut a newspaper into fragments, place in a bag, and draw out at random. Place together these pieces
in order of their appearance.   10 Holohan studied music at the Dublin College of Music, UCD, and at
the Queen's University of Belfast. He was in his late teens when he heard his first electroacoustic piece
(Doyle's *Solar Eyes*). He produced his first electroacoustic piece in 1983, *Childscapes*, utilizing a Moog
synthesizer in the third movement.

sounds) but only as an adjunct to the synthesizer and rarely as an integral or structural element in a piece.

Donal Hurley's (b. 1950) *Variations for Oboe and Tape* (1989) is a set of variations on the melody 'Think'st thou to seduce me then' by Thomas Campion, taken from the *Fourth Book of Ayres*, 1617. The melody and timbre are varied throughout, as well as being a musical commentary on the text. This piece is built around the harmonic base of the tune, with timbral and rhythmic interjections of preset synthesizer sounds throughout. A flute may be substituted for oboe. Hurley's early work indicates a fondness for preset synthesizer sounds, a chromatic harmonic base, and a strong rhythmic element (very similar to Doyle in many respects). His recordings were of excellent quality, as was his studio technique – indeed, he had the best personal studio for this type of music in Ireland.

Other composers who employed electroacoustic technology include Jerome de Bromhead (b. 1945) whose use has been one of convenience for the performers. In *Rotastasis* (1975), the electric guitar is included simply because it was available, and in *Hy Brasil* (1980), the organ is employed as the choir practised with it and thus easy to pitch their notes from it. In *Parameters* (1981), however, the tape is used as another instrument. A small section of the work is recorded, played back at twice its original speed (at the end of the work), and the performers try to follow. All three are note-based. *Drip, Drop, Drip* (1987) by John Buckley (b. 1951) incorporates many *musique concrète* elements such as recordings of astronauts, cosmonauts and water, and are used more as sound effects than as music. Michael Seaver's (b. 1967) electroacoustic output is note-based and his interest lies mainly in writing for mixed-media, especially dance. Apart from his first piece, James Wilson's (b. 1922) *The Pied Piper of Hamlin* (1967), which uses sound effects, Wilson's electroacoustic music is firmly note-based. He uses the technology as an extra instrumental timbre rather than for its pure sound potential. Eric Sweeney's (b. 1948) main use of electroacoustic music technology is to either replace or as supplement to an orchestra and/or choir. However, his *Auguries of Innocence* (1988) makes use of *musique concrète* elements (recordings of children playing and Hitler speeches), mixed with minimalist keyboard music. Ian Wilson's (b. 1964) only electroacoustic piece, *Bane* (1989), is based primarily on note relationships. The use of electroacoustic music technology (digital delay effect) indicates a simple experimental adjunct.

As can be seen from the above, there is a healthy diversity present in the early works of these Irish composers.[11] Ranging from pure sound compositions to rock music, there is no obvious school nor style of composition

11 Further details of the above works and composers are available from the Contemporary Music Centre, Ireland.

apparent – no particularly 'Irish' electroacoustic music. The dominant feature of their contribution was either as sound design for film/theatre, or in an instrumental idiom (note-based). The general trend was to apply an acoustic technique to the electroacoustic medium. There is, however, an impression of surrealism, probably due to the Irish trait for narrative and fairytales.

An *historical timeline* from 1957 to 1989 is presented here to provide an overview of developments:

1957	Victory, *The Orphans*, choir, electronic effects
1967	Wilson, J., *The Pied Piper of Hamlin*, choir, ensemble, electronics
1968	Boydell, *Errigal*, ensemble, tape
1970	Victory, *Compensations*, ca, tape
1971	Doyle, *Obstinato*, tape
	—— *Why is Kilkenny so Good?*, tape
	Victory, *Circe 1991*, radio opera
1972	Victory, *Processes*, choir, ensemble, tape
	Sweeney, *Five Italian Songs*, solo, choir, tape
	Doyle, *Emptigon*, film, dance, sculpture, ens., tape
1973	Byers, *The Nature of Gothic*, ensemble, tape
1974	Doyle, *Oizzo No*, ensemble, tape
	Hayes, *Players 2*, actress ,film, tape
1975	Doyle, *Solar Eyes*, tape
	Victory, *An Evening for Three*, opera, tape
	Hayes, *E.L.M.*, ensemble, tape
	—— *Sturm und Drang*, ensemble, tape
1976	Barry, *Beethoven WoO80*, gymnast, ensemble, tape
	Doyle, *Thalia*, tape
1977	Barry, *Nativity Play*, vcs, tape
	—— *A Piano Concerto*, pf, ensemble, tape
	Doyle, *Fin-estra*, tape
	Hammond, *Oxrxios*, rect., chorus, tape
1978	Barry, *Décolletage*, sop, tape
	Hayes, *The Second Last Remake of Stern*, mime, string-machine, tape
	—— *Discomime*, lights, tape
	—— *1001 Metropolitan Nights*, actress, ensemble, tape
	—— *Song and Trance*, mime, jazz group, tape
1979	Barry, *New Music Ireland*, radio play, tape
	Geary, *Calender*, ensemble, spkr, slides, tape
1980	Barry, *Unkrautgarten*, ballet, ensemble, tape
	Corcoran, *Balthasar's Dream*, tape
	Doyle, *Rapid Eye Movements*, tape
1981	Bromhead, *Parameters*, ensemble, tape
	Barry, *Three Fairy Tales*, actors, ensemble, tape

Hayes, *Eiskönigin*, mime, tape
1982   Corcoran, *Farewell Symphonies*, spkr, orch, tape
Hayes, *Zone*, tape
—— *Parlando*, pf, tape
1983   Bodley, *The Banshee*, voice, electronics
Corcoran, *A portrait of the artist who wanted to sing but wroteinstead*,
actor, hrpsd, slides, tape
Doyle, *Switch*, actress, tape (rev. 1985)
—— *Quiet Slipper Year*, tape (rev. 1985)
—— *Four Lucy Pieces*, tape (rev. 1985)
Hayes, *Song and Trance 2*, mime tape
1984   Alcorn, *Electronic Study 1*, tape
Hayes, *Music for Artists*, actress, model, cl, tape
Holohan, *Childscapes*, video, tape
1985   Alcorn, *Hanging Stones*, tape
—— *Electronic study 2*, tape
1987   Alcorn, *Jubilate*, pf, tape
Buckley, *Drip, Drop, Drip*, voice, perc., tape
Hayes, *Alla Soliloquy*, mime, tape (w/Hurley)
Hurley, *Alla Soliloquy*, mime, tape (w/Hayes)
1988   Barry, *St. Kevin and the Blackbird*, radiophonic tape
Victory, *Rendezvous*, opera, tape
Hayes, *Pieces of Yeats*, video, synth, tape
Holohan, *Plurabell*, tape
—— *Moonsplinters*, tape
Hurley, *Triologue*, dance, tape
Sweeney, *Auguries of Innocence*, tape
1989   Doyle, *Charlotte Corday and the Lament of Louis XVI*, tape
Hayes, *Of No Dreams Remember*, ensemble, tape
—— *Bounce*, vcl, tape
—— *The Ice Queen*, ballet, tape
Holohan, *Viaggio*, tape
—— *The Three Continents*, ballet, tape
—— *Sometime City*, film, tape
—— *Buvinda*, tape
—— *Skull Boxes*, sculpture, tape
—— *The Crane*, film, tape
Hurley, *Variations for Oboe and Tape*, ob, tape
—— *Ytrebil*, dancer, tape
—— *Collage*, dancer, tape
Johnston, *Study No. 1*, electronics
Sweeney, *Beau Est Son Nom*, nar., chor, ensemble, tape
Seaver, *The Butterfly who couldn't Dance*, play, tape
Wilson, I., *Bane*, vln, digital delay

DEVELOPMENTS IN EDUCATION

In the early 1970s, the Queen's University of Belfast (QUB) established the first fully functional university-based studio in Ireland. It initially consisted of two VCS synthesizers, a 12-channel mixer, and a Studer tape recorder. The development of the studio stagnated until Michael Alcorn, the studio's current director, was appointed composer-in-residence in 1988, and began an ongoing expansion. At the University of Ulster (UU), David Morris inherited its studio in 1980, which then consisted of a tape recorder, one microphone, and a small mixer. It was here that Alcorn and Ian Wilson composed their first pieces.

Waterford Institute of Technology (WIT) initiated its studio between 1984 and 1985. Donncha Ó Maidín developed this resource, beginning with the acquisition of an Apple Macintosh Plus computer, a Yamaha DX7 synthesizer and a Yamaha CX5 dedicated music computer.[12] Finally, the studio at Trinity College, Dublin (TCD) had its inception between the years 1988-1989, under the direction of Simon Trezise. Many of these educational facilities tried to incorporate the technology into the undergraduate and postgraduate programmes with varying levels of success.

Given that nearly all early electroacoustic music made use of institutionally-based resources, there is little evidence to suggest that the early Irish researchers had access to commercial or university facilities. There were no centres in Ireland similar to Europe or the US, which engaged in serious research into music and sound with technology. The influence of these centres in other countries is well documented, and it comes as no surprise that without such resources, the development of this genre in Ireland comes somewhat late.

It is worth noting the explosive developments in education over the last decade, especially in the postgraduate area. In 1997, the University of Limerick offered the first masters degree in music technology in Ireland. The same year TCD offered a postgraduate diploma, followed quickly by QUB, NUI Maynooth, and the Dublin Institute of Technology (DIT). The consequences of these developments are currently being felt through a vibrant and developing electroacoustic music scene in Ireland.

SUMMARY

Electroacoustic music developed relatively late in Ireland, despite several early opportunities. First explorations were close to international develop-

---

12 The author was introduced to electroacoustic music at this facility.

ments, but unfortunately not continued. Furthermore, Boydell's early appraisal of this genre had far-reaching consequences. Had he considered it a legitimate musical genre, Ireland may very well have been at the forefront of international developments.

There were a couple of key events that impacted this musical development in Ireland. Firstly, around 1978/9, the Irish Composers' Centre organised an introduction to electroacoustic music for a small group of Irish composers at Hurley's home studio. Those attending included Holohan, Victory, Buckley, and James Wilson. Secondly, in the late 1980s, Bernard Harris (then administrator of the Contemporary Music Centre) organised several workshops and seminars, which exposed Irish personnel to international composers such as Trevor Wishart, Stephen Montague, Jonty Harrison, and Rolf Eström.

Educational developments were slow to develop, with QUB being the first to have any useful facilities, and WIT the first to engage in computational musicology. Graduates are now starting to make their presence known, and this area is becoming ever more vibrant and internationally recognised.

As mentioned above, the first Irish electroacoustic piece was by Roger Doyle, who is regarded today as the senior Irish electroacoustic music composer. Paul Hayes composed the first Irish mixed-media piece, with Michael Holohan producing the first Irish installation. Special mention should be made of the composer and performer Michael Seaver, who made a substantial contribution to the early dissemination of Irish electroacoustic music, by giving regular Irish recitals of music for clarinet and tape/electronics.

There appears to be no obvious 'Irish' style of electroacoustic music. The favoured approach was the application of an acoustic compositional technique to the genre, with a sometimes very interesting collision between sound design and idiomatic instrumentation.

From slow and gradual beginnings, this genre is currently enjoying an energetic developmental period. Many international fora now recognise the work of our composers and researchers, and, given current educational initiatives, the future is promising.

3

Opera in Ireland before 1925

JOSEPH J. RYAN

One of the intriguing features of historical study is the realisation of how frequently one encounters a disparity between expectation and reality. A genius of the study is its readiness to surprise. The received wisdom is that we can and should learn from the past but when one reflects how often a train of events has taken the unsuspected route, it is not perhaps so unusual to find that discordant patterns recur.

The study of the course of Irish opera offers a good example of the gap between what one might reasonably expect and what actually occurred. The simple truth is that little enough occurred and one inevitably ends up concentrating on the reasons underlying a paucity of enterprise rather than on the enterprise itself. Throughout the late eighteenth and nineteenth centuries when wider Europe was in thrall to the spectacle of opera, music in Ireland was resolutely following its individual channel determined more by the need to corroborate the emerging nationalist sentiment than by any cosmopolitan trend. Notwithstanding the power of opera as a proselytising vehicle nor the obviously commercial visits of the touring companies, for some reason Ireland did not take the usual route in pushing forward opera as the ideal genre for the dissemination of a live political issue. Ireland eschewed the opportunity to exploit what this writer has elsewhere described as *the primary vehicle of the music of commitment.*[1] It might further be anticipated that a country that proved adept in the provision of creative literary talent would find that its musicians would naturally demonstrate a parallel dramatic interest; was it not the Dublin-born Charles Villiers Stanford who evinced the most consistent interest in opera of all creators working in Britain at the turn of the twentieth century? In order to see how unusual Ireland's case is, it is necessary only to contrast the course of opera

---

1 Joseph Ryan, 'Opera', in: W. J. McCormack (ed.), *The Blackwell Companion to Modern Irish Culture* (Oxford: Blackwell, 1999), 449.

here with that in other European states. In Russia, for example, the progression from folk music through to opera in the works of Glinka, Dargomyzhsky, and 'The Five', points to the expected course of a nationalist music. Smetana provides happy evidence of a nationalist eclosion in a smaller geographical setting and also example, most notably through *The Bartered Bride,* of the comfortable marriage of folk-opera and patriotic sentiment. It is not novel to argue that Smetana eased the way for Dvořák and Janáček nor that with hindsight one can trace through these three creators the cogent continuity of a distinctive Czech musical accent. More to the point, these masters demonstrated that favouring the picturesque did not preclude universal significance or appeal.

It is in the very nature of opera that it lends itself so readily to the emergence of a regional accent and representation of national characteristics. Opera arose as a heightened form of speech, as the highest collaboration between verse and music. It inherited the precise referential quality of the word and allied it to the aspirational otherness of music. Through the final three centuries of the second millennium when societies over the civilised world were concerned to reorder their structures in the most fundamental way opera offered the ideal vehicle for the working of particular themes that were universal. Such a genre was inevitably attractive to any committed political movement. The expectation would reasonably be that Ireland with its increasing awareness of a noble and distinct past would look naturally to opera as a principal means of celebrating this distinction and furthermore that at least some of the operas would go on to proclaim a glorious independent future that resurrected the ideals and forms of the lamented past. Such a convoluted marriage of nationalist sentiment and the pastoral with glorification of the past was the very stuff of high European romanticism.

Why should the course of music in Ireland be different? It is not that there was no audience for opera in Ireland. On the contrary, the record suggests the opposite. Scholars such as T.J.Walsh and Brian Boydell have done much in their very separate ways to bring to light the role that opera played in urban Irish life from the middle of the eighteenth century. The fruits of their research and the contemporaneous reports point to a consistent appetite for both light and grand opera. The very history of music in Dublin in the eighteenth century centres on theatres such as Smock Alley, the Theatre Royal (in its various guises) and the Musick Hall in Crow Street. Similarly the Music Hall of 1840 and the larger Ulster Hall of 1862 provided the focus of music making in Belfast while the history of opera in Cork also involves a shifting Theatre Royal with its latest incarnation in 1853 on the site of the present Opera House. Even in the more economically troubled and political fervid final decades of the nineteenth century visiting opera troupes, such as the Carl Rosa

Opera Company, guided presumably by financial imperatives, happily included Ireland's major urban centres on their annual tours. Even the briefest consideration of the repertory of this company attests that Irish audiences would have opportunity to share in the finest grand operas. Thus while light opera had its special place, it was not the sole diet of the Irish audience. Italian opera featured each season and Gounod's *Faust* was premièred in Dublin just months after its initial appearance in London and only four years after its first production in Paris. The Irish production given in October 1863 in Dublin's Theatre Royal attests to the city's enduring station as a major centre of empire capable of supporting, albeit in smaller scale, the fashions and interests prevalent in London. Brian Boydell, a judicious student of early operatic performance in Ireland, notes that:

> A remarkable feature was the short time-lag between the production of new operas in London and on the continent and their performance in Dublin.[2]

Boydell proceeds to cite Dublin's introduction in 1855 to Verdi's *Il trovatore* and *La traviata* just two years after the first performances. Just a decade earlier William Wallace's *Maritana,* which had received its first performance at the Drury Lane Theatre in 1845, was heard in Dublin's Theatre Royal. The enduring appeal of Wallace's work and that of Michael Balfe's *The Bohemian Girl* (1843) with Irish audiences was to strengthen the appeal of light opera. As late as 1920 a disdainful commentator, in the course of a review of musical activity in Dublin, noted that 'there is unqualified enthusiasm for opera, bad, good, and indifferent'.[3] It has, however, been pointed out elsewhere that such short seasons essentially 'were self-serving; they did not contribute to a wider cultivation of art music per se'.[4] Thus, the trend toward cultural distinction notwithstanding, Ireland quite contentedly continued to receive its annual share of Italianate and, increasingly, light opera through decades when various other European states were tenaciously looking to create their own indigenous operatic character.

That this was the case did not go unnoticed: one critic of the music scene in Dublin in the final quarter of the nineteenth century finds little to praise; however exception is made for the Carl Rosa Opera Company:

> ... we confess to a great weakness for it. The company is at present one of the most popular and best agencies possible for disseminating a knowledge

---

2 Brian Boydell, 'Opera', in: W.J. McCormack (ed.), *Modern Irish Culture* (as n. 1.), 447. 3 H. Travers Smith, 'A Musical League for Dublin, *Irish Statesman,* I (26 July, 1919), 119. 4 See Harry White, *The Keeper's Recital: Music and Cultural History in Ireland, 1770-1970* (Cork: Cork University Press, 1998), 105.

of good music in one of its departments among our public; and if a really intelligent love for high-class opera is ever to penetrate the minds of the many – a love for opera, which will be totally distinct from yells of delight at wonderful tenor high C's [*sic*] or at the sparkling fiorituri of fascinating prima donne – it will be through performances divorced from the star system and in the English language, 'understanded of the people'.[5]

This same critic laments the return of *hardy annuals, The Bohemian Girl* and *Maritana* proceeding to note with disfavour that the Dublin public:

vastly prefers Balfe and Wallace to Beethoven and Wagner; nor can it even be urged as an apology that in this they are actuated by patriotic considerations or prejudices.[6]

If a malaise was evident it was not confined to Irish urban centres. In a review of music in London in the first decade of the twentieth century, Stanford points to the particular situation of opera:

... every department of the art is advancing with the sole exception of the one branch which the rest of Europe has rated as the most important of all, dramatic music. For not only is it the most direct in its appeal to every class, but it gives the maximum of employment and incentive to the profession, as well as to many other crafts, scenic, poetic, and scientific. If we do not soon provide this outlet for the talent and genius of the country, the result will soon be felt in the schools, not perhaps so much in quantity as in quality.[7]

Stanford's actions were consistent with his writings. He, above all his contemporaries, persevered in the writing of opera. It is ironic that it is one of the lightest, *Shamus O'Brien*, that is the only one to have met with any degree of success.

While Stanford provides one link between British and Irish experience the touring opera companies provide yet another and they played a special role in Irish cultural life. Often presenting grand opera in the vernacular, they acted essentially as both importers and educators. They also spawned a number of local societies in centres such as Waterford, Clonmel, and Galway. Some of these were long-lived and their annual productions of light opera were a source of pride and focus for community endeavour. For pragmatic reasons the travelling companies however visited only major urban centres; outside

5 'Music in Dublin', *Hibernia*, I (2 Jan. 1882), 7.   6 Ibid.   7 Charles Villiers Stanford, 'The Case for National Opera', in *Studies and Memories* (London, 1908), 5.

of these there was little opportunity to encounter anything as exotic as opera. It is not chauvinistic but merely realistic to conflate the account of opera in Ireland with that of opera in Dublin, Cork, and Belfast. In addition to this limitation, the whole musical infrastructure – primary education, technical education, resources, venues, all the prerequisites for a healthy musical life – was deficient in Ireland. Consequently the audience base for opera was low and, as has been indicated, light opera was to prove the more popular form. Thus opera in Ireland cannot be said to be elitist as much as delimited. The record suggests that the audience for opera remained constant but also constantly low.

Despite the enduring, if circumscribed, public interest there is a noticeable dearth of original creativity in the area of musical theatre from Irish-based composers. Thomas Roseingrave's *Phaedra and Hippolitus* (1753) and Charles Thomas Carter's *The Rival Candidates* (1775) are early exceptions from Irish-born composers in an eighteenth-century dominated by imported music drama. Philip Cogan, who was to earn the respect of his fellow professionals for his technical ability, and John Stevenson – who was later to become associated in the public mind with the collaboration, and the word is chosen carefully, with Thomas Moore – combined in 1782 in the Smock Alley presentation of *The Contract*. Indeed the latter wrote quite a deal of music for the Irish stage. Another exception from a later age was John William Glover who died as his century closed in December 1899 drawing the curtain on an energetic personal contribution to the musical life of Dublin through the second half of the century. Organist of St Mary's pro-cathedral, he was the leading Catholic musical figure in an age dominated by musicians from the central Anglican matrix comprising the cathedrals of Christ Church, St Patrick's, and neighbouring Trinity College. Glover's penchant for the provision of accessible community music led him inevitably to favour choral endeavour. This populist style is evident in his major operatic venture. In 1880 he provided music for Edmund Falconer's dramatization of Goldsmith's *Deserted Village*. Set by the Shannon river in the Irish midlands in the mid-eighteenth century this three-act opera is characteristically accessible. The figure of the poet Goldsmith is employed as the narrator in a work that is tuneful but ultimately transparent as can be gleaned from the writing for the opening chorus.

During the keen political years at the turn of the twentieth century opera was sometimes seen as an alien form inimical to true Irishness. This was not the universal view but enjoyed sufficient currency to undermine further the prospect of a thriving indigenous musical drama. Opera to some was seen as decadent and at quite a distance from the noble pursuits of the Gaelic League.

> ... while the Gaiety and the Royal and the Lyric are drawing other young men and women to delight in the last flower of London or Paris corruption,

Music Example 3.1 John William Glover, *Deserted Village*, 'Sweet Auburn'

these Gaelic Leaguers meet to bring once more into honour tunes that had long been left to the peasant in the bogs or the rapparee in the mountains, together with a tongue blighted to the roots by centuries of neglect and pro-scription.[8]

Already the question of language as the true badge of nationality is suggested. Irish opera employing the native tongue was in a sense artificially inseminated arising in the main from competitions staged in conjunction with determinedly Gaelic festivals. One such fruit was *Sruth na Maoile* an *opera nuadh* (new opera) composed by Geoffrey M. Palmer with libretto by Fr Tomás Ó Ceal-laigh. The work was first given in the Gaiety Theatre in July 1923 under the auspices of Conradh na Gaeilge (The Gaelic League) an influential body founded in 1893 and primarily dedicated to language revival. Vincent O'Brien, director of the Palestrina Choir in Dublin's Catholic pro-cathedral, was centrally involved in the project and conducted this first performance

8 M [?], 'The musical season in Ireland (1899–1900)', *New Ireland Review,* xiv (October 1900), 104.

which was produced by Joseph O'Mara of the O'Mara Opera Company. The latter, a native of Limerick, had fashioned a commendable career as a tenor with the London-based Moody-Manners Company before founding his own group which regularly toured the provinces. During a delimited period in the early 1920s toward the close of O'Mara's career his company was to be the vehicle for a pertinacious attempt to fashion an indigenous opera employing the native tongue and dealing with concerns consistent with the image of an emerging independent nation. Palmer's work was characteristic of this genre. The opera is based on the legend of the fate of the Children of Lir, one of the most evocative tales in Irish mythology. It is hard to take issue with the first review given in the *Irish Times* which recorded that the *story* [is] *told in a simple and straightforward manner.*[9] This direct approach was also evident in the music where the resolution to achieve an undeniably national flavour was apparent in the use of direct quotation. Palmer, a pupil of Stanford, employed traditional airs, such as 'Silent O Moyle', whose settings, according to the same *Irish Times* critic, were 'altogether charming'.

A reading of the score attests the critic's view. *Sruth na Maoile* is cast in two acts and is preceded with a short prelude based on Moore's melody. The tale is to the fore in that the story is given syllabically with thin accompaniment. The matter of imparting the legend of the great ocean god and his children is given pre-eminence. That the tale as resurrected by the antiquarian research of the nineteenth century is conflated with a Christian message of redemption is a feature emphasised here and may owe something to Ó Ceallaigh's central influence on the shaping of the opera. The children of Lir, fated by their jealous step-mother to live for three periods of 300 years as swans, can only be restored to human form through that strange combination of the coming to Ireland of faith and devotion and the politically satisfying reunion of southern and northern sectors through marriage. The arias that are included are somewhat forced and are adaptations of airs mainly from the Petrie and P.W. Joyce collections. For instance Kathleen's aria in the second act is number 64 of the Joyce collection *Old Irish Folk Music and Songs* (1909). The same source supplies the slip jig that introduces the dance and domestic scene that open the second act.

This opera was in essence a collaboration by correspondence. Librettist and composer resided on opposite sides of Ireland and the working of the opera was carried through extensive correspondence over a period of some five years.[10] This record is revealing in that Palmer was obviously the more determined partner in the enterprise. Pressure of other work forced Ó Ceallaigh into many an apology for delay. It is also evident that Palmer provided music and

9 *Irish Times* (26 July 1923), 8.   **10** See MSS 8129 Correspondence Tomás Ó Ceallaigh to Geoffrey Molineaux Palmer in the National Library of Ireland.

direction of English text for Ó Ceallaigh to shape and translate. This moved Ó Ceallaigh to recall his working method for an earlier operatic cooperation with Robert O'Dwyer on his opera *Eithne*: '... in the case of O'Dwyer's opera I wrote everything in Irish first, this was set to music, and only a long-time afterwards was the English version produced'. That the procedure was reversed in this case with Palmer taking the musical initiative appears to have put considerable pressure on the librettist. In this respect Ó Ceallaigh's comment that 'anyhow, nobody expects high-brow literature in a libretto' is revealing.[11] In the course of the extensive exchange Ó Ceallaigh offers advice freely to his musical colleague. Notwithstanding his seemingly arbitrary use of both Gaelic and English versions of his own surname (Ó Ceallaigh/ O'Kelly), he is adamant that the opera should be in either one or the other tongue, but not in an admixture: 'I don't like compromises'.[12] The librettist also reveals that he harboured a number of reservations concerning his earlier contribution to *Eithne*. The lighter nature of Palmer's undertaking better suited his talents and even during the crafting of *Sruth na Maoile* he was pressing Palmer to consider a further collaboration on a light musical or farce.[13] Ó Ceallaigh's views are evident in the close to one letter: 'Irish Grand Opera is rather too big for us at present. Irish tunes and adaptations thereof offer great scope. What do you think?'[14]

Viewed in a broader context, this unconsciously counts as an experimental work, one that sets out to tell a traditional tale in its traditional language. The truth is that this resolve to fashion a distinctive native opera was not sustained. Early works were not built upon and the few Irish operas that emerged in the revivalist years are notable now for their rarity and considered curiosities when considered at all.

The librettist Fr Tomás Ó Ceallaigh is yet another interesting character. From Sligo on the west coast of Ireland, he had almost two decades earlier supplied the first translation of Yeats's *Cathleen ni Houlihan,* a feat that was awarded first prize at the Samhain Competition in 1904. This doubtless brought him to the attention of Robert O'Dwyer as Ó Ceallaigh was to provide the libretto for the first original opera with Irish text, *Eithne*.

One year later in the second week of August 1924 O'Mara again essayed forth with a series of Irish operas in the Theatre Royal. Palmer's work was given again along with Stanford's *Shamus O'Brien* and Harold White's *Shaun the Post.* On this occasion the series was given under the auspices of Aonach Tailteann. The inclusion of the Stanford is interesting and might appear somewhat at variance with the impetus to celebrate a noble native tradition. The composer himself seems to have wearied of the work and was set against a

---

11 Ibid. See TÓC to GMP, 13 Dec. 1919.   **12** Ibid. See TÓC to GMP, 21 November 1919.   **13** Ibid. See TÓC to GMP, 10 July 1923.   **14** Ibid. See TÓC to GMP, 12 April 1920.

revival. However his death in March of that year freed Joseph O'Mara to restage the opera with which he had gained considerable attention in March 1896 when he played the part of Mike Murphy at the première in the Opéra-Comique Theatre London. Thus the choice may well have had more to do with O'Mara's wish to recreate an acclaimed role than any desire to present a balanced view of the newly emerging Ireland. The reception afforded the work in 1896 did not translate across the sea and the three intervening decades: the Irish audience voted with its feet and the empty stalls suggested that Stanford's judgment was the wiser.[15] His shifting view of a work written to a libretto by G.H. Jessop after Le Fanu provides an early example of revisionism that is all the more interesting as the opera had offered Stanford his one true moment of broad popular success.

The final two nights of this week-long series were devoted to a new opera by Harold Robert White, *Shaun the Post*. White was a native Dubliner and an engaging character who had started his involvement with music as a result of the possession of a fine treble voice that found outlet as a chorister in the cathedral choir of Christ Church. He later served as organist in a number of city churches while enjoying some success as an occasional composer. In addition he contributed to a number of publications as a music critic where his observations provide an interesting record of musical activity in the earliest decades of the twentieth century. White set out in this opera to recreate a grand opera based on Boucicault's *Arragh-na-Pogue*, with adaptation of the libretto by R.J. Hughes. O'Mara sang the lead part of Shaun who was given a lyrical role including settings of traditional airs such as that from the County Derry. Unlike the Stanford revival, White's work which he conducted himself, attracted full and responsive houses. The contrast in public response is all the more interesting as the Stanford and White have more in common in their approach than either does with Palmer's work.

White's work is ambitious in scale; an early criticism was that it was too long.[16] Like Palmer's opera it has something of the experimental about it. Both prospered initially through direct melodic quotation; in so doing it is arguable that they opted for immediate success at the expense of the lesson from central Europe that suggested that distillation of the rhythm and character of a native music would prove more enduring. However, this is a view that is not held universally, as will be seen below.

It can be seen that this conscious determination to cultivate an 'Irish' opera centred on the years following achievement of some measure of independence when it appeared, almost a necessity, to fashion native arts that proclaimed a distinctive national personality. But the genesis of the move to a native opera lay some two decades earlier and found its first fruit in *Muirgheis* by the ele-

15 See *Irish Times* (12 August 1924), 4.   **16** See *Irish Times* (16 August 1924), 8.

gantly named O'Brien Butler. To this opera, produced in Dublin in December 1903, falls the honour of being the first opera to employ an Irish text. The nationalist credentials of the first performance were enhanced with the participation of members of the Keating Branch of the Gaelic League as the dancers. The notices in the daily journals in the first week of December 1903 proudly proclaimed *Important production – First Irish Grand Opera*.[17] The opera opened on Monday 7 December with a company of over 100 'composed entirely of local artistes'.[18] The following day's review spoke of a reasonably sized audience which was probably a reasonable return given the presence of the Brodsky Quartet in the Royal Dublin Society on the same day. However the remainder of the review did little to encourage the same for the remaining days of the week's run. The critic noted that 'it must be confessed that Muirgheas does not possess the elements of popularity'.[19] Then to add to the insult he proceeds with corporate authority to note that 'we do not think that it is more characteristically Irish than Stanford's Shamus O'Brien'.[20] The amateur status of the performers was noted with the comment that 'the chorus and the principals did their best'.[21]

The libretto for *Muirgheis* was the adaptation of *The Sea Swan* by the short-lived Nora Hopper Chesson.[22] Chesson was the archetypal Celtic Twilight poetess whose early *Ballads in Prose* (1894) were much admired by W.B. Yeats who talked of her 'birdlike little verses'. In a letter he recorded:

> I cannot resist the pleasure of writing to tell you of the great pleasure your exquisite book has given me. It is the most finished, the most distinguished volume we have had out of Ireland this decade.[23]

The admiration was more than reciprocated; Chesson's writings owed much to Yeats. She was also much influenced by the land of her father's birth, although she was born in Exeter and lived in England. However, in shaping the plot for *Muirgheis* she was helped not by Yeats but by George Moore although the result did not find favour with his friend, Edward Martyn. The plot of the opera was planned by the composer and the intention was that the work be redolent of his native Kerry. In addition O'Brien Butler's intention was that everything should be 'sung from first to last' and that:

> all are more or less stamped with the character of Irish traditional music ... The band parts yield none of that strepitous which many modern com-

---

17 See for example the *Irish Times* (5 December 1903), 6.   18 *Irish Times* (7 December 1903), 4.   19 *Irish Times* (8 December 1903), 5.   20 Ibid.   21 Ibid.   22 Chesson's name can occasion confusion. She is occasionally referred to by her maiden name and this is sometimes represented as Harper.   23 W.B. Yeats to Nora Hopper, 27 January 1895, in John Kelly (ed.), *The Collected Letters of W.B. Yeats (1865–1895)*, I (Oxford: Clarendon, 1986), 432.

posers are so fond of, but are always full enough for the requirements of the situation.[24]

Edward Martyn, a man of singular judgment and little diffidence when it came to giving of his views, thought highly of O'Brien Butler as one 'whose work is intensely national from the colour it has taken from the folk'.[25] More telling perhaps is the additional comment:

His interesting experiments, after his being saturated by the folk, entitle him to be the father of Irish composers.[26]

The assessment reveals more of Martyn than of O'Brien Butler and invites the unfortunate reflection that it was a literal saturation that ultimately is what is remembered of a composer who was to perish in the sinking of the Lusitania in May 1915.[27] *Muirgheis* is a love story that is inconsistent in treatment. After a respectable overture and strong first act the following two acts move more in the manner of a ballad opera with choruses aplenty of fairies and wedding guests and with a succession of traditional dances. The music is original throughout with the exception of one threnody that O'Brien Butler recalls hearing in his youth.[28] The composer employs a stringent economy and consciously cultivates an Irish style that, notwithstanding the technical limitations and unevenness, result in a work of some merit.

If musicology teaches the import of context and if the predominant context for music in Ireland at the turn of the nineteenth century was the prevailing nationalist sentiment, allowance must also be made for the supporting literary movement that had aspirations beyond the immediate. Thus not all compositions can be seen as utilitarian or as reactions to the mood of the moment. Michele Esposito's operetta *The Postbag* first produced at St George's Hall, London in January 1902 by the Irish Literary Society provides example of yet another form of response. Written to a libretto by the prolific poet, Alfred Perceval Graves, it provides example of Esposito's judicious choice in matters of literary alliance. This acumen was earlier evident in Esposito's success in the first Feis Ceoil competition of 1897 with his dramatic cantata *Deirdre* where the text was provided by T.W. Rolleston. *The Postbag* was followed by a second opera, *The Tinker and the Fairy* op. 53, an accomplished dramatic work in a single act. The libretto on this occasion was provided by Douglas Hyde, one of the guiding figures of the literary revival, a founder of Conradh na Gaeilge, and later destined to be honoured as the first President of the Irish

24 *Freeman's Journal* (7 December 1903), 4.   25 E. Martyn, 'The Gaelic League and Irish Music', *The Irish Review,* I (Dublin, 1911), 450.   26 Ibid.   27 For a more detailed critical assessment of *Muirgheis,* see this author's PhD dissertation 'Nationalism and Music in Ireland' (National University of Ireland, 1991), 334–341.   28 See composer's preface, *Muirgheis* (New York, 1910).

Musical Example 3.2: Michele Esposito,
The Tinker and the Fairy, 'O Tree ...'

Republic. Whereas Ó Ceallaigh can be criticized for his prolix style, Hyde is a master of the essential and Esposito is well served by the simplicity and concision of his writing. Again based on a legend with echoes of the later *Eithne* theme, the story concerns just three characters and a high-voice chorus. An old fairy woman meets with a handsome youth and is refused her wish of a kiss. She then meets with a feckless but happy tinker who enjoys none of the youth's advantages. He honours his promise to grant the fairy one wish and kisses the old woman who is transformed into a young and beautiful maid. However, their consequent embrace and promise of joy together is thwarted when the chorus of fairies call the maiden back to her own world and the tinker is left forlorn. While the parts of the fairy (soprano) and tinker (baritone) are demanding, the work can be performed with small orchestra or even with piano; the quality of the collaboration between poet and composer deserves more frequent airing than it currently receives. Notwithstanding its small scale, it is a work of integrity and focus and there is something to lament in the fact that such intelligent cooperation between cultivated artists was not built upon in the decades that followed. Esposito employs a rich harmonic palette. Thus the lyrical simplicity of the old fairy's initial lament for her aged condition is all the more striking. (Ex. 3.2)

Yet another form of response is provided by a curious opera that Sir Walter Parratt awarded the prize at the Feis Ceoil in 1903. This was W. Harvey Pelissier's *Connla of the Golden Hair*. The composer on this occasion provided both libretto and music for a work in two scenes that is scored for a quartet of principals, chorus, and full orchestra. The composer forges some unity in his creation through the use of a detailed table of *leitmotivs* that betray more than a passing debt to the more complex use of this devise to be found in Wagner. The audience for *Connla of the Golden Hair* would need to be versed in the different *leitmotivs* of a) psychological significance, b) of identification, and c) of suggestion in order fully to appreciate Harvey Pelissier's concept. This fact may well suggest why the work remains essentially a curiosity. The following phrase, for instance, is that of the Fairies: it is described as a theme of psychological significance representing ideal happiness and the endless charms of Fairyland.

Fairy theme

Musical Example 3.3: W. Harvey Pelissier, *Connla of the Golden Hair*, 'Fairy Theme'

Throughout this period there was a calculated reaction to the dominant anglophone tradition. *Muirgheis* is occasionally referred to as the first native Irish opera; an eminence dependent wholly on the use of an Irish text. Chesson's

Musical Example 3.4: Robert O'Dwyer, *Eithne*

original libretto was in English and the opera was first published in the original and it wasn't until 1910 that Breitkopf and Härtel published the work with
translation by Tadgh O'Donoghue and the proud claim to be the first Irish
opera. In reality that honour goes to Robert O'Dwyer's *Eithne* which has an
original Gaelic libretto by Tomás Ó Ceallaigh.

O'Dwyer is one of the more colourful characters in this record. Like
Chesson and Palmer, he was born in Britain of Irish parentage. He too shared
in the fascination with things Irish but unlike them he became an absolutist in
outlook; for the first three decades of the twentieth century he became the
most outspoken apologist for an insular music. Born in Bristol in 1862, he settled in Dublin in 1897 adopted the then fashionable patronymic prefix as tes-
timony of his determination to be of Ireland. For his remaining years he
evinced the zeal of the convert. *Eithne* remains his most significant composi-

tion. It tells the history of Ceart, the eldest son of the high king of Ireland, and his struggle against family treachery and his enduring love for the beautiful Eithne. It contains no spoken dialogue and is less folksy an opera than *Muirgheis.* There is a choral bias in the work that betrays O'Dwyer's other interests and while the opera has much to recommend it, it does not reveal its creator to be an inspired melodist. Even the heroine's first entry, which comes relatively late in the opera, is somewhat less arresting than might have been anticipated. (Ex. 3.4)

O'Dwyer's opera *Eithne* was first staged at the Rotunda in Dublin in August 1909 as part of the Oireachtas Festival. The latter had been founded as an adjunct to the Feis Ceoil and came about essentially from dissatisfaction at the cosmopolitan outlook of the Feis Ceoil. There is irony then in the following extract from the first review which overall is positive.

> The latter scenes of the opera are distinctively and emphatically suggestive of anything except what one would be led to associate with the purely Celtic musical style. In fact the reminiscences of Verdi and of the good old Italian method are made so strikingly manifest as to induce one to say that merely to convey the well-accustomed scena, duet, and choral refrain which recall Ernani or the Troubadore does not, because conveyed in Gaelic, constitute the work Irish in any sense or form.[29]

There can have been few observations better calculated to annoy O'Dwyer. He offers a ready target; his trenchant advocacy of a limited artistic vision and alacrity in attacking the views of others do not combine to incite sympathetic understanding. Yet the benchmark employed not only in the criticism quoted above but in many others of the day provides a fair flavour of the age. If context is at issue here, it must also move us to some empathy with the composers of the time. They lived in a fervid atmosphere of national expectation; few could be expected to have the artistic integrity or independence of a William Butler Yeats. It is for this reason that one must tread gently here while admiring even more the consistency of Esposito.

One of those who shared O'Dwyer's vision and warmly welcomed his work was the Lurgan-born Annie Wilson Patterson who holds the distinction of being the first woman to be awarded a doctorate in music from the Royal University; the award was conferred in the decade prior to her central role in the establishment of the Irish national festival Feis Ceoil in 1897. Her advocacy of a national music found outlet in her teaching in Cork, in her writings, and in occasional compositions including two operas, *The High King's*

29 *Freeman's Journal* (3 August 1909), 2.

Daughter and *Oisin*. These works are doubtless consistent with her thinking which is clearly evident in her response to O'Dwyer's opera.[30] In her role as musical commentator in the Cork-based *Journal of the Ivernian Society*, Patterson noted with approbation that *Eithne* had partially been written *in the old modes*.[31] The fact that she proceeds quickly from the particular to the general suggests that in her view O'Dwyer's opera was not the answer but merely a step towards the answer.

> In fact, from Debussy and foremost moderns of the day, we Irish may gather much of what might be done in creative departments with our native music, on the strength, too, of many traditions of our own which the dust of forgetfulness has only too long obscured. Unlike the Frenchman's, however, our music need never gain a celebrity for its 'vagueness'. Based on the definite symmetry and rhythm of our rich folk-song, the Nature-music of Ireland can well soar to the heights which shall be beyond that indefiniteness which, after all leads nowhere. We should indeed – those of us who write music for the country – endeavour to work out a distinctive school of our own. It may take generations to do so, but meanwhile laudable efforts like Mr Robert O'Dwyer's opera are worthy warm encouragement. Were more openings available, it may be assumed that more such native works would be produced, until at length, let us devoutly hope, we should unearth a masterpiece would take away for ever from Erin the reproach that she has produced nothing deserving of record in the higher phases of musical art.[32]

Patterson's vision of the composer as national labourer, as creative patriot, says much about the age and helps to explain the constraints on the emergence of a truly original vision. It is precisely this atmosphere of expectation that precluded the progression from works of real merit such as those of Esposito. In addition there was the factor that not much was expected of original composition by Irish men and women; consider, for instance the following comment of the distinguished critic Fuller Maitland during the course of a review of the life and work of his former mentor Stanford:

> ... his rare mastery of the resources of orchestra or voices, the thoroughness of his workmanship, and his remarkable skill as a teacher of composition, are qualities not generally associated even with the more brilliant natives of Ireland.[33]

---

30 No copy of her operas has been found to date.   31 'Notes on Music', *Journal of the Ivernian Society*, II (September 1909), 56–63   32 Ibid., 59–60.   33 J.A. Fuller Maitland, 'Stanford', in H.C. Colles (ed.), *Grove's Dictionary of Music and Musicians*, 3rd edn, v (London: Macmillan, 1929), 119.

Fundamental to Patterson's thesis, and one subscribed to by many, is the notion of forging a distinctive style from the elements of a venerable tradition. Some decades later John Beckett in a perceptive article in *The Bell*, argued strongly the opposite view that, essentially, what was required was not development but creativity: 'man must always change his cry, ... he can never repeat it'.[34] The twentieth century and especially the first half of that century gave rise to polarized views. That there should have been such an active debate is probably positive in itself but it proved ultimately inimical to creative industry. The truth, if there is a truth, is that a native style is more likely something innate, something that takes of the mood, the rhythm, the pacing of a song tradition but is not something that can be consciously forged. It will take rare talent to achieve such a fusion. Interested observers are inevitably drawn to the conclusion that such a talent is only likely to emerge from a people that value music and that set in place a consistent infrastructure that will support a thriving and varied musical expression.

34 J. Beckett, 'Music', *The Bell*, xvii, 2 (May, 1951), 57.

4

Modernism in Ireland and its cultural context in the music of Frederick May, Brian Boydell and Aloys Fleischmann

PHILIP GRAYDON

When Fergal Tobin wrote that 'Ireland is a very peripheral part of the western world, whose enthusiasms it has not always been in the habit of sharing',[1] he penned as good a précis of the status and concomitant stasis of Irish cultural life for the greater part of the twentieth century as any other commentator. Thus the nineteenth-century romantic-nationalist ideal of an art music wholly contingent on the ethnic repertory persevered after independence, deeming those who pursued more universal aims as being 'Anglo-Irish, or even anti-Irish', according to Aloys Fleischmann.[2]

In general, cultural life in the new state was dominated by a largely contrived, inherited vision of Ireland projected by 'artists, poets and polemicists, despite the fact that the social reality showed distinct signs that the country was adapting to the social forms of the English-speaking world and that conditions in rural [and indeed urban] Ireland were hardly idyllic'.[3] De Valera's 'Irish Ireland' curbed 'the acknowledged social-psychological power of the arts as developed in the tradition of modernism' and deemed it corruptive, especially the experimental internationalism of James Joyce who, in *Portrait of the Artist as a Young Man* (1916), wrote prophetic words for the first generation of Irish modernist composers:

> I will tell you what I will do and what I will not do. I will not serve that in which I no longer believe, whether it call itself my home, my fatherland or my church; and I will try to express myself in some mode of life or art as freely as I can and as wholly as I can, using for my defence the only arms I will allow myself to use, silence, exile and cunning.[4]

---

1 Fergal Tobin, *The Sixties: The Best of Decades* (Dublin: Gill & Macmillan, 1984), 1. **2** Aloys Fleischmann, 'Composition and the Folk Idiom', *Ireland To-day* i/6 (1936), 44. **3** Terence Brown, *Ireland: A Social and Cultural History* (London: Fontana, 1981/2nd edn 1985), 98. **4** Ciarán Benson, 'A psychological perspective on art and Irish national identity', *Irish Journal of Psychology* xv/3 (1994), 324.

According to Terence Brown, the general ideological climate was one in which:

> the theme of Irish traditions was staunchly reiterated in reviews of plays, exhibitions and concerts. An attitude of xenophobic suspicion often greeted any manifestation of what appeared to reflect cosmopolitan standards. An almost Stalinistic antagonism to modernism, … Surrealism, free verse, symbolism and … modern cinema was combined with prudery … and a deep reverence for the Irish past.[5]

It was against this background that Frederick May, Brian Boydell and later, Aloys Fleischmann, expressed the belief that the future of Irish composition lay in orientation towards contemporary developments in Britain and Europe. As Joseph Ryan notes: 'what critically distinguishes … [May and Boydell] is not only their courageous artistic stand, but that they were the first Irish composers of the modern era to study abroad and have the opportunity to be exposed to the most advanced current compositional approaches'. However, both 'were to suffer from engaging in a medium that would find little understanding, not to mention sympathy, with an audience unversed in its language'.[6] Fleischmann, who also studied abroad in a rather conservative climate in Munich from 1931 to 1933, 'demonstrated a progressive method moving from a path parallel with that taken by John Larchet to an increasing espousal of the cosmopolitan outlook advocated' by May and Boydell.

This essay also examines (in a largely unprecedented fashion) the cultural background from which each of the composers in question emerged and the milieu in which they lived. As each composer was, by virtue of his background, essentially separate from the *hoi polloi*, it was in this conscious decision that, as highlighted below, *un*conscious elements of that tradition seeped into their creative endeavour, thus lending their work a distinctive but innately drawn 'Irish note', in places.

It was May who 'led the way', as Boydell later commented, as the pioneer of Irish musical modernism by being the first composer to evade the 'folk-music trap'.[7] Born in Dublin in 1911 to middle-class Protestant parents, May attended the Royal Irish Academy of Music from 1923 to 1929, before taking an external MusB degree under John Larchet's tutelage at Trinity College, Dublin, in 1931. He continued his studies at the Royal College of Music from 1932–1935 under Vaughan Williams and Gordon Jacob; it was for Vaughan Williams's music, in addition to that of Mahler, Sibelius and Berg, that May developed an

5 Brown (as n. 3), 147. 6 Joseph J. Ryan, 'Nationalism and Irish Music', in: Gerard Gillen and Harry White (eds), *Music and Irish Cultural History*, *(Irish Musical Studies 3)*, (Dublin: Irish Academic Press, 1995), 111. 7 Denis Donoghue, 'The Future of Irish Music', *Studies* xxxxiv (Spring 1955), 111.

abiding passion which permeated the greater part of his career. A travelling studentship for his *Scherzo for Orchestra* (1933) was to have enabled him to study with Berg in Vienna in 1936. However, Mahler's disciple died in December 1935 and May consequently studied there for a short period under Egon Wellesz.[8]

Between 1933 and 1956, May's output was highly distinguished[9], but the advancement of otosclerosis (breeding tinnitus and gradual deafness) made composition thereafter impossible; his later life was continuously overshadowed by alcoholism and ill-health, both physical and psychological. He died on 8 September 1985.

As commented on by Boydell, Axel Klein rightly asserts that May 'strove for the European avant-garde, or ... was at least fascinated by it intellectually';[10] thus he was quite unlike Fleischmann, who did not wholly eschew the national outlook and, as Boydell later noted, was 'tottering on the brink for some time [until] Freddie and I dragged him into our camp!'[11] In fact, May's more subtly 'inclusive' stance is evident from his first major work, the aforementioned *Scherzo for Orchestra*.

Composed at the age of twenty-two, the work evinces an early understanding for colourful orchestration.[12] The introduction is a cataclysmic *Allegro feroce*, resplendent in texture, with powerful cross-rhythms driven by the percussion section. A short transitional section presages a dramatic *tutti* enunciating a clear pentatonic melody based in C minor which, along with its added rhythmic emphasis in May's imposition of two crotchets against three, supports Axel Klein's postulation that in comparison with his string quartet, references to the composer's Irish heritage are more overt in this work as a whole.[13]

---

8 Wellesz was to emigrate from his increasingly Nazi-controlled homeland to England, where he continued to compose but more notably forged a very successful career as a pioneering scholar in Byzantine chant studies. This interest in turn began to inform his works, which also saw a reversion to tonality compounded by an attempt to perpetuate Mahler's legacy in his symphonies. As Joseph Ryan notes, May's works after the *String Quartet in C minor* (it having been largely written before the latter's sojourn in Vienna) suggest Wellesz' influence in their abandonment of dodecaphonic tendencies in preference for a harmonic language that recalled Mahler and Reger (after Joseph Ryan, 'Nationalism and Music in Ireland' (PhD diss., National University of Ireland, 1991, 412).   **9** Sarah M. Burn, 'Ceoltóirí Éireannacha – Irish Musical Portraits: A Series of Performers, Composers and Collectors: 6. Frederick May', *NCH Calendar*, May 1993.   **10** Axel Klein, 'The Composer in the Academy (2) 1940–1990', in: Richard Pine and Charles Acton (eds.), *To Talent Alone: The Royal Irish Academy of Music 1848–1998* (Dublin: Gill & Macmillan, 1998), 420.   **11** Boydell in Michael Dungan, 'Everything except team games and horse-racing', *New Music News* (February 1997), 11.   **12** This could have been due to the influence of Gordon Jacob (1895–1984); some forty years later, the latter still remembered May: 'A small, rather schoolboyish figure packed with musical talent. His music had its own character even then, and his manuscript showed decision. He was certainly among my really talented pupils' (cited in O. S., T. [Tomás Ó Suilleabháin ?: see *n*. 40 below]: 'Spring Nocturne – a Profile of Frederick May', *Counterpoint* ii (1970), 14). Jacob was an acknowledged authority on orchestration and its technique, and wrote several books on the subject during his forty-year tenure at the Royal College of Music (1926–66).   **13** Klein (as n. 10), 421.

Example 4.1: May: String Quartet in C minor I, bars 1–8

This yields to a lyrical, second major theme presented in the violins and answered by the first clarinet. Although Joseph Ryan seems justified in pinpointing the influence of Mahler at this juncture[14] (certainly in the opening of the first presentation of the theme), Klein's above-mentioned assertion also holds fast, as evidenced in the second part of the theme and its clarinet answer, by their use of 'gapped' scales, and in their various guises throughout.

14 Ryan, 1991 (as n. 8), 405.

The *Scherzo* was, in many respects, a 'supranational' piece; yet despite the influence of Vaughan Williams, and without recourse to pastiche or Stan-fordesque stage-Irishry, its distinctly 'ethnic' elements succeeded in subtly representing its composer's cultural identity without compromising his mod-ernist stance. An even greater degree of refinement in this regard was achieved in May's next work, the avowedly internationalist String Quartet in C minor, partly composed in Vienna in 1936. Hailed by Boydell in 1985 as the 'first really significant composition by an Irish composer – certainly of the present century',[15] its revolutionary status was confirmed by the work's arresting opening which one could be forgiven for mistaking as an exercise in Second Viennese school-serialism. (See Ex. 4.1)

However, this approach is eschewed in favour of a less constrained atonal-ity.[16] Notwithstanding its internationalism, its innate 'Irishness' shines through in the 'brighter' sections of the piece. The first motif of the third movement, as Klein has noted, 'with its multiple variants in the course of the piece is a clear reference to his Irish heritage',[17] without a hint of 'hat-tipping'.

Example 4.2a: May: String Quartet in C minor III, bar 477

The same can also be said of a later, equally tranquil section, which in into-nation rather than construction leaves one with a subtle scent of its composer's nationality. (See Ex 4.2b)

In common with his colleagues Fleischmann and Boydell, May was influ-enced not only by his cultural environment, but also by the natural or physi-cal one. It was this concern that fuelled a later work: the *Spring Nocturne* of 1937. It begins impressionistically with a dark Winter setting which gradually brightens with the coming of Spring. Although it is in no way (as with most

15 Boydell, Brian: Script for 'A programme commemorating Frederick May, who died on 9 September 1985 [*sic*]', prod. Dan McHale (1st broadcast RTÉ Radio 1, 9/1985), 1.   16 Ryan, 1991 (as n. 8), 412. 17 Klein (as n. 10), 421.

of May's works) overtly Irish, there is a certain atavistic quality to the piece, underlined by the first statement of the main theme. This plaintive, wide-spanning melody in C major with a simple but effective use of the flattened third (incidentally, a characteristic of Irish ethnic music) stands testament, perhaps,

Example 4.2b: May: String Quartet in C minor III, bars 570–576

to May's apparent wish (like Fleischmann and Boydell) to write nationally (or rather *naturally*) – reflective, yet contemporary music.

May's next major work was the *Lyric Movement for String Orchestra* of 1939. Fanny Feehan, although discounting the modernist effect of the composer's Austrian studies, quite justifiably contended that '... it is most definitely related to Strauss or Mahler from the point of view of the richness of its string sonorities'.[18] It also contains 'Irish' allusions (rather than references) and a distinctly 'Irish' turn-of-phrase. May's largest and most ambitious composition followed in 1941. The expressionistic *Songs from Prison* for baritone and large orchestra relate the story of a political prisoner who gains solace from watching swallows building their nest outside his cell window. However, his happiness is cut short as the prison guards deliberately destroy the nest. May's settings were appended in the guise of a final poem that linked the fate of the swallows with that of the millions persecuted by Hitler during the Holocaust.[19] This obvious anti-Fascist resonance could also be interpreted as acting for May on a closer level also: 'the creative torpor, the dead weight of tradition, imprisons the compositional spirit in Ireland'.[20]

May's firm opposition to the prevailing nationalist idiom did not, however, prevent him from directly succumbing to it. Although probably spurred by financial difficulties, he did in fact avail of Radio Éireann's commissioning scheme for arrangements of Irish 'folk' music, most notably contributing the *Suite of Irish Airs* in 1953.[21] However, a voice quite alien to that which he had actively espoused, characterised by 'an expression without marked personality or commitment', is heard immediately from the opening of the first movement, *Ga Gréine* (The Sunbeam). (See Ex. 4.3)[22]

Indeed, May's 'marked personality and commitment' had steadily waned by this time, and *Sunlight and Shadow*, composed in 1955, was his last work. Hailed by many as his best, it did not prove to be May's last word – in 1974, he commented:

> I have great respect for Vaughan Williams ... He seemed to think salvation [from the domination of Wagner and his ilk] lay in English folk music. I'm not sure if he was right ... I think he recognised earlier than most composers that *there was a danger that the international market would be overtaken by serial and atonal music, leaving no room for national flavour* [my italics]; and this is why he tried to establish an English national musical tradition.[23]

18 Fanny Feehan in: Hugh MacDiarmid, 'A Tribute to Frederick May', *May*: String Quartet in C minor, (Dublin: Woodtown, 1976), [*iii*]. **19** Fanny Feehan, 'Frederick May: The Forgotten Genius', *Sunday Tribune*, early 1980s [?]. **20** Harry White, *The Keeper's Recital: Music and Cultural History in Ireland, 1770–1970* (Cork: Cork University Press, 1998), 136. **21** Ryan, 1991 (as n. 8), 426. **22** Ibid., 427. **23** May in: Kent, Kay: 'Kay Kent talks to Frederick May', *Irish Times*, 12 December 1974.

Music Example 4.3: May: *Suite of Irish Airs*, bars 1–9 (strings only)

Surely if the reason behind May's repudiation of the modernism he so cogently evinced in the *Scherzo*, the string quartet and the *Songs from Prison* is sought, one should look no further than the above statement. However, the crux of the issue was to follow:

> If I hadn't been afflicted in this way, I'd have liked to try to bridge the national-international gap myself. This is something that Seán Ó Riada never quite managed to do ... there was always a dichotomy between his Irish music and the work with which he achieved international recognition. The gap is a hard one to bridge for an Irishman.[24]

That May noted and would have endeavoured to bridge such a 'gap' is a sure indication of his (understandably) bi-cultural leanings. For unlike the afore-mentioned Ó Riada, who seemed to find self-advertised, personal and musical fulfilment in a quasi-mystical 'Gaelic' lifestyle and identity, perhaps May

---

[24] Ibid. One could, of course, apportion this description to May himself (which may have been the reason for his raising such a point, certainly in reference to the second part of the statement). Indeed, the similarities inherent in the viewpoints and career fortunes of both composers is alluded to by Harry White (see White, 1998, as n. 20, 135–6).

(during his 'active' years) increasingly saw himself as the nexus between a 'European' and an 'Irish' compositional mindset. Thus his efforts to promote himself as such in the face of cultural stagnation and official ignorance are all the more noble; Charles Acton's description of May as 'our Sibelius *manqué*', though regrettable in its resonance, is thus most apt.[25]

However, perhaps it is better to remember him for what he *was*, rather than what he could have been: 'a fervent advocate of cosmopolitanism who ... hoped to ignite belief in the search for an individual style, free from the constraints of national stereotypes'.[26]

The youngest of the triumvirate, Brian Boydell, was born in Dublin on 17 March 1917 and educated at the universities of Cambridge and Heidelberg, the Royal College of Music and the Royal Irish Academy of Music. After gaining external MusB and MusD degrees from Trinity College, Dublin, in 1942 and 1959 respectively, Boydell went on to become professor of music there from 1962–1982, revolutionizing both the tenure and character of the post, and creating an honours school of music. His retirement saw him gain recognition as an esteemed historical musicologist, publishing two books on music in eighteenth-century Dublin.[27] He died on 8 November 2000.

Boydell was born to a Protestant Anglo-Irish family of the rising upper middle class.[28] In the inter-war period, the Anglo-Irish usually distanced themselves from the new Irish *bourgeoisie*, preferring to perpetuate the look eastwards for their moral and social values, their political views, and for the education of their children. As Boydell commented: 'For families of my background, the usual thing to do was to send your son to school in England: to learn good manners and get rid of the awful "brogue".'[29] A brief period in Germany followed, although he later admitted: 'I was too steeped in cultural interests, and too immature to be politically aware (except in disturbing retrospect) of what was going on [there] at that time.'[30]

After obtaining first class honours in natural sciences at Cambridge, Boydell's musical education began in earnest at the Royal College of Music in 1938, where he studied voice, oboe and composition, the latter under

25 Charles Acton, 'Frederick May: an appreciation', *Irish Times*, 10 September 1985. 26 Jeremy Dibble, 'The Composer in the Academy (1) 1850–1940', in: Pine and Acton (as n. 10), 417. 27 Brian Boydell, *A Dublin Musical Calendar 1700–60* (Dublin: Irish Academic Press, 1988) and *Rotunda Music in Eighteenth-Century Dublin* (Dublin: Irish Academic Press, 1992). 28 I follow here the detailed account of Boydell's cultural background (based on an interview) in: Daniel Murphy et al., *Education and the Arts* (Dublin: Trinity College, 1987), 219–229. 29 Boydell in: 'All my Enthusiasms', prod. Anne Makower (1st broadcast RTÉ Network 2, 1/1998). 30 Boydell quoted in: Axel Klein, 'Irish Composers and Foreign Education: A Study of Influences', in: Patrick F. Devine and Harry White (eds) *The Maynooth International Musicological Conference: Selected Proceedings, Part One, (Irish Musical Studies 4),* (Dublin: Four Courts Press, 1996), 281.

Patrick Hadley and Herbert Howells. However, his studies were curtailed a year later by the outbreak of the Second World War, and as he revealed:

> When I came back to Ireland after being educated in England you could-
> n't get a good job unless you spoke Irish. I had the greatest difficulty in
> being accepted as an Irishman because I had the wrong type of voice ...
> I'm always slightly embarrassed about my background ... And I had quite
> a struggle right throughout my life ... trying to identify myself with the
> people that I really felt I belonged to. So I saw the 'other side of the coin'
> and really 'sat on the fence'.[31]

Boydell's avowed position of 'sitting on the fence' meant, in effect, that he expressly went 'neither one way or the other'[32]; thus he asserted himself as a cosmopolitan Irishman of eclectic interests. Juggling painting and music as potential careers he chose the latter, and in 1949 won the Radio Éireann Chamber Music Prize for his String Quartet No. 1 op. 31, which along with the orchestral *In Memoriam Mahatma Gandhi* (1948), can be considered among the composer's major early works. These works saw the maturation of Boydell's musical language through his employment of the octatonic scale,[33] a feature that was to characterise his style as his career progressed.[34] The next decade witnessed what was perhaps (notwithstanding the achievement of the first quartet) one of the most accomplished works of Boydell's *œuvre*: the Violin Concerto op. 36 of 1954.

Described by Fleischmann as 'brittle [and] energetic with moments of quiet',[35] the work exhibits a quirky, undercurrent admixture of *Mitteleuropa* and innate, ethnic Irish elements, giving a vivid and pungent vitality to its musical language. An early 'moment of quiet' for the soloist (after the 'energetic' opening) sees the plaintive second theme which, akin to a similar moment in May's quartet, is unmistakably Irish (bars 92–94).

> There is one particular little figure which keeps cropping up in my music,
> and I notice it keeps cropping up in Irish folk music. It's completely uncon-
> scious, it just happens. I think I use the sort of characteristic Irish melis-
> mata unconsciously ...[36]

This theme, cast in the Dorian mode beginning on the note c" over a bare harmonic backing, is then enunciated an octave higher and added to, before a reversion to its original register is appended by an example of the 'character-

---

31 Boydell, 1998 (as n. 29).   32 Ibid.   33 An eight-note scale that alternates tones and semitones.   34 Gareth Cox, 'Octatonicism in the String Quartets of Brian Boydell', in: Devine and White (as n. 30), 266.   35 Fleischmann, Aloys: 'Brian Boydell', *Hibernia* xxxii/9 (1968) (Music Supplement).   36 Brian Boydell in: Charles Acton, 'Interview with Brian Boydell', *Éire-Ireland* v/4 (1970), 105.

istic Irish melismata' at bar 103. As Axel Klein comments, the effect of an old Irish lament is thereby evoked.[37]

Music Example 4.4: Boydell: Violin Concerto I, bars 102–104
(solo violin and strings only)

The above-mentioned melisma of the work's first movement, which pointed strongly to its composer's nationality, is what helps to add a new depth of expression to the second; indeed, Boydell himself once remarked upon the *Lento* as being 'very Irish'.[38] The opening features an exotic, octatonic melody for the soloist contributing to an overall sonority that evokes Bartók, before being 'capped' by the now familiar melisma.

Another striking example of the use of ethnically-'inspired' material is in the String Quartet No. 2 op. 44 of 1957. Cast in two movements, the work starts in a mood not unlike the first quartet, with a tentative motif for solo viola 'answered' by a similar line in the cello 'in which the harmonies, with their bare fourths and fifths', as the composer described, 'owe something to the flavour of certain types of mediaeval music'.[39] This leads to a phrase-ending

37 Axel Klein, *Die Musik Irlands im 20. Jahrhundert* (Hildesheim: Georg Olms Verlag, 1996), 227.   **38** Boydell in: Acton, 1970 (as n. 36), 105.   **39** Brian Boydell, 'Boydell: String Quartet No. 2', programme notes for 'Brian Boydell: 80th Birthday Celebration', National Concert Hall, John Field Room, Tuesday 25 March 1997.

with a definite 'Irish' character in its 'gapped' sonority, as it draws to a close (bars 6–10). The cello re-enters with the above-mentioned theme suffixed by the 'Irish melisma':

Music Example 4.5: Boydell: String Quartet No. 2/I, bars 1–15

The same high level of craftsmanship is also evident in Boydell's more pictorial works. 1966 saw Yeats' poetry, in addition to that of other figures from Ireland's revolutionary period[40], providing the inspiration for *A Terrible Beauty is Born* op. 59. The work, for SAB soli, SATB, symphony orchestra and speaker, was commissioned by RTÉ for the commemoration of the 1916 Easter Rising. Boydell's transition from *enfant terrible* to *doyen* of the musical establishment was, by that time, virtually complete in order to quantify the offering to him of the commission; but its significance was nevertheless telling. He commented:

> I am always interested in challenges. A particular challenge was the 1916 music, *A Terrible Beauty is Born*. That interested me enormously because … I was so much excited by the fact that I was offered the commission at all, being Protestant Anglo-Irish and a pacifist to boot.[41]

Boydell's relish for challenges is also evident from his forays into the world of film and radio music[42] A fruitful working relationship with Paddy Carey for a number of documentary films provided the inspiration for Boydell's *Symphonic Inscapes* op. 64 (1968), revealing how it 'grew out from feelings about the Irish countryside' and his particular interest in archaeology.[43] Using the apt term of Gerard Manley Hopkins,[44] Boydell succeeded in crafting an evocative, imaginative and yet *mostly* abstract work; though a work based on the 'feeling' of Ireland's natural terrain by a sensitive artist is bound to be subjective in places. Thus even though *Symphonic Inscapes* is one of Boydell's more 'uncompromising' works in musico-linguistic terms, it nevertheless is permeated by that unconscious ethnic Irish influence that so naturally and tellingly pervades his output. A slow section that occurs early in the piece exemplifies this trait (bars 192–7): here a variation of the cornerstone 'open' motif of the introductory bars is found in the harp and brass; this prefaces a hexatonic melody in the oboe, accentuated by its syncopated beginning and lyrical melodic contour.

In conclusion, it should be evident that the cultural context for Boydell's modernistic and highly personal style had a profound and, in some respects, desired effect on his output. This was, in essence, the secret of his art: it was

---

40 Francis Ledwidge (1887–1917), Thomas MacDonagh (1878–1916), George Russell (1867– 1935), George Sigerson (1836–1925) and Thomas Kettle (1880–1916). It should be noted that a significant contribution to Boydell's selection of poetic texts, especially in this work, was made by his friend (and co-member of the Dowland Consort), Tomás Ó Suilleabháin. The aforementioned ensemble was founded and directed by Boydell, and was particularly active in the 1960s. **41** Boydell in: Acton, 1970, (as n. 36), 103. **42** Ibid., 103. **43** Boydell in: 'Music and the Musician', prod. Jane Carty (1st broadcast RTÉ Radio 1, 7/1974) **44** In his lyrics, Hopkins (1844–89) attempted to evoke the essential quality of his subject, its individuation or 'inscape' as he termed it, by the use of internal rhyme, alliteration, compound metaphor, and the use of 'sprung rhythm', i.e. the use of a combination of regular numbers of stresses with freely varying numbers of syllables.

his emphatic cosmopolitanism that makes instances of the 'Irish note' in Boydell's music all the more indirect and enriching.

The third and last composer for discussion is Aloys Fleischmann. In 1980 he made the telling admission: 'The folk idiom is pretty strong in my early work, and I suppose it is still there.'[45] For Fleischmann, the advent of musical modernism in Ireland presented its own personal challenge to him as man and musician: the striking of a path between tradition and innovation. Although perhaps not an uncommon crisis for any twentieth century artist of note, it is the fashion in which he dealt with this matter that makes him a fascinating figure.

Born in Munich in 1910 to immigrant musician parents who had settled in Ireland, Fleischmann became a quintessential Corkonian in later life and professor of music at University College, Cork, from 1934–1980. He died after a short illness in 1992.

His pluralist attitude to matters musical was symptomatic of an education divided between Cork and Munich[46]; this fuelled an early compunction to assert his cultural identity with Ireland and things Irish, thus initially making his line considerably softer than those of his compatriots. However, his youthful ardour for a 'Gaelic art-music' using 'contemporary technique' while 'rooted in the folk music spirit' was quelled by the late forties as his compositional *modus operandi* became increasingly dichotomous in nature. Thus Fleischmann 'donned' two 'hats': a fairly diatonic, populist style exemplified in orchestral works with/without audience participation, that fulfilled commissions for public events, and were indicated by titles with 'Irish' connections, was counter-balanced by a more individual, detached and abstract voice found in the smaller-scale works which espoused modernism and cognisance of contemporary technique.[47]

It is with acknowledgement of this dichotomy that one must approach his music. At the outset of his career, Fleischmann adopted an Irish pseudonym (Muiris Ó Rónáin) for his first major work: the *Piano Suite* (gaelicized as *Sreath de Phiano*) of 1933. Fleischmann even persuaded its publisher, Chester, to print the performance directions in Irish, in addition to the conventional Italian. This very visual indication of where Fleischmann's sympathies lay was further underlined by his *raison d'être* for leaving Germany: 'I was never so enthusi-

---

45 Fleischmann in: 'The Arts: Profile of Aloys Fleischmann', prod. Dan Collins (1st broadcast RTÉ Radio 1, 7/1974). **46** Joseph J. Ryan, 'Fleischmann: *Piano Quintet*', sleeve notes for CD 'Frederick May: String Quartet/Aloys Fleischmann: Piano Quintet', Marco Polo 8.223888 1995 [1995]. **47** I follow Axel Klein's reasoning here with regard to the logic behind Fleischmann's compositional career. See Axel Klein, 'Aloys Fleischmann', in: Walter-Wolfgang Sparrer and Hans-Werner Heister (eds.), *Komponisten den Gegenwart* (edition text + kritik, Ninth Supplement, February 1996); *idem*: 'The Composer in the Academy (2) 1940–1990', in: Pine and Acton, 1998 (as n. 10) 419–28 (esp. 426); and Klein, 'Aloys Fleischmann: An Inspiration', in: Ruth Fleischmann (ed.), *Aloys Fleischmann (1910–92): A Life for Music in Ireland Remembered by Contemporaries* (Cork: Mercier, 2000), 309–13. See also Séamus de Barra, 'The Music of Aloys Fleischmann: A Survey', ibid., 325–48 (esp. 339–344).

astic about Ireland and its traditions as I was in Munich. I wouldn't for the world stay [there], the Celtic pull was too strong.'[48]

This affinity with 'Celticism' formed the backbone of Fleischmann's output for some years afterwards. But it was the mythology, history and literature of Ireland that resonated more throughout his corpus; 'It seemed vital', he wrote, 'to delve into the Hidden Ireland[49] and out of the heroic tales and romances to create an idiom which would express in music some of the essence of this rich untapped literary tradition'.[50]

The *Piano Suite* saw an attempt on its composer's part to demonstrate the possibilities of diatonic modal writing in a compositional climate which, in the wider European sense, had embraced serialism.[51] This description, allied with Fleischmann's own opinion of his early style as being 'terse and austere … not too esoteric'[52] encapsulates the musico-linguistic 'setting' here perfectly. At a glance, one notices the transposed Aeolian mode beginning on E outlined in the right-hand at bars 1–5 and a characteristic 'Irish' rhythm at bars 2, 3 and 7 while the placing of a duple rhythm against this syncopated figure serves to highlight its 'quirkiness'. Bars 9–12 see Fleischmann conscious of European pianistic heritage, certainly in terms of technique, where the figuration of Liszt is recalled in the rapid, wide spacings interspersed with a derivation of the rhythmic 'tag' outline above. (See Ex. 4.6)

Axel Klein's comment in regard to the rhythm of the work as a whole, that 'one feels the jig sooner that one hears it',[53] is especially apt in regard to the opening of the fifth movement.

Another of Fleischmann's early works to reflect the 'Celtic' note was the *Piano Quintet* of 1938. However, the dropping of the Gaelic pseudonym for his first Irish première 'as himself,' and the adoption of a more abstract form, also signified an increased catholicity of styles and influences in its make-up. The pensive opening of the *Allegretto* that starts the work establishes its dialogic construction while the rhythm underlines its more gentle Irish 'flavour'. As Joseph Ryan comments, the work is 'eclectic with a range of echoes from Stanford to Delius …';[54] the influence of the former is certainly apparent in the

48 Michael Dervan, 'Unflagging Energy': Interview with Aloys Fleischmann, *Music Ireland* (5/1990), 7.   **49** *The Hidden Ireland: A Study of Gaelic Munster* was a book by Daniel Corkery (1878–1964). First published in 1924, this study of Irish poetry and culture in eighteenth-century Munster was a curious influence on Fleischmann; its espousal of a narrow sense of cultural separatism, as promulgated by the Irish Ireland movement, would seem to have flown in the face of his avowed pluralist approach to music. However, it is telling that Corkery was one of a considerable number of the contemporary cultural *intelligentsia* to have frequented the Fleischmann family home during the composer's youth. (Sean Dunne, 'A life given to music', *Cork Examiner*, 15 January 1986).   **50** Séamus de Barra, 'Fleischmann the Composer', *New Music News* (September 1992), 7.   **51** Anthony Quigley, 'Fleischmann: *Piano Suite*', sleeve notes for LP 'Charles Lynch/Piano Vol.1' NIRC [New Irish Recording Company] NIR 001 1971.   **52** Fleischmann in 'Books and Bookmen: Interview with Aloys Fleischmann', pres. Des Hickey (recorded RTÉ Radio 1, 2/1978).   **53** *'Man spürt den Jig eher als daß man ihn hört.'*: quoted from Klein, 1996 (as n. 37), 187 (my translation).   **54** Ryan, 1995 (as

Music Example 4.6: Fleischmann: *Piano Suite* I, bars 1–11

euphonious section in D major that begins at bar 34 and follows the introduction, while Fleischmann's later 'modernist' works are foreshadowed in the astringent harmony and fragmentary texture found later in this movement. (See Ex. 4.7)

To paraphrase Ryan, Fleischmann's overall approach in this and later works was one founded on a conscious proposition to represent the Irish condition.[55] Although his next work of note, *Clare's Dragoons* (1944), was resolutely nationalist in orientation and populist in its musical language, as his career progressed his modernist 'hat' was increasingly worn. One of the first clear

n. 46)   **55** Ibid.

Music Example 4.7: Fleischmann: *Piano Quintet* I, bars 211–214

examples of this departure was the song-cycle *The Fountain of Magic* of 1946, which included bitonal elements and the use of varying metre while maintaining a semblance of traditional thematic development by use of short melodic and rhythmic units.[56] The composer's *Introduction and Funeral March* (1960), later extended and in this guise named *Sinfonia Votiva* (1977), displayed a more serious, contemplative side of his compositional character that contrasted with the many slight, commissioned works for mostly non-professional ensembles of the fifties and sixties.

Fleischmann continued this tendency towards modernism into the seventies but the resultant works were not all necessarily serious in nature. This fact was perfectly exemplified by *Cornucopia* for horn and piano, commissioned for the Dublin Festival of Twentieth Century Music in 1970. Presented in a version for orchestra a year later, the erudite wit underlying the broad interpretation of the work's title results in solo-writing of melodic and inventive fecundity befitting of the 'horn of plenty' in its title. The imaginative opening asserts a harmonic language and resultant sound-world which were notably advanced of anything heard heretofore in the composer's output:

A further commission for the above-mentioned Dublin Festival of Twentieth Century Music was *Tides* (1973) a song-cycle for mezzo-soprano and piano that, like *Cornucopia*, was adapted for orchestra a year later but with the addition of a harpsichord. In the first setting of four, 'King and Queen', man is seen as a ritual image; the use of harpsichord bespeaks telling acknowledgement of its revival in twentieth-century music while lending a new and somewhat eerie quality to the orchestral colour. The vocal writing is characterized by understatement, which later leads to heightened expression. The

---

56 Klein (as n. 47) 9.

Music Example 4.8: Fleischmann: *Cornucopia*, bars 1–6

Music Example 4.8 (*continued*)

third setting, entitled 'A Dream of July', is, as Boydell asserts, 'serene as a girl in a Botticelli painting'.[57] This description is underlined by the writing for both voice and solo violin: the Bergian lyricism of the latter showing that 'modern' music need not be shorn of beauty.

The broad wit that circumscribed the above-mentioned *Cornucopia* of the early seventies was brought to the fore in Fleischmann's compositional swan-song, *Games*. Composed in 1990 (two years before his death), the piece was scored for choir, harp and percussion. Despite Fleischmann being an octogen-erian at this stage, it astonished the audience at its première in Cork with its 'vir-tuosity, vigour and vehemence'.[58] Indeed, the second movement, 'The Nail', is testament to this acute observation in its sheer momentum and visceral energy:

However, his ineffable humour shines through at the movement's close with a whimsical spoken ending. The fact that *Games* probably stands as Fleischmann's last work is telling; it was, perhaps, his way of indicating where his true stylistic leanings lay after a compositional career characterised by a public/'private'-populist/modernist dichotomy.

Though open to innovation and less often making use of clear 'Irish' refer-ences after the forties, the youthful respect for tradition that spurred his early quest for a 'Gaelic art-music' did, it seems, remain with him throughout his life. Perhaps his admission of 1980 – to reiterate: 'The folk idiom is pretty strong in my early work, and I suppose it is still there' – can thus be viewed as a tacit acknowledgement of an underlying 'debt' to the ethnic repertory; his monu-mental posthumous publication, *Sources of Irish Traditional Music 1583–1855*, certainly attested to his scholarly interest in the subject.[59] As Séamus de Barra writes: 'Aloys Fleischmann was keenly aware of his position as one of the first group of native composers to live and work in Ireland': '… how to be Irish in a larger European context [was] a question that lost none of its urgency' for him.[60]

To conclude, I think 'cultural context' begs further examination. It was, per-haps, inevitable that any lasting engagement between Irish art music and mod-ernism would entail a solution to the 'national question' in Irish composition: in various periods and to varying extents, each composer provided their own answer. As adverted to above, May and Boydell were the first to consciously by-pass it, even if the pitiful lack of a support system for music and its prac-titioners led to competent, if uninspired, 'folksong' arrangements for com-mercial gain on the part of the former which were worlds apart from his masterly string quartet. For Fleischmann, a bid to coalesce elements of the

57 Boydell in: 'Sixty Years of Irish Radio: The Irish Composers', prod. Jerome de Bromhead (1st broad-cast RTÉ Radio 1, II/1986).   58 Burn, '5. Aloys Fleischmann', (as n. 9)   59 Aloys Fleischmann, *Sources of Irish Traditional Music 1583–1855* (New York: Garland, 1997).   60 de Barra (as n. 50), 7.

Music Example 4.9: Fleischmann: *Games*, I bars 1–25

ethnic tradition with inherited art music techniques, and a realisation of their inherent incompatibility, led to a conscious adoption of two, fundamentally dislocated styles.

But it should be obvious, too, that their familial and social backgrounds were also vital in creating who and what they were. This important factor is most clearly evidenced in Fleischmann and Boydell. Fleischmann, as already seen, though raised in the country, was not even Irish by birth, despite his hypothetical wish to the contrary; thus his name and aforementioned bifurcated compositional character displayed a plurality that remained with him throughout his life. Boydell's cultural background was similarly apart from the Irish social mainstream. However, it was his concomitant 'West British' accent and manner that caused him to feel alienated. Thus the concept of a 'multiplicity of Irishness' comes to the fore: such an abstraction was not as common a currency as it is in today's more pluralistic society.[61] May, also

61 Pine, 'Maturity, 1922–1998', in: Pine and Acton (as n. 10), 345; The original quote from Pine's essay is:

Music Example 4.9 (*continued*)

nominally Protestant, probably endured similar difficulties; in early independent Ireland, relatively few Protestants were regarded as 'truly' Irish unless (like Douglas Hyde) they were outspokenly pro-Irish culture, or (like W.B. Yeats) they expressed a strong *public* Irish identity.

'When May wrote in 1935 of cultural life and cultural practitioners being equally fragile and vulnerable, by virtue of the fact that a nation did not exist, that there was a "a multiplication of private languages, but no vehicle for communication", such a sense of identity was not available to him' (Pine's own quotation is from Frederick May, 'Music and the Nation', *Dublin Magazine* xi (July–September 1936), 51).

Music Example 4.9 (*continued*)

However, it should be noted at this juncture that while all three composers
were in their various ways outside the norms of a highly conservative Irish
society, they were not outcasts; nevertheless, they felt drawn, as a consequence
of their avowed artistic modernism, to wider European musical (and cultural)
concerns. In their determined 'internationalism' (in the most literal sense of
the term), May, Boydell and Fleischmann courageously, if unconsciously,
adhered to the 'dictum' that (to paraphrase Michael Kennedy) there is no such
thing as Irish music, only music by Irish composers.[62]

'Music seems to be a key to identity because it offers, so intensely, a sense
of self and others, of the subjective in the collective'.[63] Cultural identity, it
seems, was a concept that concerned the triumvirate, even from their youth.
Another binding factor was that their experiences or awareness of Nazism
(during their respective periods of foreign study) brought the effects of
'extreme' nationalism into sharp relief, thus informing their aversion of similar practices as applied to culture (and especially music) in Ireland. As Axel
Klein asserts: 'Fleischmann's Munich, Boydell's Heidelberg and May's
Vienna were overshadowed by this fatal ambition.'[64]

62 Michael Kennedy, 'Foreword to the Second Edition', *National Music and other Essays*, Ralph Vaughan
Williams (arr. Kennedy) (Oxford: Oxford University Press 1963/2nd edn. 1986), viii.   **63** Simon Frith,
'Music and Identity', in: Stuart Hall & Paul du Gay (eds.) *Questions of Cultural Identity* (London: Sage,
1996), 110.   **64** Klein (as n. 30), 281.

May, Boydell and Fleischmann's achievements as the harbingers of Irish musical modernism, in light of the cultural context, are manifold. In their inclusive view of creativity in Irish music, and their conscious look to Europe, they succeeded in de-shackling composition from the folk idiom. That their music is imbued with (on the whole) subtle 'Irish' hints is merely concomitant of their nationality and the nature of the modernism they introduced from the thirties to the fifties which was characterised by 'stylistic tensions' prevalent in this period – 'elements which contribute to the creation of any identity'.[65] For May, Boydell and Fleischmann, being artistically 'modern' constituted being *both* Irish and European: in a phrase, forging the universal without repudiating the particular.[66]

65 Fiona Clampin, "'Those Blue Remembered Hills'": National Identity in English Music: 1900–1930', in: Keith Cameron (ed.), *National Identity* (Exeter: Intellect, 1999), 75.   **66** Derived from comment ascribed to Fleischmann by Ryan, 1995 (as n. 46).

5

Interval cycles and inversional axes in Frederick May's String Quartet in C Minor

ROBERT W. WASON

In 'a tribute to Frederick May', which appears right after May's own programme note at the opening of the score to this quartet, Hugh MacDiarmid
writes that an earlier critic is correct 'in discounting the modernist effect of
[May's] studies in Austria'.[1] Both MacDiarmid and the earlier critic (Fanny
Feehan) would prefer to see May as a 'landmark in Irish music because [as
she puts it], "he was the first Irish composer to work without leaning on a
background of the Irish mode".'[2] Whether the 'modernist effect' arose from
May's studies in Austria is itself debatable, as we shall see shortly, but completely 'discounting the modernist effect' – especially in the quartet at hand,
which 'established [May's] position among Irish composers'[3] – risks serious
misunderstanding of this work, for 'modernist' compositional techniques identified with such apparently disparate composers as Webern, Berg and Bartók
figure prominently in the quartet.

Though this work was premiered in 1948, it was actually composed much
earlier, near the end of May's student career. On graduation from Trinity
College, Dublin, in 1931, May went on to the Royal College of Music in
London, where he studied with Gordon Jacob and Ralph Vaughan Williams
for an additional three years. After the RCM, his *Scherzo for Orchestra*, written and premiered in 1933, won him a travelling fellowship, and he planned
to study in Austria with Alban Berg. But alas, Berg died, completely unexpectedly, in December 1935, just before May arrived in early 1936. The young
composer instead undertook studies in Vienna with Egon Wellesz, a student
of Schoenberg's from the Berg-Webern generation, but also Professor of
Musicology at the University of Vienna and a recent recipient of an honorary
doctorate (Oxford, 1932). Given Wellesz' cosmopolitan point of view (he

---

1 Frederick May, *String Quartet in C Minor*, Score, Dublin: Woodtown Music Publications, 1976. It
should be noted that Feehan was referring specifically to May's *Lyric Movement for Strings* (1943),
Feehan, *Hibernia*, 6 October 1971. 2 Ibid. 3 Kitty Fadlu-Deen, 'Frederick May', in: Stanley Sadie
(ed.), *The New Grove Dictionary of Music and Musicians* (London: Macmillan, 1980), vol. 11, 851.

grew up in a wealthy Viennese family with international connections), his own music, and his activities on behalf of contemporary music throughout Europe (he was one of the founders of the ISCM), he must have been an ideal intermediary between the Second Viennese School and this young foreign student.[4] Wellesz understood – and probably took great interest in – the "national" characteristics of music, and the task confronting an 'Irish Composer'. But whether or not Wellesz was the 'right' teacher for May, there can be no doubt that Berg would have been fascinated with the work that May was involved in when he arrived in Vienna: his *Quartet in C Minor*. As George Perle has shown, the notion of the 'interval cycle' is absolutely basic to Berg's music. A further development of this technique is the 'inversional axis', resulting from the simultaneous use of two interval cycles that are inversionally related (Perle's 'P and I cycles' and 'sum dyads')[5]. These techniques compete with more conventional tonal techniques in May's quartet.

The compositional history of this three-movement quartet – and even its date of composition – is not entirely clear. In the foreword to the score, May claims that 'this work was written in 1936, shortly after I had returned from a period of study in Vienna ...'[6] This claim seems to have given MacDiarmid the notion that May learned his modernist compositional techniques during his Austrian study. But in his own note, May goes on to say that 'the middle section of the impetuosamente [the middle movement] was suggested to me by the death of Alban Berg, [24 December 1935], which occurred while I was at work on the music.'[7] Such a claim strongly implies the existence of the first half of the second movement prior to Berg's death, and, very likely, the whole of the first movement as well, given the close relation of these movements with regard to thematic material and compositional technique. Finally, a little further on in the same note, May remarks that 'the slow final movement, incidentally, was the first to be written.'[8] If this movement existed even before the first and second, then clearly most of the piece was written before May arrived in Austria; in claiming that the piece was 'written in 1936'[9], May must have been referring merely to the writing of the final draft of the work. Two more recent sources likewise assume that the piece was largely written before May's study in Vienna.[10] One, Joseph Ryan, goes so far as to see his Viennese study with Wellesz as the crucial event that took him *away* from modernism and back in the direction of Mahler, recapitulating Wellesz' own artistic develop-

4 Robert Layton, 'Egon Wellesz', in: Stanley Sadie (as n. 3), vol. 20, 334–7. **5** George Perle, 'Berg's Master Array of the Interval Cycles', *Music Quarterly* 63/1 (January 1977), reprinted in: Perle, *The Right Notes* (Stuyvesant, NY: Pendragon, 1995), 207–35. **6** May (as n. 1). **7** Ibid. **8** Ibid. **9** Ibid. **10** Joseph Ryan, 'Nationalism and Music in Ireland' (PhD diss., National University of Ireland, 1991), 405. See also Philip Graydon, 'Modernism in Ireland and its Cultural Content in the Music and Writings of Frederick May, Brian Boydell and Aloys Fleischmann', MA thesis (NUI Maynooth, 1999).

ment.[11] Indeed, the very fact that May would desire to study with Berg in the first place implies that his modernist proclivities were part of his compositional technique well before he actually set foot in Vienna.

As the title and key signature imply, May did intend the piece as a 'tonal' work (though much of it might be termed 'pitch-centric' in current music-theoretic parlance); the techniques by which 'tonality' or 'pitch-class centricity' are produced in the piece vary considerably, however, and May's documented compositional influences offer some help both in addressing them and providing a more general context. In an interview from the early seventies, first on the list of May's 'most admired composers' was 'Beethoven of the late quartets.'[12] It seems not unreasonable to conjecture that Beethoven's op. 131 Quartet in C# Minor may well have been the model for May's first conception of the work, which ultimately became the last movement: key, mood, thematic profile and its quasi-fugal unfolding – all these features may be adduced in support of this conjecture. Example 5.1a provides the theme of the last movement of May's quartet; 5.1b shows the opening of Beethoven's op. 131:

Music Example 5.1a: Frederick May, String Quartet in C Minor,
bars 477–478

Music Example 5.1b: Beethoven, String Quartet in C# Minor, op. 131, bars 1–4

The rest of May's list is also of interest: when we read 'Bartók and ... particularly his exploration of the string quartet form', it is tempting to place the opening of Bartók's First Quartet (which also seems to evoke op. 131) in the line from Beethoven to May, though the pieces Bartók was writing during May's formative years call to mind the interval cycles and inversional axes. Certainly the final form of the Quartet, which begins in C minor and ends in C# minor, evokes Mahler, who appears on May's list, and was the all-important influence on Wellesz. It is as though the final 'transcendent' C# minor of

11 Ryan (as n. 10), 412.   12 'Kay Kent talks to Frederick May', *Irish Times*, 12 December 1974.

the last movement emerges from the worldly turbulence of the opening C minor, a 'directional' tonal plan that Mahler would certainly have endorsed.[13] 'Directional tonality' plays an important role within movements as well: for example, in the first movement, the strong arrival in C minor – the 'structural downbeat' of the work (bar 17) – quickly yields to further working out of the same theme (now with a consequent added) in C# (bars 22–30; the consequent occurs with the upbeat to bars 28 and 29) and then in D (bars 30–40; this time the consequent is extended sequentially in bars 41–43, followed by a gradual dissolution of D in bars 44–53). Moreover, the final ordering of movements (sonata, scherzo and *lento espressivo*) recalls Mahler, though without a 'final movement'.

The relatively clear tonal structure of the last movement suggests that the interval cycles which open the final version of the piece (in a largely non-tonal environment: first movement, bars 1–16) may well have begun as by-products of a more traditional tonally conceived composition. Example 5.2 provides a graphic interpretation of the theme of the last movement given in Example 5.1a. Observe, in particular, the compound melodic structure of the second half of the theme: the lower line fills out the typical chromatically-filled descending tetrachord in C# minor from c#'– g#', while the upper line elaborates the third (e–g#) of the diatonic ascending pentachord, c#"– g#'.

Music Example 5.2

Though this analysis seeks to normalize the theme within a conventional C# minor, there can be no doubt that the prominent (and unresolved) F# in the second half of the first measure suggests an underlying pentatonic (and folk-influenced) structure as well. The second half of the theme gives rise, at later points in the third movement, to diatonic lines juxtaposed with chromatic lines in contrary motion (see for example, bars 497–503, and its reappearance in the recapitulation, bars 597–601, where the effect is heightened by double counterpoint). But at no point do pure chromatic contrary-motion structures take over, though such events are crucial to the first and second movements, as we shall see shortly.

---

13 Extensive contributions to the study of 'directional tonality' appear in a collection of articles on tonal practice in late nineteenth-century music that emerged from an international conference on the theme 'Alternatives to Monotonality'. See William Kinderman and Harald Krebs, eds., *The Second*

INTERVAL CYCLES, THEIR COMBINATIONS, AND INVERSIONAL AXES

In a seminal article, George Perle shows the following music from Berg's *Wozzeck*, which provides an actual musical demonstration of the combination of four interval cycles, and one non-cyclic line (the top one). Incidentally, it is clear that May knew this piece[14]:

Music Example 5.3: Alban Berg, *Wozzeck*, II, bars 380–381

Perle began his article with a chart of interval cycles that Berg included in a letter of 27 July 1920 to Schoenberg, in which Berg writes out a uni-intervallic succession of each of the twelve 'simple' intervals, arranged from an octave to a semitone in progressively decreasing order. (Berg assigns the

Practice of Nineteenth-Century Tonality (Lincoln and London: University of Nebraska Press, 1996). **14** May is quoted as saying, 'I must say that I could never really understand the doctrine of the Schoenberg school ... It certainly produced some wonderful work, like Berg's *Wozzeck*, and so on; but if you look at the subject matter, it is all of the most horrifying nature'. Kent (as n. 12).

traditional diatonically-based names to each, but frequent notational 'bumps' – e.g., A♭ to F# in the 'whole tone' progression – show that he is thinking in an equally tempered 12-tone pitch-space.) Most importantly, he carries each interval iteration through at least to the point that it reaches the same pitch class from which it began, but now in a different octave. The chart (and its many empty spaces and 'etc.'s) show that the length of the 'repetition-cycle' of each interval (paired with its inversion) is different, as determined by the divisors of twelve equally-tempered tones: $12/6 = 2$ (2 'tritones' divide an octave); $12/4 = 3$ (3 'major thirds'); $12/3 = 4$ (4 'minor thirds'); $12/2 = 6$ (6 'whole-tones'); the cycles of minor seconds/major sevenths and perfect fourths/fifths are all of length 12, the result of dividing 12 (and multiples of it) by intervals of 1, 11, 5 or 7 semitones.

The idea of reaching the octave (or some multiple of the octave) is important to this use of interval cycles. I would suggest that the reaching of the octave suggested the traditional 'scale' to composers looking for analogies to traditional tonal practice, and that the notion of scale in turn replicates the general tonal conditions of 1. statement of tonal centre, 2. departure, and 3. return to tonal centre. Thus, just as a traditional diatonic scale is more than a 'seven-note collection', so too is the 'whole-tone scale' more than a 'hexachord', etc., in this context. The all-important difference from traditional tonality, of course, is that the diatonic scale, with its many properties that tend to reinforce the notion of a tonic (a dominant that divides the octave in such a way as to give clear priority to the lower fifth over the upper fourth, the leading tone, etc.) gives way to a succession of intervals of equal size. A further development of this technique is the *combination* and alternation of interval cycles, still producing octave duplication. Thus, the interval-3 cycle may be interpreted as 1+2 or 2+1 resulting in the 'octatonic scale', or the interval-4 cycle may be 3+1 or 1+3, recently dubbed the 'hexatonic scale', to cite the most prevalent of these.[15] At the outset (of the octatonic scale, in particular), the alternation of interval type may seem to simulate the directed motion of the diatonic scale, but this quickly recedes as the repetitive pattern takes shape. In such constructs, pitch-class priority depends purely on a sense of 'pattern completion' and closure brought about by memory of the opening pitch.

Another way in which the matter of pitch-class priority has been addressed in such cyclic contexts is the notion of 'inversional axis'. In general, we can define an inversional axis as the 'centre' of two simultaneously unfolding lines (of pitch-classes) that are *inversionally* related. In the present context, each line may be a cycle, or a combination and alternation of cycles. In fact, just as

---

15 See, for example, Richard Cohn, 'Maximally Smooth Cycles, Hexatonic Systems, and the Analysis of Late-Romantic Triadic Progressions', *Music Analysis* 15/1 (March, 1996), 9–40.

Berg's chart implicitly combines *different* interval cycles proceeding in the same direction (by convention, 'P'–or prime-cycles), it is possible to combine different cycles (and combinations of cycles) that are inversionally related ('P' and 'I' cycles). However, for purposes of the present discussion, we focus entirely on combining interval cycles of the same type that are inversionally related. Of those, we are most interested in the 1-cycle–the 'chromatic contrary motion structures' that I alluded to earlier. In essence, there are only two ways to do this: one scheme results in all of the 'even intervals' (measured in semitones) between parallel components of the cycles; the other results in only the 'odd intervals'. Example 5.4a shows the Even Cycle; Example 5.4b shows the Odd Cycle, as we shall call them.

Music Example 5.4a: Even Cycle

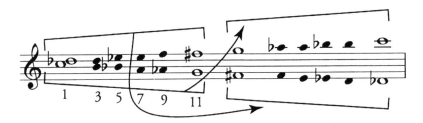

Music Example 5.4b: Odd Cycle

The 'centre' of the Even Cycle is obvious: the unison and octave (0s) that are formed from some arbitrarily chosen starting point and its tritone (further registral expansion only increases the sense of 'pitch doubling' here). In its formation of these 0s, the Even Cycle would seem to have potential for use as a tonal surrogate. (By constructing Example 5.4 so that it is symmetrical around pitch-classes C and G♭, the example is directly transferable to May's quartet.)

In contrast, the Odd Cycle presents a complete redistribution of the total hexachordal pitch-class content after the midpoint of the cycle, as shown in the example. By analogy to the Even Cycle, we can consider the 'centre' of the Odd Cycle to be the semitone and major seventh (intervals 1 and 11), but its effect as a 'tonal axis' is certainly equivocal. Not surprisingly, the Odd Cycle is basic to twelve-tone operations that seek complete saturation of all 12 pitch-classes (e.g., Schoenberg's 'inversional combinatoriality' of rows, and his prohibition of octave doublings). The Even Cycle, on the other hand, is an important contributor to tonal centrism in Bartók, but curiously, it is also at home in 'twelve-tone music', where it can produce a kind of 'twelve-tonal centrism', as in the more famous works of Webern, or Dallapiccola, for example.

INTERVAL CYCLES AND INVERSIONAL AXES
IN THE OPENING OF MAY'S QUARTET

The remainder of this article will concentrate on an application of the theory we have just discussed through a close reading of the first sixteen bars of May's String Quartet in C Minor. A score may be found on pp. 92–3. (I will refer to this passage below merely as the 'opening'; we shall leave a discussion of its formal significance to the end of this article.) Little justification of this myopic view is necessary: however the first sixteen bars may have evolved in the compositional process, there can be no doubt of their striking effect, their importance in setting up the rest of the piece, and their recurrence – literal and transformed – at important junctures in the work. We conclude with a few remarks on the possible implications of our analysis for a more comprehensive understanding of the work.

The very beginning of the piece presents an important conflict: C/Db. Though spelled Db, its presentation in bar 1 suggests 'C#', a chromatic inflection between C and D natural, and momentarily we might suspect a conventional (diatonic) tonal context. If, in fact, B and D do represent a dominant chord, however, they give way quickly to a chromatic filling-out of the c"–c'" octave, partitioned rhythmically into interval 3s, suggestion a 'hexatonic' C–Eb, E–G, Ab–B, division. However, the resolving C in bar 3 quickly changes to an interval-4 partitioning of the C–C octave, filled in by whole tones on down beats (C [Bb] Ab Gb E D C). All of this still seems to support the idea of C as the primary tone, but Db intrudes on the last beat of bar 4, seemingly anticipating a varied restatement of the opening, four-bar idea.

Bar 5 begins with what seems at the outset to be a 'counterstatement' of the opening 4-bar phrase, but instead, it continues to develop the contrary motion lines of the opening five beats of the piece. Upon comparison of the music with the two inversional schemes presented in Example 5.4, it is apparent that the Odd Cycle (Example 5.4b) more closely approximates the actual music, though up to the end of bar 6 it is also possible to interpret it as derived from the more conventional contrary motion scheme presented below, in Example 5.5 (which might recall the opening of Schubert's *Quartettsatz*):

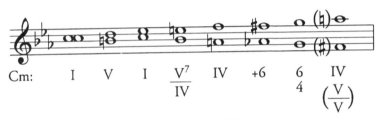

Music Example 5.5

Bar 7 clarifies, however: the bar presents the complete Odd Cycle unequiv-ocally, starting from interval 1, and moving to its tritone (downbeat of bar 8), underscored by the *crescendo* and arrival of *ff*. Most importantly, the Odd Cycle has the effect of equalizing C and D♭ – of elevating the earlier implied conflict to a much more audible one. As this conflict gradually comes to the fore, this three-bar, compressed continuation (bars 5–7) of the opening four-bar phrase propels the music to the downbeat of bar 8, and what will be, in fact, the largest registral expanse of this opening sixteen bars: the cello's low C to the violin d♭‴. This immediately overlaps with new activity.

Bar 8 marks the first appearance of a texture that will be prominent in the rest of this 16-bar segment, and elsewhere in the work: the first violin, second violin, and viola proceed in parallel major first inversion chords, while the cello moves in contrary motion to the prevailing first violin line. Thus the passage, like the previous music, reduces to two-part counter-point, though the top part is now 'filled out'. Example 5.6 presents the octave-length succession of first inversions with the bass-line in contrary motion (aligned according to the Odd Cycle) of bars 8–9 out of rhythm:

Music Example 5.6

Comparing Example 5.6 to the music, it is clear that the rhythmic setting and repetition obscure the simplicity of the technique; moreover, as the semiquavers reach the quavers and the down-bow marking in bar 10 (second half of third beat), May switches to the Even Cycle, which the music holds to through the first quaver of bar 10. This change is quite clearly articulated by register expanse and rhythmic motive, and will be linked-up by the listener to Even-Cycle events to come shortly.

The second quaver of bar 10 (down bow) marks a return to the Odd Cycle, and a continuation of the same pattern demonstrated by Example 5.6 (the upper lines start a minor third higher, the lower line a minor third lower). This likewise fills an octave : e'–e" in the first violin, and a–A in the cello, and at the expected point (bar 11, second half of beat three), the music switches again to the Even Cycle, though one that is apparently symmetrical around B/F, not C/F#. Why? Here, I suggest that we must keep in mind longer-range linear connections in this *Allegro*: thus I would maintain that the first violin eb" (bar 10) connects to db" (end of 11), and thence back to eb" (bar 12); all of these are supported by the cello A. In this context, the db" is a 'neighbour' to the surrounding Ebs, which initiate contrary-motion Even-Cycle activity in bar 13, reverting to the downbeat clarity of bar 7 for the first time, this time emphasizing the Even Cycle. As part of the move towards the arrival of C in bar 17, Even-Cycle motivic activity is now in descent, in direct contrast to the previous ascent of the Odd Cycle. Example 5.7 shows the first-inversion form of the Even Cycle; chords are displayed in ascending motion to make clear the relationship of Example 5.7 to Examples 5.4a, 5.4b and 5.6. Examination of the score will show that all vertical formations are taken from this cycle, though their ordering in the actual music is now quite different:

Music Example 5.7

Thus, the conflict of C/Db is moving towards solution in favour of C. Indeed, bar 12 even contains two C first-inversion triads pitted against the obligatory C bass, but placed rhythmically so that they are 'passing chords' that elaborate contrary motion 2-cycles (whole-tone lines from the scale that does not contain C) at the crotchet level.

Bar 13 initiates a counterstatement and eventual dissolution (through fragmentation) of the material of bar 12 and the upbeat to it. This time, the crotchet level 2-cycle lines are from the other whole-tone scale: the one that does contain C (and G♭), in effect preparing still further the strong arrival of C in bar 17.[16] Indeed, they approach a seemingly inevitable octave C, as is shown in Example 5.8:

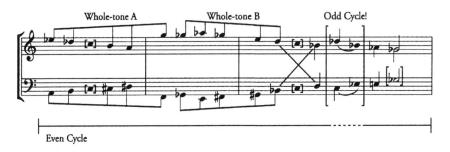

Music Example 5.8

But just as they are about to converge on C on the third beat of bar 14, the first violin moves instead to D♭, causing a return to the Odd Cycle on C/D♭ and revival of the C/D♭ conflict.[17] Bar 15 rectifies the situation with an immediate move back to the Even Cycle, pitches chosen to be as tightly packed around G♭ as possible. Indeed, the dichotomy of Odd Cycle on C/D♭ at the greatest registral expanse of this passage presenting the C/D♭ conflict in starkest terms (opening of bar 8), versus the penultimate convergence through the Even Cycle to the smallest registral expanse (the unison g♭' of bar 15) epitomizes the drama of this extraordinary opening gesture. Thus we come to the end of our close reading.

But what is the larger function of this passage: is it the 'first theme', or an 'introduction', in a movement that seems to invoke the conventions of 'sonata form'? This is more than an idle question of 'formal analysis', for it speaks to some difficult issues, including, for example, the very different compositional techniques that lie at the base of bars 1–16, as opposed to bars 17–55. Though the opening 16 bars return literally – and untransposed – at the beginning of the 'recapitulation' of the opening movement (bars 238–55), we remain uncomfortable not thinking of them as introductory, given the sense of tonal (and structural?) downbeat that arrives in bar 17. True, we can call upon the famous 'Tempest' Sonata (op. 31/2) of Beethoven, in which the

---

16 Incidentally, the Woodtown score contains quite a number of mistakes; one of these is apparently the first violin e♭" on the upbeat of 3 in bar 13; f" would seem to be called for. The Vanbrugh Quartet agrees in their recorded performance (Marco Polo 8.223888).   **17** The first violin d" should be d♭".

'structural' (and certainly the tonal) downbeat of the first movement does not arrive, arguably, until the transition to second theme enters (bar 21). But Beethoven's bars 21ff seem clearly transitional in their simplicity of motivic structure and modulatory progression (given stylistic conventions, they are not 'melodic'). May's quartet presents us with the opposite situation: the opening 16 bars are 'simple' motivically (and hence 'unmelodic'), and 'headed towards' C, as our close reading demonstrates, while bars 17ff present a melody that clearly states a modal key area, though admittedly it continues according to the directional tonal plan described earlier. At present, my preferred characterization of the opening is that it acts in a way not unlike the famous 'fourth chords' of Schoenberg's *Kammersymphonie*, op. 9 (perhaps yet another influence), a passage that recurs at important junctures in the piece as a sort of 'refrain', but is very different from other 'thematic' music from a compositional-technical point of view. (The passages are also similar in that they are based on interval cycles.) This notion of a 'refrain' might be made to account for the appearance of the opening at bar 60 in the 'exposition', where it seems to signal the entrance of a 'second theme' (bar 80) – a passage that also returns, though much abbreviated, in the recapitulation (bars 276–80). Yet another instance of the opening as a formal 'signal' is the clear statement of the Even cycle around C that begins the 'development section' (upbeat to bar 114).

As is obvious from the somewhat scattered remarks with which I close, much work remains before we can claim to have a satisfactory analysis of this piece. Such work will surely expand and refine – or refute – my tentative sonata analysis, but it will also have to explore the 'modal' tonal language in this piece and others by May, and the interaction of that language with the more non-tonal techniques I have described here.[18] Certainly the exploration of May's modal language will engage the question of May's relation to indigenous Irish music as well, but I leave that to Irish ethnomusicologists. In concentrating on my limited topic, I only hope to have made a secure if small step towards the level of understanding that May's music merits.

---

18 In what is the most substantial writing on this piece to date, Axel Klein takes an 'organic-motivic' approach to the analysis of the piece, showing, for example, the pervasiveness, throughout all three movements, of the cello semiquaver motive first presented in bars 2–3. See his *Die Musik Irlands im 20. Jahrhundert* (Hildesheim: Georg Olms Verlag, 1996), 189–95.

Music Example 5.9: Frederick May, String Quartet in C Minor, Opening

Music Example 5.9: *contd.*

6

An Irishman in Darmstadt: Seóirse Bodley's *String Quartet no. 1* (1968)

GARETH COX

Having once been the most avant-garde Irish composer of his day, Seóirse Bodley now finds himself in the role of elder statesman following the recent demise in the 1990s of a whole generation of senior Irish composers that included Aloys Fleischmann (1910–92), Gerard Victory (1921–95) and Brian Boydell (1917–2000). He was the first Irish composer to become intimately acquainted with (and accept) the post-war avant-garde aesthetic and his three summers spent at the Internationale Ferienkurse für Neue Musik in Darmstadt in the 1960s introduced him to the exciting (if often cerebral) developments in international contemporary composition. This article deals with one of the final works of what could be described as his 'Darmstadt Period' of the 1960s, namely his *String Quartet no. 1* of 1968, a piece which represents not only the peak of his personal modernism but also marks a watershed in his compositional career between two styles.

Before 1968 there are few examples of compositions written in the string quartet genre in post-war Ireland.[1] Notable quartets include Brian Boydell's two octatonic quartets of 1949 and 1957 (and his third written just after Bodley's in 1969),[2] Gerard Victory's String Quartet of 1963, and John Kinsella's (b. 1932) two String Quartets of 1960 and 1968. Mention should

---

1 Other string quartets include A.J. Potter (1918–80), Fantasie nos. 1 & 2 for String Quartet (1957 & 1958), Bernard Geary (b. 1934), String Quartet no. 1 (1960), and Proinnsias Ó Duinn (b. 1941), *Essay for String Quartet* in 1961 and a String Quartet in 1962. It may also be noted that the English composer of Irish descent, Elizabeth Maconchy (1907–94) wrote twelve string quartets between 1933 and 1979 and a Sonatina for String Quartet in 1963.   2 See Gareth Cox, 'Octatonicism in the String Quartets of Brian Boydell', in: Patrick F. Devine & Harry White (eds), *The Maynooth International Musicological Conference 1995, Selected Proceedings, Part One (Irish Musical Studies 4)*, (Dublin: Four Courts Press, 1996), 263–70; Hazel Farrell, 'The String Quartets of Brian Boydell, MA thesis (Waterford, 1996); Philip Graydon, Modernism in Ireland and its Cultural Context in the Music and Writings of Frederick May, Brian Boydell and Aloys Fleischmann', MA thesis (NUI Maynooth, 1999); and Axel Klein, *Die Musik Irlands im 20. Jahrhundert* (Hildesheim: Georg Olms, 1996).

also be made, however, of one important pre-war quartet, namely Frederick May's (1911–1985) String Quartet in C minor of 1936[3].

Bodley was born in Dublin in 1933 and his distinguished career as composer, pianist, conductor and academic has followed an uncomplicated path, from studies in Dublin and Stuttgart to an academic post in the Music Department at University College Dublin where he retired as Professor Emeritus in 1998 after nearly forty years. Stylistically, his compositional career has been more eventful as he progressed from a fairly predictable tonal/chromatic/modal language in the 1950s, to serial and aleatoric excursions in the 1960s, before developing an idiomatic style in the 1970s with the juxtaposition of avant-garde elements and aspects of traditional Irish music.[4]

He won a scholarship in 1962 and used it to attend the Internationale Ferienkurse für Neue Musik in Darmstadt the following year, returning again in 1964 and 1965. Darmstadt was for many years the European (and many would argue, also the international) post-war home of avant-garde music[5] and Bodley was exposed there to the most complex forms of post-Webern integral serialism, aleatoricism, and electronic music. Although the compositional fervour in Darmstadt appears to have subsided somewhat by the early 1960s after Wolfgang Steinecke's death in 1961 as the format of the Summer Courses became more academic under Ernst Thomas, the influence on Bodley's compositional thinking was nevertheless significant. He had there the unforgettable opportunity to hear many of the leading composers of the day such as Boulez, Pousseur, Berio, Stockhausen, Babbitt, Ligeti, Kagel, and Maderna analysing their works and techniques in lecture/workshop series: The wide-ranging lectures in 1963–1965 included: 'Notwendigkeit einer ästhetischen Orientierung' (Boulez), 'Questionmétier – Frage Handwerk' (Pousseur), 'Instrument und Funktion' (Berio), 'Analyse: Gruppen für 3 Orchester' and 'Komposition, Komplexe Formen' (Stockhausen), 'The Structure of Musical Systems' (Babbitt), 'Klangtechnik und Form (Analyse von *Apparitions, Atmosphères,*

3 See Axel Klein (as n. 2) and Joseph Ryan, 'Nationalism and Music in Ireland', PhD diss. (National University of Ireland, 1991). May's quartet is also the subject of an article by Robert W. Wason in this volume. 4 For biographical details and comments on his studies in Stuttgart with Johann Nepomuk David, see Malcolm Barry, 'Examining the Great Divide', *Soundpost* (October–November 1983), 15–20; Bodley in interview with Charles Acton, *Éire-Ireland* 5 (1970), 117–33; Gareth Cox, 'German Influences on Twentieth-Century Irish Art-Music', in: Joachim Fischer, Gisela Hoffler, Eoin Burke (eds.), *Irish-German Connections*, (Trier: Wissenschaftlicher Verlag, 1998), 107–14; Klein (as n. 2); and Klein, 'Aber was ist heute schon noch abenteurlich?: Ein Porträt des irischen Komponisten Seóirse Bodley', *Musiktexte* H. 52 (Januar 1994), 21–5. 5 See Gianmario Borio and Hermann Danuser (eds), *Im Zenit der Moderne: Die Internationalen Ferienkurse für Neue Musik in Darmstadt 1946–1966* (Freiburg im Breisgau: Rombach Wissenschaften, Reihe Musicae, 1997) and Metzger & Riehn (eds.), Darmstadt-Dokumente I in: *Reihe Musik-Konzepte Sonderband 1946–1966* (Munich: edition text + kritik, 1999). See also Rudolf Stephan & Lothar Knessl et al. (eds), *Von Kranichstein zur Gegenwart: 50 Jahre Darmstädter Beiträge zur Neuen Musik 1946–1996* (Stuttgart: Daco Verlag, 1996).

und *Aventures)*' (Ligeti), 'Analyse des Analysierens' and 'Komposition und Denkkomposition' (Kagel), 'Komposition in Sprache' (Hans G Helms), 'Klangvorstellung und Realisation: Satzlehre und Instrumentaltechnik' (Boulez), and 'Komposition und Klanggestalt' (Maderna).[6] Presumably Siegfried Palm's lecture on 'Notationsprobleme für Streichinstrumente' could have shaped his thinking somewhat as regards his future quartet. He also attended the concurrent conferences on topics such as 'The Notation of Contemporary Music' (1964) with papers by Earle Brown, Pousseur, Ligeti, Kagel, Caskel, Dahlhaus, Roman Haubenstock-Ramati, Aloys Kontarsky, and Siegfried Palm, and 'Form in Contemporary Music' (1965) with Adorno, Boulez, Earle Brown, Haubenstock-Ramati, Kagel, Ligeti, Rudolf Stephan, and Dahlhaus and avidly noted his frank opinions in the programme booklets at the concerts of contemporary works performed during the two-week courses. Small wonder, then, that his influences were so eclectic.

All this stimulation could not but have a radical impact on his musical language. He has described his period at Darmstadt as 'a most exciting and stimulating time' and made him feel that 'serial and post-serial music was almost the only way that music could develop'.[7] However, he has also said that he was not so much influenced by other composer's music but rather by aspects of their techniques and the lectures by composers explaining and analysing their works.[8] It was therefore more the *spirit* of Darmstadt that inspired him rather than any specific composer or language and he was to spend six months free from composition rationalising what he had learnt. He embarked on a series of the most avant-garde works that he was to write and which Anthony Hughes would describe as the 'most adventurous Irish music of the decade'.[9] The works from this period include *Prelude, Toccata and Epilogue* for piano (1963), *Chamber Symphony no. 1* for flute, bassoon, harp, vibraphone and strings, (1964), the song cycle for soprano and orchestra *Never to have lived is best* (1965), *Configurations for Orchestra* (1967), *String Quartet no. 1* (1968), and the *Ariel Songs* (1969).

Bodley recalls that the string quartet was informally commissioned by the leader of the RTÉ String Quartet, David Lillis, during the interval of a concert.[10] It was completed in September 1968 and premiered a few months later by the RTÉ String Quartet on 6 January 1969 at the Dublin Festival of

---

6 All taken from the *Darmstadt Internationale Ferienkurse für Neue Musik, Programme Booklets*, 1963–1965.   7 Axel Klein, 'Irish Composers and Foreign Education: A Study of Influences', in: Devine and White (as n. 2), 282.   8 Bodley in conversation with the author, 2000.   9 Hughes, Anthony, 'Bodley', in: Stanley Sadie (ed.), *The New Grove Dictionary of Music and Musicians* (London: Macmillan, 1980), vol. 2, 838.   10 He also said that David Lillis particularly remembered the ending of his quartet at the recording as it marked the final farewell of the original RTÉ String Quartet and the last time they played together (Bodley in correspondence with the author, 1999). According to Bodley the Quartet were later pressing him to write another one for them (Acton, as n. 4, 130).

Twentieth-Century Music[11]. It was performed twice subsequently, in Belfast and in Newcastle, and recorded by the New Irish Recording Company in 1973 (as number NIRC LP NIR 006) but never released. There are two interpretations on cassette in circulation (both by the RTÉ String Quartet) and both of which are available from the Contemporary Music Centre, Ireland:[12] One is a live recording of the premiere and the other is of the unreleased recording just mentioned, the latter being truer to the composer's intentions. The score is only available in a manuscript photocopy from the CMC and the RTÉ Library has a set of parts. All in all, it is a work much better known by title than by performance, perhaps because, as Malcolm Barry suggests, it 'represents a peak of abstraction unique in Bodley's output'.[13] A programme note for the premiere was supplied by the composer himself: in it he stated that he thought of 'the first movement as September Music no. 1' and that he intended it to be 'the first of a series of projected works which somehow reflect the significance of that month [for him], not only that month externally [but] also an attitude'.[14] The String Quartet[15] is in two movements of contrasting duration: the first should last about 2½ minutes and the second about 11 minutes.

The short **First Movement** has only 64 bars and can be formally divided into five sections. Metrically there are 34 changes of time signature within the 64 bars, mostly 2/4, 3/4, or 4/4 and, although there are no tempo indications, each section, as can be seen from the following table, has a different metronome marking which gets faster throughout (slowing, however, in the final section). Sketches indicate exact timings in minutes and seconds for each subsection of beats, for instance the final section is subdivided into the following beats: 6, 21, 9, 36:

First Movement:
Section I	bars 1–2 (2)	♩ = 48 (8 beats)
Section II	bars 3–10 (8)	♩ = 60 (24 beats)
Section III	bars 11–21 (11)	♩ = 72 (56 beats)
Section IV	bars 22–43 (22)	♩ = 144 (77 beats)
Section V	bars 44–64 (21)	♩ = 96 (72 beats)

The pitch material is derived from the following row and his sketches show that he clearly intended the row to be subdivided into three discrete tetrachords;[16] however, although the pitches 1–4 and 9–12 are fixed, the pitches 5

11 This is why it is sometimes listed as 1969. The senior music critic of the *Irish Times*, Charles Acton, whilst freely admitting that he was out of his depth in attempting to come to terms with the language, conceded however that there were 'a few moments and passages of quite lovely illumination of an otherwise misty prospect'. *Irish Times*, 7 January 1969.   **12** 19 Fishamble Street, Temple Bar, Dublin 8.   **13** Barry (as in n. 4), 18.   **14** Dublin Festival of Twentieth-century Music, Programme Booklet, 1969.   **15** I wish to thank Seóirse Bodley for generous access to his sketches.   **16** John Kinsella's less rigorous Second Quartet

& 8 can be moved or omitted and the pitches 6 & 7 omitted or reversed if desired. Thus the row retains most of the serial rigour whilst also permitting a certain amount of flexibility:

Music Example 6.1: Seóirse Bodley, String Quartet no. 1, Prime Row

The extremely disjunct row exhibits all interval classes except ic6, the tritone, and includes three each of the ics 2 & 4 between the eleven contiguous pitches. The three tetrachords mentioned belong to the prime forms 4–4, 4–7 and 4–4 and their interval vectors show their lack of tritone intervals, [21110] and [201210] respectively. The pc set 4–4 will act as a referential point in the second movement (e.g., Section II in the second movement begins with the pc set 4–4 sonority in all four strings and displays 4–4 and 4–7 at prominent moments during the section). The row matrix is presented here to facilitate row identification:

	I	I	I	I	I	I	I	I	I	I	I	I	
	0	2	1	9	11	6	10	7	5	8	4	3	
P0	C	D	Db	A	B	F#	Bb	G	F	Ab	E	Eb	R0
P10	Bb	C	B	G	A	E	G#	F	Eb	F#	D	Db	R10
P11	B	C#	C	Ab	Bb	F	A	F#	E	G	Eb	D	R11
P3	Eb	F	E	C	D	A	C#	Bb	Ab	B	G	F#	R3
P1	Db	D#	D	Bb	C	G	B	Ab	Gb	A	F	E	R1
P6	Gb	G#	G	Eb	F	C	E	C#	B	D	Bb	A	R6
P2	D	E	Eb	B	C#	Ab	C	A	G	Bb	F#	F	R2
P5	F	G	F#	D	E	B	D#	C	Bb	Db	A	Ab	R5
P7	G	A	Ab	E	F#	C#	F	D	C	Eb	B	Bb	R7
P4	E	F#	F	C#	Eb	Bb	D	B	A	C	Ab	G	R4
P8	G#	Bb	A	F	G	D	F#	Eb	C#	E	C	B	R8
P9	A	B	Bb	Gb	Ab	Eb	G	E	D	F	C#	C	R9
	0	2	1	9	11	6	10	7	5	8	4	3	
	RI	RI	RI	RI	RI	RI	RI	RI	RI	RI	RI	RI	

The pitch material of Section 1 begins with the aggregates of the untransposed prime row P–0 and a transposed version of the retrograde inversion RI–10 within its two bars (although in the RI–10 aggregate pcs 3, 5 & 6 are

repeated): P–O: C (vc) D (vln1) Db (vln2) A (vc) B (vla) F# (vc) Bb (omitted)
G (vla) F (vc) Ab (vln2) E (vla) Eb (vln1); RI–10: G & F# & D & F & Eb & C
& E (vln1) B (vln2) C# & A (vla) Ab (vc) Bb (vln1). The section ends with the
interval class 4 (as the major third dyad) in all three lower string parts; this ic4
will prove to be a feature of the entire movement which, despite the serial
nature of the pitch selection, gives some parts a quasi tonal feel: For instance,
of the nearly 300 intervals, 33% are permutations of ic4.

Music Example 6.2: Seóirse Bodley, String Quartet no. 1, Movement I, Section I,
bars 1–2

Section II shifts up a semitone in the bass and begins with an upward striving
in the first violin over more than three octaves. Besides the preponderance of
ic1 (particularly noticeable in the violins in canon in bars 3 & 4), the emphasis in this section is also on the tonal interval class, ic3 (e.g. vlnI: bars 4 & 5).
The beginning of this section uses I–1: C# (vc & vla) B & C (vc) E (vla) D

Music Example 6.3: Seóirse Bodley, String Quartet no. 1, Movement I,
Section II, bars 3–10

(omitted) G (vln1 & 2) E♭ (vln 2) F# (vln1 & 2) A♭ (vln 2) F & A & B♭ (vln1) and then R–6, R–3 and R–8 can be traced throughout the rest of this short section.

However, I am less concerned with highlighting the various permutations of the row throughout the movement. As Christopher Fox has noted, 'generally, the aesthetic purpose of Darmstadt serialism is not that the series should occupy the musical foreground; rather the serial principle is the method whereby musical transformations can be achieved'[17]. Instead I wish to suggest that Bodley was allowing his ear to rule his pen, i.e. writing in many ways intuitively and governed by what Malcolm Barry has succinctly described as his tension between ear and historical consciousness.[18] The quartet is essentially linear and melodic and it is interesting to note that Bodley has stated that, although his radically different second string quartet written almost 24 years later in 1992 differs in style and texture from his first, both share 'beneath the surface disparities, a common emphasis on melody, and rejoice in the ability of strings to carry a singing melodic line'.[19] The movement also begins and ends on C (with a cadential-like rise through B♭–B–C in the first and second violins).

The structure of this movement could be interpreted as a Webernesque variation form with the five sections corresponding to five variations on the row material with the theme being the row itself (no section can therefore be designated as a theme as such). Each variation becomes more substantial as the movement progresses and is clearly separated (except between IV & V) by either a *fermata* or rests. They all display an individual character: the first presents the pitch material in two aggregates of the Prime (0) and Retrograde Inversion (–10) in two short bars and reveals straight away Bodley's preoccupation over the entire piece with multiple modes of string timbre: the first violin begins with a minim (tied to a semiquaver) started *non-vibrato* leading to *molto vibrato*, followed by two semiquavers played *col legno battuto*, a semiquaver (with acciaccatura) *sul ponticello tratto*, and a final semiquaver (of the quintuplet) plucked *pizzicato*, with the remainder of the section bowed *al talone* with *normal vibrato*. These playing techniques are also employed across the other parts in approximately the same order (although the slide up a quarter-tone in the second violin is the only instance of microtonal elements in the entire quartet, apart from some *glissandi* in the second movement). The second[20] section begins with an imitative (quasi canonic) idea in the violins

of the same year is divided into four trichordal sets (tracing major and minor dyads: B, C, D – A#, C#, A – E, G#, G – D#, F, F#).   **17** Christopher Fox, *Darmstadt and the Modernist Myth*, New Music, 1999, www.hud.ac.uk/schools/music+humanities/music/newmusic/Darmstadt_myth.html   **18** Barry (as n. 4), 17.   **19** RTÉ Programme Booklet (May 1993).   **20** Despite the fact that the sketch pages for Section II of the first movement has 'clarinet and piano?' written at the top, Bodley has stated that he never intended

and uses *Klangfarbenmelodie*, the third explores numerous possible permutations of the quintuplet rhythmic cell before ending with a short cello solo and a *sff* heptad, the fourth includes many large leaps and again imitative features and leads without a break into the fifth which uses serial dynamics (his sketches also show evidence of these attempts to construct series of dynamics such as '*ff, f, mf, mp, p, pp*' or '*sf, ff, f, mf, pp, p*'). If any composer's influence comes through strongly it is surely that of Pierre Boulez, in particular his serial and pointillistic techniques as employed in *Polyphonie X* (1951) and *Structures* Books I & II (1952 and 1956–61), seminal works which would have been discussed, at least informally, at Darmstadt. Bodley has stated that when writing the Quartet he started with a technical approach which was 'very much concerned with this whole idea of irregularity of rhythm and the question of musical impulse behind it ... the whole thing did grow ... very much from a musical impulse.'[21]

Of course, Bodley was open to other non-musical influences (as he says, it was the Sixties after all![22]) and in his sketches he has twice noted the word 'Ikebana' – the Japanese traditional art form of flower arranging – as he was impressed and influenced at the time by its concept, proportions and ideals. Ikebana, which purports to bring nature and humanity together, is based on a triangular pattern of three points which represent Heaven, Man, and Earth, thus allowing for creative expression although governed by certain structural parameters. In 1970 he mentioned that he had 'the greatest respect for much of the Japanese traditional art ... a Japanese flower arranger has to learn a very strict discipline and spontaneity tends to come after the discipline has been learnt'[23]

The **Second Movement** is considerably more substantial and complex than the first and is divided into eleven metrical and ametrical sections of varying length (the duration of each section is taken from the composer's sketches):

Section I	45 seconds	Section VII	67 seconds
Section II	90 seconds	Section VIII	110 seconds
Section III	67 seconds	Section IX	22 seconds
Section IV	22 seconds	Section X	67 seconds
Section V	90 seconds	Section XI	45 seconds
Section VI	45 seconds		

the material to be for anything else but a string quartet. Similarly, on one of the pages for Section III of the same movement, the words 'blocks = orchestral = style with either instruments producing more than one note at a time (piano) or many instr. (orchestra)' refer rather to a texture sought. Bodley in conversation with the author, 2001. **21** Acton, 1970 (as n. 4), 128. **22** Bodley in conversation with the author, 2001. **23** Acton, 1970 (as n. 4), 124–125.

It begins with a tetrachord derived from the pitches 8 through 11 of the RI–1in the first violin (presumably again because he wishes to emphasize ic4 and the C with which the first movement began and ended), followed by R–10 in the cello (the C# being the final pitch of RI–1 and the first of R–10), and spread through the second violin, cello again and viola. The music in the connecting boxes are to be played consecutively, an idea which was apparently influenced by an account of the basics of Critical Path Analysis which Bodley had read about in the *Radio Times*.[24] It is an organisational method of prioritising the planning of a project where certain parts are dependant on others and therefore must be completed in a sequence (i.e., a Critical Path Action and a Non-Critical Path Action). For instance, I–6 begins in the first violin and continues down through the second violin part to the cello before completing the row back on the E♭ in the first violin (where RI–2 commences). Bodley has noted in his sketches that the Critical Path can be divided between instruments and can contain more than one part (e.g. just before Section IX the Critical Path is spread over all four parts consecutively).

D could be considered to be a referential pitch for this movement: it begins and ends on this tone and the opening D is emphasised in the first violin under a prolonged *fermata* while the second violin also holds a D leading to the first violin's long trill on D at the end of the section (with an octave C 'clashing with the second violin at one point). Even the repeated E♭–D dyads in the second violin which follow this octave D 'resolves' to a D acciaccatura. There are also five very prominent and accented dyads E–D in the first violin in the bars before and after Rehearsal No. 2b, a dyad which also ends Section V and occurs in the penultimate bar of the movement. Dare one indulge in a little *Augenmusik* here and stretch the pitch centricity argument a bit further to point out that the second violin's emphasis of A♭ five times just before, and at the beginning of, Section V, and again in bars 5 & 6 of Section VI in the first violin, both towards and at the middle of the piece, constitutes a tritonal point equidistant from the two Ds? Perhaps not.

Section XIII contains a prominent passage in the first violin which Bodley alludes to in his programme note remarking that it reminds him of a seagull he saw flying over the sands as he was cycling along the Howth Road in North Dublin in his teens.[25] Bodley has marked in his sketches for this section 'Bird!!! (flies away)' and notes the word 'Bird' again for the final section. The three exclamation marks indicate perhaps his self-consciousness at his audacity in using such non-Darmstadtian (if there is such a word) programmatic elements. His notes for this section also clearly differentiate between the higher region of the solo line which should contain many tremulos and trills and a

---

24 Bodley in correspondence with the author, 1999. 25 See n. 19.

Music Example 6.4: Seóirse Bodley, String Quartet no. 1, Movement II, Section I

lower region which should have darker sounds and generate 'a certain tension'. The solo violin (or seagull?) begins playing in bar 2 of the section on a high D♭ over a cluster accompaniment of D,E,E♭. A similar passage returns muted in Section XI.

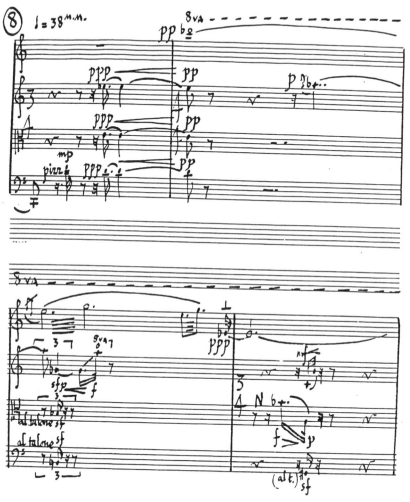

Music Example 6.5: Seóirse Bodley, String Quartet no. 1, Movement II, Section XIII, bars 1–4

Darmstadt had also undergone a reaction to a rather contrived integral serialism and embraced the indeterminacy of John Cage and others. This clearly had an impact on Bodley as well and the second movement displays some

Music Example 6.6: Seóirse Bodley, String Quartet no. 1, Movement II,
Section III, bars 1–9

such aleatoric elements: hexachords (or 'reservoirs of tones'[26]) are presented in boxes, mainly for the lower strings as a textural device in Section III: bars 1 & 7; Section IIIb: bar 3; Section IVa: bar 3; Section VII: bars 4 & 7; Section IX: bar 2. They are to be played in random sequence whilst observing any of the given dynamics. The following example from Section III also shows a semi-free, second violin line in bar 7.

Another influence of Darmstadt is his inclusion in the score of a very detailed table of signs. Apart from standard instructions such as *sul tasto*, *sul ponticello*, *al talone*, or a Bartókian snap, the following exact string techniques are demanded:

⊥	= Non-vibrato
⩔	= Molto vibrato
⊥ → ⩔	= Move from non-vibrato to molto vibrato
N	= Normal vibrato
⟨⩔⟩	= Sudden crescendo with vibrato

Courtesy markings for the performers in this very complex second movement are also inserted, for instance he marks the end of notes (or in some cases, the beginning of notes), relative to other parts with arrows and beats in ametrical bars are indicated with vertical strokes. Ascending and descending arrows through beams indicate a quite exact progressive *accelerando* or *ritardando* and are used over longer passages in, for instance, the entire Section V of the second movement to good effect. The square fermata sign ⌐•⌐ is used for a pause of approximately 2½ seconds (and variations thereof) and the ⌐⊓ sign indicates a pause or rest *ad libitum* (Bodley sometimes instructs the player to play everything under bracket in the time of the pause). However the plethora of agogic, timbral and dynamic instructions can make the work seem a little overcrowded occasionally and it sometimes appears as if Bodley had learnt *too* much in Darmstadt and is trying to fit too many techniques into a single work; this can detract from the rhythmic energy which he is clearly striving for and clouds some lyrical moments.

This work has not been heard in concert for over 30 years and, although aspects of the work can appear a little unconvincing, another public perfor-

---

26 Bodley sketches.

mance is surely long overdue. Not only is it the last major work which Bodley was to write purely in the experimental 'Darmstadt' idiom before exploring his own more individual language, it also represents a milestone in twentieth-century Irish string quartet writing and avant-garde composition in Ireland. However, nothing could be a clearer statement of his future intentions than the C major beginning and end of *The Narrow Road to the Deep North* for Two Pianos of 1972 and, although many of the techniques and dissonances from the String Quartet still abound, his attempts to ensure, as he himself said, 'something which is *audible to the listener*'[27] [my italics] speak volumes about his desire for communication. It is therefore hardly surprising that he was to relinquish some of the dissonant and extremely complex language of the Sixties for a more accessible (and ultimately neo-tonal) style and for what might be described as Irish music as heard through Darmstadt ears.

---

27 Acton, 1970 (as n. 4), 128.

7

Some observations on form-building processes in twentieth-century music: shaping time in Ian Wilson's *Rich Harbour: Concerto for Organ and Orchestra*

MICHAEL RUSS

INTRODUCTION

This essay uses a recent work by Ian Wilson to explore some issues of form building in twentieth-century orchestral works. Analysis of twentieth-century music, and the construction of theories about it tend to focus heavily on pitch relations: pitch-class set theory, theories of scales and genera, twelve-tone theory and so on. Yet, with the weakening, and in some cases the abandonment, of the tonal system, music has had to rely on other parameters for shape and direction. Arguably, the theoretical emphasis on pitch-class (and to a much more limited extent on rhythmic innovation) has tended to detract attention from register and the temporal positioning of pitches at precisely the moment when these elements take on a greater significance. Form has been given very little attention, whether at the level of the phrase or on a larger scale.[1] Perhaps as result, much analysis of twentieth-century music seems impoverished: extensive exploration of sets and genera, for example, often leave us thinking 'so what'. One reason for this is the gap between analysis and perception. In the study of form and formal procedures, perception is at the core. 'The idea of an inaudible musical form would be a contradiction in terms. Structure is the aspect of the work directed at the composer, form that which is directed at the listener.'[2] Our obsession with poesis has perhaps led to an over-obsession

---

1 There are, of course, notable exceptions. Three are: Edward Cone, 'Stravinsky the Progress of a Method', *Perspectives of New Music*, i/1 (Fall 1962), 18–26, reprinted in: Benjamin Boretz & Edward T. Cone (eds.), *Perspectives on Schoenberg and Stravinsky* (Princeton: Princeton University Press, 1968), 156–64 (in which Cone outlines 'stratification, interlock and synthesis' as important constituents of Stravinky's formal method in *Symphonies of Wind Instruments*); Derrick Puffett, *Debussy's Ostinato Machine*, Papers in Musicology no. 4 (Nottingham: Nottingham University Press, 1996); and Derrick Puffett, 'Berg, Mahler and the Three Orchestral Pieces Op. 6', in Anthony Pople (ed.), *The Cambridge Companion to Berg* (Cambridge: Cambridge University Press, 1997), 111–144. The title of this paper owes something to David Epstein: *Shaping Time* (New York: Schirmer Books, 1995); Epstein's book, however, does not concern itself with twentieth-century music.   2 Carl Dahlhaus, 'Form' (trans. by

with structure and an under-emphasis on form, genre and archetype. In the broadest sense formal structures deal with the ways in which composers shape time in their work. 'If we are talking about form, then we should – generally speaking – remember the trivial fact that it is nonsensical to sacrifice the outline of the whole to the structure of the details, the concrete musical shape to the preparation of abstract components, and the result to the method.'[3]

Discussions of formal structure in twentieth-century music often fail to move much beyond the identification of principal sections and the attribution of the form to a pre-existing model, where that may be appropriate. In academic circles views of formal structure which have their origins in nineteenth-century theory have been remarkably persistent in the twentieth, despite the forceful challenge of Heinrich Schenker.[4] Schoenberg's view of form as evident in *Fundamentals of Musical Composition*[5] clearly followed A.B. Marx.[6] Marx's formal theory rested on the definition of a small range of basic formal archetypes, for example, song forms, rondo and sonata. The essence of formal teaching in his model is melodic and thematic and rests upon the division of the work into constituent sections. This contrasted with eighteenth-century teaching as found, for example, in Heinrich Koch, where the focus was on harmonic periods. Schenker's challenge to nineteenth-century 'formenlehre' was based on a more organic view of form, one that through the projection of the Ursatz across the work seems to bridge its natural divisions. (Schenker did not, of course, concern himself with music outside the eighteenth and nineteenth-century Austro-German mainstream).[7] Organicism was important to Schoenberg too, but in his conception this arose out of the force of the initial idea, and its development through essentially motivic processes. In his own music he tended, as did Berg and Webern, to cast his music, outwardly at least in the 'traditional' forms.

This short essay is not the place to assemble a theory of twentieth-century form. But, using Wilson's work as an exemplar, we may be able to raise a number of issues with regard to formal structure that are of interest beyond the work in hand. Because Wilson is essentially an intuitive composer who is not inclined to develop abstract systems, his music is well matched to the type of investigation carried out here.[8] Much analytical attention has been focused

Stephen Hinton) in *Schoenberg and the New Music: Essays by Carl Dahlhaus*, trans. by Derrick Puffett and Alfred Clayton (Cambridge: Cambridge University Press, 1987), 261. **3** Ibid., 261. **4** Berry's widely available text is a good example. Wallace Berry, *Form in Music* (Englewood Cliffs, New Jersey: Prentice Hall, 1966). **5** Arnold Schoenberg, *Fundamentals of Musical Composition*, Gerald Strang (ed.,) (London: Faber, 1967). **6** See Janet Schmalfeldt, 'Towards a Reconciliation of Schenkerian Concepts of Form with Traditional and Recent Theories of Form', *Music Analysis*, x/3, (October, 1991), 233. **7** Heinrich Schenker, *Free Compostion (Der Freie Satz)*, trans. by Ernst Oster (ed.), (New York and London: Longman, 1979), 128–144. **8** Wilson has published an article on this work and also discussed the concerto with the author. See 'Ian Wilson: "Rich Harbour"', *Choir and Organ* (January

on innovative and often very small-scale works from the beginning of the century written by a relatively small number of composers who have, for reasons which have yet properly to be articulated, been defined as canonic. Much music by composers working in the latter part of the century and particularly those writing works on a relatively large scale remains unexplored. Using a work by Wilson for the purposes of this essay will perhaps go a tiny way towards redressing the balance.

EVALUATING FORM

Writing of statistical and aleatoric forms of the 1960s, Dahlhaus made an observation that rings true beyond its immediate subject: 'To expect a discussion about musical form to produce definitions and prescriptions would be naïve. It is by no means certain what form in music is, and any attempt to formulate rules would provoke nothing but derision.'[9] Nevertheless, as Adorno implies, form should be at the core of analytical activity: 'analysis, as the unfolding of the work, exists in relationship to the work itself and to its genre or compositional archetype'.[10] By the work itself, Adorno means its inner driving force, its singularity, and while the word 'form' is not actually used here, the influence of nineteenth-century theory means we readily conflate form with genre and archetype. All three words indicate a generic set of requirements or assumptions about how the composition will behave against which we can evaluate the individual work. Here we are touching on a fundamental aspect of musical perception and aesthetics. We wish to define, find vessels in which to contain things, yet at the same time we harbour a wish for the individual composition to break the mould, and we often attach value to works to the extent that they do. Forms are tools to categorise and give shape and meaning (they are models against which deviations can be measured), but we suspect formalism to the extend that it can be seen to be 'wanting to incarcerate music in schematic patterns.'[11]

The definition of form is essentially a heuristic activity that aids the process of interpretation. But a structure such as ABA should not only be regarded simply as a disposition of elements in time, but also as a starting point for an exploration of how the two elements, A and B function in relation to one another: how for example is B a consequence of A and A subsequently of B? 'The pattern is not a representation of the form but an instrument towards its understanding.'[12] To evaluate form we must understand the dual purpose of

1996), 24–27   **9** Dahlhaus (as n. 2), 258.   **10** Theodor W, Adorno, 'On the Problem of Musical Analysis', trans. by Max Paddison, *Music Analysis* i/2 (July, 1982), 178.   **11** Dahlhaus (as n. 2), 248. **12** Ibid., 263.

the material within a composition. It must both serve its role within the formal structure and be expressive and meaningful. The study of form can all too easily lead to a false distinction between form and content. Form is pointless without content and content has no meaning unless it has form.

Determining whether elements are fit for their formal purpose is made problematic by the lack of any clear theory of formal functions. While we may perceive certain aspects of formal construction (introduction, statement, continuation, transition, development, repeat, recurrence, restatement, dissolution, liquidation), what makes these materials fit for their formal purpose and their positioning appropriate, is often a matter of conjecture and speculation.[13] As these categories of material exist in many different works, what we need to determine is what it means to be one of them in the particular work. We need to evaluate the 'balance between detail and context, between heterogeneous and homogeneous' in the various aspects (time, emotional states, activity and so on) of the particular work.[14] To be more specific, the idea of the musical period is founded on the concept of balance and complementation, but what do these terms mean in a non-tonal environment?[15] Degrees of difference play an important role too. Clear difference may be important in the articulation of the form, but too much difference may simply lead to a focus on the details and character of the individual section, rather than its relationship to the whole. Balance and difference may take on different meanings as we progress from one structural level to another. At the level of the phrase it may still be possible to hear the operation of a macro rhythm, That the duration of phrase x is balanced by phrase y is still a possibility, and from this we may also perceive (structural) downbeats of differing weights. Move beyond the length of the phrase and while we may perceive that in broad terms the length of A is greater or lesser than B, difference is all we perceive and not large-scale rhythm.

STATIC AND DYNAMIC VIEWS OF FORM;
THE ROLE OF SECONDARY PARAMETERS

A formal structure will have static and dynamic aspects. Defining a form is more than simply identifying the component parts and their disposition across the work; more than the 'plan which gives order and coherence.'[16] Descriptions of sectional content, the proportions of elements, their relative

---

13 These elements are among those that constitute Adorno's 'material theory of form'. Adorno (as n. 10), 185.   14 Dahlhaus (as n. 2), 264.   15 I am using the term complementation in its formal sense rather than its meaning in pitch-class set theory.   16 Berry (as n. 4), 436. On the matter of static and dynamic, energising and subsident elements in music see also Wallace Berry, *Structural Functions in Music* (Englewood Cliffs, New Jersey: Prentice Hall, 1976), 1–26.

sizes, the degree of symmetry and asymmetry in the form as a whole, all belong to an essentially static view. Dynamic elements create a sense of movement towards (intensification) or abatement from (subsidence) and also of stasis. Berry: 'little if anything is more vital in musical form than the controlled maintenance and effective change, subsidence and direction of motion. Failure to move with conviction and direction is one of the most common and crippling effects of ineffective music.'[17] These dynamic processes that as well as shape the internal components of the form sometimes cut across their boundaries.

It is easy to equate these two views of form with the 'formenlehre' (static) and Schenkerian (dynamic) views of form discussed above. However, in a non-tonal environment without the structuring force of tonality and voice-leading, the music comes to depend to a greater extent on so-called 'secondary' parameters, as we will discuss below. Despite this difficulty, creating large musical spans that can sustain themselves without obvious sectional divisions remains a goal towards which many composers aspire, not least Wilson, who in works since *Rich Harbour* has sought to create less section-alised structures than the one we describe below and who in the present work is keen to dovetail sections and not to create abrupt internal contrasts that will break as it were the flight of the music.

How motions towards and from are controlled is one major facet of formal construction, another is the way in which the form is articulated by the composer for the listener. As Dahlhaus comments: 'A single section may be articulated in different ways, all of which are meaningful. Yet it is improbable, even if not impossible, that a large number of sections will form a coherent whole if the articulation of the individual sections, on which the connection between sections, depends, is left to the listener.'[18] Again 'secondary' parameters play a larger role in twentieth-century structures, and the processes of articulation, as with intensification and abatement, become the product of the interaction of all musical parameters. This is a more complex analytical and theoretical issue than it might seem, since the parameters of music are difficult to define (is rhythm a parameter or the product of a number of other parameters including duration and meter?), are different in kind, and behave differently. In comparing parameters there is no sense of a common scale. To take two extremes: scales of pitch are axiomatic but of timbre impossible; pitch is a relative concept, timbre absolute (the one amenable to analysis, the other only to description). Similarly, duration may be measured against the underlying beat, but dynamic is never precisely quantifiable. The parameters of music are all intertwined in complex ways. At one extreme, pitch and duration might seem to have some independence, to a limited degree they may be

17 Berry (as n. 4), 447.   18 Dahlhaus (as n. 2), 2.

changed without affecting others, but other parameters are much less free. Melody (if melody is a parameter) cannot be independent of rhythm, nor rhythm independent of aspects of dynamics. For Dahlhaus, timbre is entirely the result of the interaction of all other parameters and is therefore a 'sound quality, not a parameter, since it does not fulfil the condition of being a variable independently of other parameters'.[19]

So the role of these 'parameters' in the form-building process will differ sharply. Pitch, duration and meter will remain at the core, shaping the progress of the music both in the foreground and over larger spans. However, in the case of pitch, gesture and the exploitation of register take on greater importance as the influence of tonality and voice-leading diminishes. Dynamic and texture (notably the relative density of activity) also play a more active role. Melody, as we will explore below will play quite different role, behaving not so much as a parameter, but emerging at certain moments as a point of focus, of crystallisation. Timbre and dynamic may be 'restricted to elementary, rudimentary formal connections. They are either similar or different and antithetical, and nothing else.'[20] But included in these antitheses may be important articulatory roles. In the present work, clear changes of timbre and texture often announce the arrival of a new section, or articulate the segments within sections. Furthermore instruments can take on roles in the form-building process by virtue of their historical usage: brass and percussion may 'announce', for example. Nevertheless, Dahlhaus argues: 'it is scarcely conceivable that something could be composed which concisely and unambiguously performed the function of a continuation or complement merely by making use of timbres or degrees of loudness. Despite the experience of his orchestral piece 'Farben' (No. 3 from the *Five Orchestral Pieces* op. 16) Schoenberg seems to have held a similar view. In 1926 he wrote: 'For the true product of the mind – the musical idea, the unalterable – is established in the relationship between pitches and time-dimensions. But all other things – dynamics, tempo, timbre and the character, clarity, effect etc., which they produce are really no more than the performer's resources, serving to make the idea comprehensible and admitting of variations'.[21] Berg made a similar remark: 'the necessity [of performing piano reductions of orchestral works because of the unavailability of orchestral performances] becomes a virtue. In this manner it is possible to hear and judge a modern orchestral work divested of all the sound-effects and other sensuous aids that only an orchestra can furnish'[22] But the set of priorities that underlies such a view is an early twentieth-century exten-

19 Ibid., 252.   **20** Ibid., 254.   **21** Arnold Schoenberg, 'Mechanical Musical Instruments', *Style and Idea: Selected Writings of Arnold Schoenberg*, ed. Leonard Stein (London: Faber, 1975), 326. My attention was drawn to this remark by Dahlhaus. See Dahlhaus (as n. 2), 254.   **22** Berg quoted in Kathryn Bailey, *The Life of Webern* (Cambridge: Cambridge University Press, 1998), 97.

sion of the nineteenth-century German line of thought that privileges the abstract idea and its working out. It sits uncomfortably at the beginning of the twenty-first century when the presentation of an idea has become as important as the idea itself.

Completed in June 1995, Wilson's *Rich Harbour: Concerto for Organ and Orchestra* is a large single-movement structure lasting a little under half an hour.[23] The inspiration for the work came in a visit to a small graveyard at Caldragh in County Fermanagh. Wilson became interested in 'how to approach musically that most final of subjects, death, and what lies beyond'. He decided that the concerto should take 'the character of a meditation ... with the organist as protagonist. I could imagine the soloist wandering in Caldragh, seeing different aspects come into relief or go out or focus, and this affected the way I approached the structure'.[24]

Wilson's work involves four types of material ('x', 'a', 'b', 'c'). 'x' is found in interludes and comprises 'more peaceful background material'; 'a' material represents 'a struggle to reach the unobtainable' it is frenetic, vituosic, generally highly mobile, and spread across the full range of registers; 'b' materials are slower, more restricted harmonically, and fragmented melodically 'the darkest I have ever written';[25] 'c' materials are more optimistic and uplifting. On the surface Wilson's work appears to have many of the traits of twentieth-century modernism. Its musical language is at times harsh and dissonant and shape and gesture are potent forces. There are points of tonal focus and there are patches of diatonic material, but there is no sense of working towards a particular tonal goal in this piece.[26] C often appears at crucial moments but this may have more to do with C being the lowest pedal tone on the organ than any particular desire for C-centredness, E and B♭ also appear to take on a referential status from time to time. While there are extensive passages of octatonic writing (particularly in the 'a' sections), Wilson's use of the octatonic scale is very free. He does not capitalise on the octatonic routines made possible by the symmetrical partitioning of the scale and most obviously evident in the work of Stravinsky, and non octatonic pitch-classes are freely mixed with the octatonic. There is some exploration of non-functional diatonicism too. Aside from octatonic and diatonic passages, much of the writing seems

---

23 The Concerto won first place in a competition for an organ concerto organised by the Irish Arts Council and RTÉ, the Irish state broadcaster. **24** Wilson (as n. 8), 24. **25** Ibid., 26. Wilson's fascination with darker materials continues as in his recent *Abyssal* (2000). **26** For this reason I regard the work as non-tonal.

to employ a freely chromatic language determined intuitively, rather than by means of any system. In particular, there are a significant number of many-voiced chords that appear to be structured intuitively, determined by ear at the piano, rather than according to any particular system. Some are octatonic, others diatonic, and many seem freely determined.

FORMAL STRUCTURE

In his essay on the work Wilson indicates that the form is ordered according to the following 'archetype':[27]

x1(1) a1(30) b1(80) A2(104) x2(179) b2(226) c1(290) x3(318) B3(341) a3(389) C2(433) x4(528)

In practice this scheme is not itself archetypal but is an elaboration of one that is: ab, abc, abcd which is open to endless extension. In his compositional application Wilson adds a series of interludes ('x') which serve both to open and close the work as well as providing internal punctuation. He also reverses the order of the final 'ab' and the work is foreclosed before we reach 'd'. Wilson also identifies through capitalisation the sections that represent the 'apotheosis' of each type of material. The 'a' material has its apotheosis earlier, the 'b' and 'c' material much nearer to the end. Thus from the middle of the work there are two different processes in hand: 'b' and 'c' are still working towards their apotheosis while 'a' is already spent and will be recalled between 'B3' and 'C2'. What was otherwise a rather sterile pattern is much enriched by such processes.

The lengths of sections ranges from 23 to 95 bars, but the pulse variation is actually quite restricted ($\downarrow$. = 42 to $\downarrow$ = 112/116) and variations in speed tend to be achieved through the note values employed. Particular strands are not identified with recurrent tempi, although the fastest material is associated with the 'a' strand and the slowest with 'b'. The fastest metronome speed indicated is in 'a1' ($\downarrow$ =112–116) and the slowest in 'b2' ($\downarrow$. = 42). Within sections there is a tendency for tempi to remain broadly the same. 'C2', the climax of the 'C' cycle and of the work, is the longest in terms of number of bars; 'A2', the early climax within the 'A' cycle, is the next largest. 'B3', climax of the 'B' section has fewer bars, but a slow tempo. Following tradition, there is quieter central part to the work which begins with 'x2' and as the work progresses, there tends to be more emphasis on melody, particularly from 'c1' onwards.

Wilson subtitles the work 'Concerto for Organ and Orchestra'. This invites us to consider the relationship with the conventions of the concerto genre.

---

27 Wilson (as n. 8), 24. Wilson does not indicate the bar numbers or number the x sections; I have done so for ease of reference.

Clearly there is a soloist who has opportunities for virtuosity and moments where he/she is pitted against the orchestra. There are passages where the organ takes on a very distinct persona and where both organ and orchestra may appear to over-react to certain events (as in the cadenza at the end of 'C2'). The organ is also provided with cadenza-like moments and climactic materials that allow it to contribute fully to the emotional life of the work. If we are to take Adorno's advice and try to determine the core of the work we are examining, 'the paradox, so to speak, or the 'impossible' that every piece of music wants to make possible' then it is surely Wilson's desire to construct a concertante work for organ with the range of expressive states of a three movement structure within a single movement.[28] Wilson's solution involves four strands running through the work, each of which must evolve and become, yet the work should still be perceived as one over-arching whole (if it is not, then there would be little point in the single-movement structure).

One perspective we might use better to understand this form, is to consider how far the three principal strands are parallel plots. In literature, Tolstoy's *Anna Karenina* famously involves two plots running simultaneously and Margaret Atwood's recent *Blind Assassin* has three, with interludes (in the form of fictitious press cuttings).[29] In novels the parallel plots set each other in relief, and we await not only the outcome of each, but the collective impact of the novel as a whole when each strand has run its course. However, in literature it is easy to separate the plots through their respective characters, locations (spatial and temporal) and so on. In music this is more difficult; if the materials become too distinct then the work becomes fragmented and may degenerate into the episodic. Clearly this was not Wilson's intention. He wished to 'make the work sound organic and overcome the rather fragmentary nature of its structure'.[30] He also felt a need for 'dovetailing many of the episodes in order that they lead naturally into each other in terms of mood, tempo, and also on occasion melodic and harmonic progress'. To do this he employs a 'memorable motif which appears at the beginning and returns at strategic points in conjunction with whatever material is present [which] also helps to achieve a sense of continuity'.[31] However, in making the statements he does, Wilson is revealing a very old set of aesthetic values. These relate to the work of art being an organic whole: 'wholeness, unity, logic, coherence – all relate clearly to the principles of aesthetics as formulated during the eigthteenth century, notably by Shaftesbury and Baumgarten'.[32]

There are of course alternative sets of values with respect to formal construction. Russians have long made a virtue of the episodic, fragmented and

---

28 Adorno (as n. 10), 181.   **29** Margaret Atwood, *The Blind Assassin* (London: Bloomsbury Publishing, 2000). This novel was the Booker Prize winner for 2000.   **30** Wilson (as n. 8), 24.   **31** Ibid.   **32** Arnold Whittall, 'Form' in: Stanley Sadie (ed.), *The New Grove Dictionary of Music and Musicians*

discontinuous. The sudden abandonment of lines of thought and the taking up of others is the essence of much Stravinsky as Cone demonstrated in his famous analysis of *Symphonies of Wind Instruments*.[33] But as Cone points out, even Stravinsky felt a need to work towards a goal and to invoke some kind of synthesis. In the *Symphonies* it is the final chorale. The idea of chorale, or chorale-like music, as a crystallisation, the goal towards which we work is familiar from works as diverse as Beethoven's Ninth Symphony to Debussy's *La Mer* and perhaps, as we discuss below has its origins in the recitative/aria polarity. Wilson follows this model in arriving at a chorale as the work moves into its final stage in section 'C2'.

THE MIDDLE

Although each section in Wilson's work tends to be united by a broadly common speed and the distinctiveness of its material, there is great variety in the modes of internal organisation and the sections conclude in a variety of ways with a variety of degrees of closure. Before exploring the sections that begin and end the work in detail, I will consider briefly the range of modes of sectional organisation employed by Wilson. The degree of internal sectionalisation and articulation, and the way in which some sections have a strong sense of intensification and abatement while others proceed in a more restrained way, are issues of interest here. Two fundamental problems with the formal model used by Wilson are firstly, how to distinguish between the climax of the work as a whole and the climaxes of the 'a', 'b' and 'c', cycles, and secondly, how to create different degrees of closure at the sub-section and sectional level.

Some sections subdivide and are clearly articulated internally, the 'a' sections in particular. 'A2' contains five sections with further subdivisions, there are many internal points of contrast and the section progresses in short-lived waves of intensification and abatement, while becoming increasingly frenetic and rhythmically complex as it progresses. 'a3' is similarly constructed and like 'A2' contains cadenza-like elements. Repetition and ostinato, familiar structuring devices in a non-tonal environment are much in evidence in this work.[34] In the first part of 'b1' a series of largely diatonic chords are heard in different rhythmic and metric arrangements as though viewed from different perspectives. Here we have a feeling of varied repetition without any strong sense of growth and intensification. The second part of this section is built over an ostinato that evaporates as the section ends. By contrast 'b2', based on the same diatonic chord sequence, has a stronger sense of growth and

(London: Macmillan, 1980), vol. 11, 709.   **33** Cone (as n. 1)   **34** See Puffett, 1996 (as n. 1)

intensification. This is achieved through incremental writing: as layers are added to repeated chords the sound becomes more chromatic, denser and more intricate. 'C1' comprises a continuous ostinato in strings and a series of melodic fragments that span the entire section. The effect of the ostinato is to mitigate the section's internal contrasts.

The 'x' sections are either introductory or interludial. As befits the latter role, 'x3' is a section in which clearly articulated phrases in solo violas intensify or abate only gently and strong internal contrast (in any parameter) is entirely avoided (the melodic statements are also remarkable for their lack of repeated elements). Some degree of intensification is only offered towards the end when high violins join the violas, there is then a gradual downward abatement. 'x2' is a simple rounded structure beginning with a series of quiet, distant chords and a simple diatonic melody. Its recall of materials from the introduction indicates that its role lies outside the arguments of the principal 'a', 'b', and 'c' strands. In 'x2' the work's principal motif reappears, heralding the return of deep rumblings from the introduction (see discussion of 'x1' below). The E♭ minor focus of this material jars with the E minor of the chordal outer sections creating a degree of harmonic tension and expectation.

The climax of the 'a' cycle, 'A2', comes relatively early in the work, and must not appear to be a premature climax to the work as a whole. One technique used to avoid this is to ensure that climaxes within the section are short-lived. When a chorale-like homophonic harmonic version of the principal motif appears in bar 117, massively scored in brass and with a powerful organ counterpoint in rapidly-changing chords using as many notes as the organist has fingers and feet, it evaporates after only three bars. Similarly the return of the opening material of 'a1' at bar 143 is short lived, giving way to a brief, vigorous, intense cadenza on a rising octatonic scale in the bass: a cadenza that will reappear at the end of the work (see below). But this is not the end of 'A2', a powerful ascending bass line in trombones with rapid counterpoints in bassoons and low strings ensues; but again this fades after six bars and further variants ensue.

The closure of sections is achieved to a great variety of degrees and in a number of different ways. It is necessary to distinguish here between three terms. Abatement is regarded simply as a diminution in intensity, closure is the instigation of a process or processes that imply that termination of a section is imminent, while ending is simply curtailment without clear preparation through closural processes. Sometimes abatement is simple and uncomplicated, as with the dying away of a five-part octatonic chord in the strings punctuated by strokes in the tubular bell that get gradually further apart at the end of 'A2'. This section is carefully dovetailed into the next by overlapping the octatonic pentachord and the first chord of the 'x' section that follows (with which it shares four invariants including the bass note C). The bell also continues to sound for two more strokes in the new section but is marked 'Lontano'. Other sections conclude with much lengthier abatements usually involving descending motion (an exception is the conclusion of 'x3' with its upward decremental chord).[35] 'A3' employs a different process of abatement in that it concludes with a reference to the main motif of the piece harmonised with diatonic tetrachords (bar 423). The repetitions of this motif lengthen in note values until they come to rest on a sustained chord that dovetails into the next section. During this passage the accompanying downward chords of accretion in the woodwind and a glockenspiel solo are gradually stripped away.

Another strategy Wilson employs is to leave ideas foreshortened or open-ended. So, for example, at the end of 'b1' a trombone melody is curtailed and open-ended crescendos are heard dissolving into brief silences, creating expectation for the next section.

The substantial closural passage of 'B3' (bars 377–388, Example 7.1) that follows the climax of the B sections, employs two principal procedures of abatement: melodic fragmentation and descent of register. As is typical, the abatement is not organized in an entirely regular way, so the exact point of closure is not predictable, but unlike the closure of 'A2' there is a clear feeling that these materials are spent and must terminate.[36] The dynamic and the number of voices remains fixed during the course of the abatement which is announced by two events: rapid descending chromatic material in organ manuals (with a slight lengthening of note values towards the end) and the crystallization of the strings onto a diatonic hexachord over a pedal B. This chord is transposed down through two octaves, transpositions drawn to our attention by the use of glissandi. At bar 382 a thematic fragment focused on C begins, creating a strong dissonant conflict with the B pedal (and a further conflict with C# in the string hexachord). This thematic idea is initially extended over 2 bars and given a weakly complementary consequent phrase. Given this four-bar mini-period and the clear downbeats at bar 382 and bar 384 we expect clear articulation at bar 386. But there is a delay of two beats before the idea from bar 382 is repeated three times, in increasingly curtailed form an octave lower (at bar 388 only the initial three Cs are left). The thematic fragment is first given a winding chromatic accompaniment, but this straightens out as the passage progresses until it twice (bars 386 and 7) becomes a descending chro-

---

35 It is possible to define two types of chord in this work that either acquire notes incrementally or shed them in the same way. The chords may either add notes in a consistently upward motion or a consistently downward one. I term these chords as either upward/downward accretive or upward/downward decremental chords.   36 Schoenberg's term 'liquidation' comes to mind here. See Arnold Schoenberg, 1967 (as n. 5), 58.

Music Example 7.1: Ian Wilson, Organ Concerto, bars 378–389

matic scale arriving on C#. At the end we realise that the C# is an upper chromatic neighbour, and the long B pedal a leading tone to the C that sounds alone (except for a bass drum roll) at the beginning of 'a3' (bar 389). One bar later a completely new texture confirms the onset of a new section and the closure of the old.

At the opposite extreme to this lengthy closural passage, we have 'c1' which, rather than going through a period of abatement or liquidation, seems simply to end. The music freezes or crystallises on a chord with nine pitch classes, formed from subsets in wind and organ of two octatonic collections. The strings persist with their ostinato for one bar, and then simply stop. A held tone leads us into the 'x' section that connects with 'B3'. Freezing or crystallising onto a chord is a characteristic of this work and several sections appear to end with large chords with five or more pitch classes. At times these chords seem to summarise the pitch content of the previous section or refer to the endings of other sections. As observed above, 'A2' a predominantly octatonic section, ends with an ocatatonic pentachord. It is built on C, an important point of tonal focus in the work so far. This chord shares 4 invariants with the octatonic chord at the end of 'b2' (not otherwise an octatonic section). Each section, except 'x3', from this point to the end of the work, concludes with a large chord. The nine-voice chord that ends 'c1' has already been mentioned, 'b3' ends on an A major hexachord (pitch class A has been a point of tonal focus in a number of the previous endings). 'a3' ends on a simple diatonic tetrachord (C major plus F) recalling those employed in 'b1' and 'b2'.

In the final 'x' section, 'x4', a curious feature is the way in which the final chords of the first two statements summarise the content of the music prior to them. So, the final chord of the first statement is the union of the earlier ones plus C (again we see this note being used as a destination). The total set is a six-note subset of the E♭/Cminor scale. The union at the end of the next phrase is then the entire seven-note E♭ major collection. At the end of the third phrase we never reach the expected summarising chord (E♭ major minus C), this has the effect of leaving the passage distinctly unclosed. (The missing C does occur prominently in the organ pedals at the beginning of its final cadenza.)

As well as the tendency for sections to end with large chords there is also one for sections (and the work as a whole) to progress towards melodic outpourings. These may be seen as another form of crystallisation. The idea that extended and highly-structured melody follows naturally from more fragmentary, more discursive, music, flows out of the ancient recitative / aria distinction. That a statement of ideas that takes rapidly changing twists and turns, somewhat akin to the way in which our thoughts might change from moment to moment, should lead to a more sustained and more focused outpouring of emotion, is a well-established musical convention. In *Rich Harbour* a chorale occupies bars 453–78 and comprises the main part of 'C2', the apotheosis of the 'C' sections and arguably the work as a whole. On a smaller scale there is often a tendency for sections to precipitate melody. Both 'b1' and 'b2' are sections in which melody emerges in the latter part (trombone in 'b1' and cor anglais in 'b2'). The solos share some similarities, but it is the role and positioning of the melodic outbursts that is significant. The effect of these short melodic statements is to make the material that leads up to them appear preparatory.

THE BEGINNING

The opening sections of the work ('x' and 'a1') allow us to illustrate many of the techniques and procedures used in a little more detail. (Ex. 1 shows 'xl' and the beginning of 'al') We can also reflect on some more generic issues. In the case of 'x' how do we recognise the opening material as 'introductory'? How fit are the contents for the purpose of opening the work, and do they suit the later roles of 'x' as interludes or transitions? In the case of 'a1', how do we recognise this section as a 'beginning' of the main part and a 'statement' of both materials and an expressive state identifiable with the A sections? As well as serving these purposes for the work as a whole, the sections must also have meaning, content and structure in themselves. In order to define the opening 'x' 'section as an introduction, Wilson employs a familiar musical trope: 'creation myth' music.

After an initial horn call, the music slowly emerges out of the depths, moving up through pitch space and gaining in complexity in a musical metaphor for the shift from darkness towards light. Among the other striking examples of this technique are of course the opening of *Das Rheingold*, Stravinsky's *Firebird*, Bartòk's Sonata for Two Pianos and Percussion and Ravel's Concerto for the Left Hand. Self-evidently such music can only be found at the beginning of a work.[37]

Although instrumentation and colour, as discussed above, are not parameters in the strict sense, they do play an important formal role in 'x'. There is a clear polarity in this section between brass and string timbres, which helps to articulate the essentially tripartite internal structure of the section. Furthermore, brass and percussion are also employed in their traditional 'signalling' role. The opening held B♭ in the horn clearly performs this function, and at three points percussion are used in a similar way. Oddly, the tonal focus on B♭

---

37 The 'Praeludium' to Berg's *Three Orchestral Pieces* op. 6 approaches the metaphor in a different way: indeterminate, unpitched percussion sounds at the beginning giving way to sounds with precise pitch (another way in which timbre may play a structural role).

Music Example 7.2: Ian Wilson, Organ Concerto, bars 1–29

and the polarity between B♭ and E established at the beginning of 'x1' (a polarity reinforced by timbral changes), is not a significant part of the later tonal argument. B♭ is prominent in the closing stages of the work and in the final chord. But C is more often heard as a goal tone. The contents of the opening section are tied to the remainder of the work through the first presentation of an important motif that will reappear in a number of guises in a variety of

Music Example 7.2 (*continued*)

sections. It is a simple and memorable idea in the tuba in bars 8–10 and horns in bars 25–29. In this sense, while acting as an introduction, the section also acts in an exposition. It is this very motive that will return too in stark form in the closing moments of the work. This is an interesting dual function: the creation-myth troping of these materials casts them as introductory, yet the materials are actually crucial to the core argument and to the ending. The upward-moving scale patterns in the strings (bars 12–24) also play, in modified form, an important role in the latter part of the work.

Turning to the more dynamic aspects of this opening section and its closure, the strings enter in bar 4 with low almost fugal material. This transforms into repeated upward-moving scales organised in groups of 7,7,9 quavers (cellos and basses) and 6,6,8 quavers (second violins and violas). After each three-element group the tessitura rises higher (see Example 7.2). Such a pattern can go on indefinitely, and implies no specific point of closure (although there is an increasing feeling that an end must come). The effect is one of intensification and motion towards an unpredictable goal. No corresponding process of abatement is provided, simply a cut-off at the end of bar 24. A bass drum roll in bar 22 signals the imminent ending of this passage. A passage of brass chords introduced by a tubular bell stroke, is then inserted. It serves to close the central part of 'x' simply by contrast in nearly every parameter (and by returning to the brass sounds of the opening). But is the function of this passage to close 'x' as a whole, or act as a transition into 'a1'? This little passage has low-level internal closure in that the horn's statement of the work's main motif is a balanced entity in which the held final note (C) seems loosely to balance the opening three (as so often in Wilson's music, the constantly changing bar-lengths deny feelings of exact balance). But, the five-bar statement is too short to feel complete in itself, and ends with a crescendo and drum roll that lead us into 'a1'.

The slow-fast contrast between sections 'x' and 'a1' has the effect of 'x' being perceived as introduction and the forceful first entry of the organ tends inevitably to make 'a1' sound like a 'solo exposition'. The new section begins with a strong downbeat emphasised by an organ pedal cluster and the bass drum. There is also an immediate emphasis on C (the first time this pitch receives strong emphasis). A number of other elements serve to give this section its statemental quality as the first of the 'a' sections. The section has a tightly organised internal structure (it is an intricate assemblage of smaller forms) and a greater sense of completeness than the introduction. Its fifty bars divide equally into A+B 25+25 (even given the ever-changing bar lengths there is a 92.5 crotchets followed by 95.5 crotchet division of the section). However, this approximate symmetry (which is probably difficult to perceive with any degree of exactitude) is not replicated on the smaller scale within each 25-bar sub-section.

Each subsection divides in three. In bars 30–54 the three divisions constitute a bar form: 'm+n' 30–35, 'm+n' 36–43, 'o' 44–54). The phrases 'm' and 'n' have little internal sense of direction, little sense of either intensification or abatement, and it is the way they are contrasted and built into forms that gives them significance. The use of octatonic writing mitigates against any strong sense of tonal direction. A question that arises here is whether the paired phrases ('m+n') constitute a period. In eighteenth and nineteenth-century music, the period formed the main building block and may be defined as 'a pair of parallel phrases, the second ending in a cadence which is more final and positive in effect than that of the first. Usually the two phrases are in parallel construction – i.e. of the same motivic material, although this is not always the case'.[38] To this definition we may add that the two phrases are usually regarded as complementary, they should come together to form a larger whole. Wilson's two phrases are the same length. The main component of 'm' is a vigorous idea in the organ, ascending rapidly through three octaves, and flexible in rhythm; phrase 'n' is by contrast more static, unfolding two downward chords of accretion in repeated quavers. Wilson's phrases are neither articulated by cadences, nor parallel in construction. While there is a sense of balance and contrast there is no strong feeling of complementation. However, although there is not a coming together of these phrases they become linked by virtue of their varied repetition (the repetition of a unit will always have the effect of defining it as a recognisable segment). The varied repeat of 'm+n' is less balanced than the original, in that 'n' is no longer a downward chord of accretion, but is a single hexachord in a higher register, all the notes of which are stated simultaneously. Its diatonicism contrasts with the chromatic/ocatatonic material that goes before it; the effect is to reduce any sense of closure.

The onset of new material at bar 44 marks the move to 'o'. This is, following the bar-form model, a longer and more continuous outcome with a more consistent texture, registration and harmonic language (the passage is almost exclusively octatonic) until bar 51 where we are led clearly to the second half of 'a1'. The outbreak of melody in 'o' (there are several in counterpoint) helps create a feeling of consequentiality, particularly when the horn draws out a fragment at the beginning.

Example 7.3 shows the closing bars of 'a1', a classic example of abatement/collapse suggesting imminent termination, if not the exact point of closure. The move towards closure is much clearer and more decisive than that of the 'x' section. The final abatement takes place from bar 73, but the termination is prepared much earlier, when the music crystallises onto a melodic idea in bar 61. The closure of 'a1' is achieved through downward chords of accretion, but with an abatement of the number of notes in successive chords

---

38 Berry, 1966 (as n. 4), 16.

Music Example 7.3: Ian Wilson, Organ Concerto, bars 71–81

until, in bar 76, only one note sounds. The dynamic also abates. A falling melodic idea emerges low in the organ that shortens in length with each statement, creating a strong feeling of liquidation or collapse and the convergence of all three lines (including a falling bass line), onto a single note, once again C, the lowest note of the pedal board. As usual, the process takes place in bars of irregular length. The next section begins quietly with only a slight overlap, dovetailing the two sections together with C as a common tone.

Music Example 7.3 (*continued*)

THE END

Although the final minutes of the work are loaded with materials connected to an approaching end (chorale, cadenza, quiet epilogue) processes of closure and abatement are less in evidence than in earlier sections. It could be argued that Wilson's work does not close, it simply ends. The longest section in the work ('C2') is built to a high state of tension, which the work finds it impossible to dispel through processes of abatement such as those described above. At bar

453 'C2' reaches a climactic chorale in organ with strings and woodwind playing repeated upward scales: a familiar-enough strategy as we approach the end
of a large orchestral work. Here the tension is generated not by tonality but by
a range of contextual factors including the persistent use of upward moving
devices and the increasing dynamic. The chorale concludes on a huge eleven-
note chord (bar 478); a cadenza follows. Traditionally a cadenza connects V6/4
to its 5/3 resolution, thus releasing harmonic tension and assisting the work to
move towards its eventual closure. Wilson's cadenza, not propelled by any such
harmonic progression, is unable to dispel the tension generated by the end of
the chorale.

The cadenza, set off by an *fff* (*in aria*) brass chord, is unable to dispel the
tension largely because it is comprised predominantly of rising six-voice
quaver scales deriving from the rising figures in wind and strings that accompanied the chorale. Again the scales become higher and they are also in irregular groupings, factors that tend to work against any sense of closure. The introduction of percussion marking the beginnings of each upward pattern serves
only to heighten tension, as the percussion gets louder, so the quavers are
divided into semiquavers (Example 7.4). Far from trying to achieve a sense of
closure, Wilson lets the music literally get stuck on its final and highest chord
(although the organ pedals have once again achieved a low C). Wilson's
describes this moment by saying that the 'organ stops abruptly, as if realising
it has 'gone too far'.[39]

The organ stops, but the percussion persist in desolately thumping out their
irregularly spaced downbeats and do not fade, but keep the *fff* dynamic. The
effect of this is to leave the work emasculated. The final 'x' section is left to
draw some sort of conclusion, but does not effect closure, it rather conveys the
impression that the energy of the work is spent and that it is almost an after-
thought. This section comprises four elongated, simple, stark diatonic har-
monisations of the piece's central motif (a motif closely associated with the 'x'
sections). It leads to an abbreviated repetition in the organ of the short octatonic
cadenza at the centre of section 'A2' with its irregular bass rhythm that proceeds up a rising octatonic scale (bar 549, Example 7.5). This juxtaposition of
diatonicism and octatonicism at the end of the work summarises two important aspects of its harmonic construction, but summary and recall do not close.

The entire work ends (see Example 7.5) by freezing on an octatonic chord
that had prominence, but was not the concluding chord, in the previous
cadenza (it appears immediately before the *ritardando* in bar 150 and was the
first, rather than the last, of the three chords that conclude the cadenza in bar
151).[40] Ending by recalling, but not otherwise developing, bringing new light

---

39 Wilson (as n. 8), 27.   40 The top note of this chord should be D♭ not D, and the analysis proceeds
on the assumption that the A♭ in the double bass ceases to sound on the downbeat of bar 550.

Music Example 7.4: Ian Wilson, Organ Concerto, bars 503–533

on or closing more decisively, part of an earlier event and freezing on a chord whose significance to the work as a whole is no greater than that of many others is to end with a feeling of faint reminiscence and leaves the work without definitive closure. Oddly too, the ending does not focus on C, perhaps the most important goal tone identified in the earlier sections of the work. Instead the E♭ triad prominent at the end of the statement of the main motive remains a component in the final chord.

41 Wilson (as n. 8), 24.   **42** Bailey (as n. 22), xx.

Music Example 7.4: (*continued*)

CONCLUSION

In the course of this essay the connections I have drawn have been with works of the European mainstream and with the preoccupations of composers from the earlier part of the twentieth century. Although Wilson is from Northern Ireland, he does, I believe, see himself very much in a European context and his approach to form and the aesthetics that inform it seem to confirm this. In this essay I have explored a number of broad formal issues in Wilson's work; issues that stem from his rejection of the three-movement form that he says 'holds little attraction for me'.[41] His approach, while rooted in the formal and aesthetic principles of the eighteenth century, involves solutions to formal problems that are clearly those of the twentieth century. Kathryn Bailey has recently identified a tendency in Webern's early atonal works (the *Five Orchestral Pieces*, op. 10 for example) for the music to polarize between extremely rapid compressed pieces with frenzied gestures and extremes of dynamic, and slower pieces in which time and activity stand almost frozen and suspended.[42] To contrast sections 'A2' and 'x4' will indicate how Wilson achieves such contrasts within his single span; thus fulfilling a desire to create a single movement that fulfils what is expected of a concerto.

Music Example 7.5: Ian Wilson, Organ Concerto, bar 546–551

8

A post-war 'Irish' symphony:
Frank Corcoran's Symphony No. 2

JOHN PAGE

I am a passionate believer in 'Irish' dream-land-scape, two languages, polyphony of history, not ideology or programme. No Irish composer has yet dealt adequately with our past. The way forward – the newest forms and technique ... – is the way back to deepest human experience.[1]

The intention of this discussion is to examine the significance and nature of a specific post-war 'Irish' Symphony, namely Frank Corcoran's Second Symphony, within the broader symphonic context. The examination of the specific work itself shall form the final part of the discussion and shall be preceded by a general view of the 'Irish Symphony' in the second half of the twentieth century, focussing briefly upon the output of three major twentieth-century Irish symphonists: Gerard Victory, Seóirse Bodley and John Kinsella. The notion of a peculiarly 'Irish' Symphony is something that shall be explored through the ensuing discourse and indeed the rejection and redefinition of the idea 'Symphony' by some Irish composers shall be an important adroit aside within the overall investigation.

   There appear to be two fundamental questions that must inform any such discussion. Firstly, what does it mean for a composer of the late twentieth century to write a work entitled 'Symphony', and secondly, what, if anything, does it mean to be an Irish composer writing such a work? The symphony is a complex compositional problem for any post-war composer. The traditional view of the symphony as a complex and extended work of 'serious' intent may still hold, but the manifestation of such motivation engages the obvious problems of how to organise compositional material into a significant structure of weight-bearing capacity. In other words, we immediately invoke visions of an extended and coherent work dealing with the expectations of symphonic form and nomenclature. Herein lies the quan-

---

1 Frank Corcoran in an interview with Michael Dervan, *Irish Times*, 22 September 1995.

dary for many symphonists – to write a work entitled 'symphony' still means to confront a mass of canonic expectation, being in itself a potent and enduring symbol of the Western Art music tradition. The reactions to this elemental issue have redefined the post-war symphony and have led to a typical lack of consensus regarding the symphonic genre.

In broad outline there have been three types of response to this condition. Firstly, we find a group of symphonists who have engaged with the Symphony as a viable means of serious musical expression and with whom this discussion is most interested. Secondly, there appears to be a compositional response that emanates from those whose natural disposition may be described as symphonic, but for whom the entitling of a work as 'Symphony' is an impossible shackle that in some way prescribes and even interferes with the creative process and its subsequent reception. The final response to the post-war symphonic condition is most extreme and involves a rejection, conscious or not, of a symphonic method. For these non- (if not anti-) symphonic composers the notion of the Symphony has no relevance to their compositional workings.

In Ireland this situation can be seen in a comparison of the output of several composers. The symphonic stance shall be examined, as previously stated, through the symphonies of Victory, Bodley, Kinsella and particularly Corcoran. The fundamental question surrounding a national identity of a post-war symphony – can such a work be described as peculiarly 'Irish'? – is one that is answered in very different ways by the composers in question. The abstract and formal nature of symphonic writing has by its nature never really been a vehicle of national expression, although there have been many successful attempts to integrate symphonic expression with a feeling of national identity, Jean Sibelius being an obvious and striking example. The post-war symphony though has become a more abstract musical proposition and indeed the notion of an 'Irish Symphony' is one that in essence does not exist as an integrated formal category for those composers engaged in the genre. There are elements of national identity in the inspiration and material that form the foundation for such works, but for these composers the Symphony is a serious work written to express weighty concepts that may have specifically Irish elements (such as the use of folk melody, instrumentation or text) but are essentially formally abstract.

For the second and large group of composers the title 'Symphony' forges an intrinsic and irrevocable link with a canonic tradition that has only an indirect relevance to their own compositional practices. Both Raymond Deane (b. 1953) and Kevin O'Connell (b. 1958) share a similar and not uncommon view regarding the actual title 'Symphony' as an archaic and somewhat anachronistic construct that remains the symbol of a tradition that has no place in their

2 See Victory's own explanatory notes that are included in the score of the work.

musical imaginations and creative processes. The conclusions of such a particular reading of the Symphony have led such composers to abandon the expectations of the title itself for the freedom of a new nomenclature in which the work itself exists as an unfettered and unexpectant entity.

It is possible that the motivations for such a revisioning of the Symphony may lie in the perception of the Irish identity as being clearly outside of the musical tradition that has produced and nurtured the Symphony. It may be easier for an Irish composer to reject the Symphony as a non-indigenous idea, something to which an Irish composer has no right of inheritance and therefore no duty to maintain. It may also be merely a manifestation of the enduring post-war *Weltgeist* that has, in general, globally deconstructed such traditions and categorisations rendering redundant the need and desire to label, an era in which the individual art work exists solely on its own terms.

The symphonic concept, the actual compositional method itself however, has remained for some such composers, both Deane and O'Connell included, a vital component of their creative process. O'Connell describes his two-movement piece, *North* as having elements of symphonic construction and Deane's recent work, *Ripieno* displays facets of symphonic organisation. Both pieces, however, decidedly evade traditional symphonic expectation, and although Deane chooses a quasi-formalistic title for his work, both compositions are not symphonies in title or concept.

Beyond the redefinition of the symphonic concept and the rejection of the actual designation 'Symphony' and its concomitant tradition, there exists a purely non-symphonic response to the post-war predicament. The music of Gerald Barry (b. 1952), for example, is a radical distancing from the traditional symphonic ideal. The prescribed functional attributes of the Symphony do not apply in such music where there is no direct or indirect engagement with the symphonic tradition. Such a compositional position lies clearly outside of the idea of Symphony and creates a new vision of musical organisation that avoids association with symphonic practice and its attending arguments. Such a distancing may or may not be described as anti-symphonic but it is clear in either case that the Symphony in any definition has no part to play in the creativity of such composers.

Of the four Irish symphonists under discussion, Gerard Victory (1921–1995) remains one of the most prolific and diverse of twentieth century Irish composers. Within such a large corpus lie four symphonies. The First Symphony (1961), subtitled '*Siomfóin Geárr*', is a short three-movement work that follows a traditional formal plan. The most obvious feature of this work is the clever use of orchestral colour, something that characterises all of Victory's symphonies and is clearly evident in the Second Symphony (1977), 'Il

Rocorso' (The Return), another three-movement work based upon Italian philosopher Giambattista Vico's three-phase theory of cyclical history. Entitled 'Refrains', the Third Symphony (1984) is also in three movements, and is a highly complex work lasting some forty minutes. As the title suggests it contains a sequence of recurring motives, particularly prevalent in the first movement. There is no programme as such, but Victory himself describes a musical conflict deriving from deliberate opposition of contrasting musical styles.[2] The Fourth Symphony (1988) is a continuous and more condensed work lasting just over twenty minutes. It is a fusion of two different sketch works: *Greek Festival* and *The Nightwatch*. Again, orchestral texture and colour are the identifying marks of the work, but these are of a complexity that surpasses the previous symphonies. Thematic invention appears to become subservient to sonority and it is doubtless this use of instrumental texture and sonority that informs Victory's symphonic style, where the symphonic differentiation of blocks of sound provides the necessary contrasts to create such complexity of structure, a particular feature of post-war symphonic construction.

Seóirse Bodley's (b. 1933) symphonic writing dates back to 1958 and a period of study in Stuttgart under Johann Nepomuk David. The First Symphony, which was completed in Dublin in 1959, is a continuous twenty-minute piece divided into four sections and owes much to the mainstream European tradition. The Second Symphony uses Ireland for its direct inspiration and is entitled 'I have loved the lands of Ireland' (quotation from Colum Cille) accompanied by a significantly parenthetical 'Symphony No. 2'. Written in 1980, some twenty years after the First Symphony, 'I have loved the lands of Ireland' is described by Bodley himself as a 'post-modern Irish symphony'[3], an attempt 'to delineate the essence of the emotional and psychological history of the Irish people'. Bodley claims the work to be 'a symphony in the sense of being a musical statement of depth and size, rather than because of any adherence to particular formal structures', hence the parenthetical title. *Ceol* (Symphony No. 3) of 1981 is a much shorter work lasting only twenty-five minutes in comparison with the forty minutes of 'I have loved the lands of Ireland.' It is again based upon literary texts, this time by the Irish poet, Brendan Kennelly. The Fourth Symphony (1990–1) marks a clear departure from Bodley's two previous symphonic works. No longer directly inspired by text, it is in four movements and is highly abstract in nature. Symphony No. 5, 'The Limerick Symphony' of 1991 subscribes to more traditional symphonic expectations and the folk idiom that was subtly integrated into the Fourth Symphony here appears in a more obvious guise.

---

3 All Bodley citations concerning 'I have loved the lands of Ireland' (Symphony No. 2) are taken from the composer's own programme notes.

The diverse nature of Bodley's symphonic works is clearly apparent. From the inspiration of the European *avant-garde* in the First Symphony through the Irish text inspired Second and Third to the more abstract and finally integrated Fourth and Fifth, Bodley's symphonies outline a musical progression spanning over thirty years. The importance of text in Symphonies No. 2 and 3 signifies the close relationship that pertains in those works between a literary and mythical tradition and perception of an Irish identity. This combination of symphonic thought and Irish identity is a vital aspect of these works, and the subsequent process of distillation and embedding of the folk idiom in the Fourth and Fifth Symphonies, which were written after a ten year gap, appears to be an attempt to integrate both formal symphonic expectations and the perception of Irish tradition.

By far the most prolific of twentieth century Irish symphonists is John Kinsella (b. 1932). His eight symphonies extend over a concentrated twenty-year period and what follows is a brief description of only a few. For Kinsella, the Symphony is fundamentally a large orchestral work engaging serious subject matter, a flexibly universal construct. Essentially his symphonic style relies upon a traditional idiom in which symphonic structural expectations are fulfilled. The similarity of formal conformity found in the first two symphonies is abandoned with the somewhat more unorthodox construction of the Third Symphony (1989–90), entitled '*Joie de Vivre*'. The work is formed as two movements proper, framed and separated by a Prologue, Intermezzo and Epilogue. The integrated structure of the work, effected in no small part by the points of reference that connect the three above-mentioned sections, is followed by another strictly four-movement work, akin to the formality of the first two symphonies but inspired by a more programmatic, and indeed, Irish concept – 'The Four Provinces'. The Fourth Symphony (1990– 1) is a forty-five minute piece and comprises four movements, each inspired by one of the four Irish provinces. The wholly Irish subject matter is further illustrated by the subtitle 'The Birmingham Six'.[4] In the Fifth Symphony (1991–2), entitled 'The 1916 Poets', Ireland continues to be the source of inspiration, but unlike the somewhat vague and abstract description of provincial location found in the Fourth Symphony, here we find a more concrete realisation of 'Irishness' through the poetry of the 1916 rebels.

The engagement with nationalist thought through symphonic form finds a voice here, as in Bodley's Second and Third Symphonies, and is an aspect of the nineteenth-century symphonic tradition that seems to reinvent itself in the imaginations of certain Irish symphonists throughout the twentieth century.

---

4 This sub-title refers to a major miscarriage of British justice in 1974 when six Irish men were wrongly imprisoned for suspected involvement in an IRA pub bombing in Birmingham. They were finally released 17 years later.

The idea of a generic category entitled post-war 'Irish' symphony is therefore an impossible one. As has been seen, many Irish proponents of the symphonic genre have found the concept of an 'Irish' symphony untenable, and
have relied upon the traditional abstract definitions whilst remaining open to
the possibility of using Irish material for inspiration in folk melody, texts or
events. This then seems to be an answer to our earlier question. It obviously
does mean something to be an Irish composer creating symphonies, but it is
not necessarily a compositional process or model. The symphony remains an
abstract idea, a way of dealing with important musical issues, even if employing particularly Irish material.

In turning to the music of Frank Corcoran (b. 1944) we find the abstract
symphonic definitions taken to a new realm. The notion of an 'Irish' symphony has no concrete association for Corcoran, but his intense fascination
with the past evokes a pre-historical Irish psyche, the manifestation of which
is vital for his music. Corcoran has written four symphonies to date and each
deals with the post-war symphonic predicament in very different ways from
those symphonists previously discussed. Corcoran has spent most of his compositional life in Germany, and this has unquestionably affected his response
to the problems facing the post-war composer. Much of Corcoran's compositional practice can be traced back to the Piano Trio (1978). Here, Corcoran
explored the concept of 'Macro-counterpoint', a technique that remains an
important element of his compositional style. The process itself, as Corcoran
has stated, is not note against note; rather level against level, a controlled
superimposition of musical layers of such complexity that the resultant texture resembles the aleatoric counterpoint of Lutoslawski, a distinct influence,
as well as the micro-counterpoint of Ligeti. It is somewhere between these
prominent positions that Corcoran sees his own style residing.

In summary, Corcoran views 'the problems any extended, musical art-work
poses as that of structure, expression, aura, semantics and historical palimp-
sest'[5]. This is essentially his symphonic concept, a construct that he simply
defines as 'sounding together' (Greek allusion rather than Viennese tradition),
the old etymological stance that moves towards the emancipation of sound
structure. In agreement with Adorno[6], Corcoran commends music's desire to
break free from the castrating social label of entertainment, in an attempt to
validate the eternal questions that music poses: 'Can music express? Have a
real message? Manipulate our minds? Illustrate? Mirror? Reveal? Does it do

---

5 All Corcoran citations, unless otherwise noted, are taken from two unpublished sketches for the insert
notes of the Marco Polo/Naxos CD of Symphonies Nos. 2, 3 and 4, entitled 'Unscrambling My
Symphonies' and 'About my Symphonies Nos. 2, 3 and 4.'   **6** For Adorno's perspective on modernist
art and its opposition to commercial isolation and the culture industry, see Theodor Adorno, *Aesthetic
Theory*, Gretel Adorno and Rolf Tiedermann (eds), trans. Robert Hullot-Kentor (Minneapolis:
University of Minnesota Press, 1997).

Music Example 8.1: Frank Corcoran, Symphony no. 2, I, Opening

so, some of the time? If yes, how? Does it matter?' With a resounding Yes, Corcoran answers his final question: music does matter, and the expression of music in symphonic form is vindicated in its ability to deal with such fundamental interrogation and exploration of musical structure. In the *Symphonies of Symphonies of Wind Instruments* (1981) Corcoran takes the *Symphonies of Wind Instruments* by Stravinsky as a defining point of departure, both in its clearly etymological definition of 'Symphony' (sounding together) and in its presentation of blocks of timbral units.[7] This is music about music and Corcoran's macro-counterpoint produces a density and complexity that on occasion surpasses the obvious metred, Stravinskian thoughts.

The Second Symphony (1981) is central to the present discussion and confronts fundamental issues for the post-war symphonic composer, hence the focus upon this specific work. The implications of structure, manipulation of time and timbre, order and chaos and primeval violence form the basis of Corcoran's approach. The Symphony lasts some 23 minutes and comprises two movements entitled 'Soli' and 'Tutti' respectively. The structure of the entire work proposes a symphonic dialectic depicting chaos in the first movement as an unfettered, non-metric flow of events, held in place by the passage of particular time periods, followed by the metric, notational ordering of said events and material in the second movement. The contrast of 'Soli' and 'Tutti'

---

7 The works share the same instrumentation.

Music Example 8.2: Frank Corcoran, Symphony no. 2, I, bars 50*ff*.

could be described as a social ('Tutti') ordering of primordial ('Soli') individualism, a poignant reflection on post-war society in general.

The opening section has a primal violence, effected in no little part by the
technical originality of the double-bass writing. (Ex. 8.1)

The effect of playing behind the bridge, a technique first deployed by
Corcoran in his Piano Trio (1978), is fragmented and volatile, described by

the composer himself as the barking of seals and human suffering. Throughout the first movement the clear division of timbral choruses (traditional orchestral sectional divisions) functions as a structuring device that also continues the contrast and isolation that characterises the work. These units return either identically or in varied guises but they rarely overlap; in fact there is only one occasion of such timbral and material interaction at letter R, where the brass, wind and percussion combine in a collision of chaos and order. (Ex. 8.2)

Here the wind and horns are metred in 3/4, the first such temporal organisation in the work, whilst the remaining brass play in *diversi tempi*, also the first such marking in the piece. The occurrence of such a violent juxtaposition creates the point of climax from which the movement quickly retreats, ending with a varied recurrence of the opening bass material.

The function of the percussion section in the first movement is distinct from the other sectional units. Each division of the movement is accompanied by a percussive entry, heralding the section with use of either tamtams, cymbals, gongs and cowbells (one exception is the return of the opening basses at letter H_3). This structural use of percussion is further enhanced by the introduction of the timpani just before letter M. From this point to the end, and particularly through the collision point and climax at letter R, the percussion act as a temporal, if not metric foundation which undoubtedly prefigures the organisation of the second movement (note the tempo marking of $\quarternote = 50$ in both the metred wind and horns and percussion).

The whole issue of time is presented here as a primitive periodic division of the music, within which the actual rhythmic and metric articulations are left imprecise and individualistic, in keeping with the movement's title. In the smeared string chorales (at letters C, E, I and U) the method of playing: behind the bridge, tremolo, *senza/con molto vibrato*, harmonics and glissandi all within slower time periods (four or five seconds as opposed to one) with fewer events in each period all contribute to a significant increase in imprecision. The wind and brass passages (from letters F to H_3) are also marked by an imprecision in performance, but unlike the string chorales, the intervallic patterns and the increased number of events per time period produces a more organised and definite texture (Ex. 8.3)

It is worth noting that the imaginative use of string technique is also found in the wind and brass writing – the tuba flutter-tonguing and markings for trombones and horn to play the highest note possible at letter F are clear examples of the constant striving for imprecision.

It is impossible to describe a unified and coherent theory of pitch organisation in such an intentionally imprecise movement, but in general the

Music Example 8.3: Frank Corcoran, Symphony no. 2, I, Letter G*ff*.

pitch material follows the distinctive divisions of the timbral units. Each section derives pitch material from an individual collection of pitches, ranging from seven-note groups to the full chromatic spectrum at the climax point, letter R. Within these groups there are prominent pitches such as at the opening where the notes D, E and F# appear at strategic points within a group of seven notes (D, E♭, E, F, F#, B♭, B). At letter A, the brass unit describes another group of seven pitches (D, E♭, E, F, G♭, G, A♭) where the bass motion from D to A♭ marks a definite quasi-cadential transition within the unit. Within the imprecision of the string chorales there is a gravitation towards the note E, particularly in the basses, as a point of repose. Indeed this bass note E loosely functions throughout the entire symphony as a point of arrival (the second movement begins with the basses playing low E and at the end of the symphony the bass note E is again found, now displaced three octaves higher).

Within the complexity and nature of the movement it may not be possible or desirable to discern a definitive pitch strategy, but there are certain junctures throughout the movement in which individual pitches have a specific functional role providing an added and obscure structuring element to the chaotic depiction.

The contrast between the two movements is striking. The first movement ends with the imprecise sounds of the opening only to be followed by an intense and chromatic macro-counterpoint in the strings. The effect is aleatoric, almost chaotic, but the control is precise and ordered and the staggered horn entries only heighten the overall smeared effect. The metric and rhythmic order of the second movement is obsessive with a more homogenous sense of texture between the timbral groupings. There are still moments of isolation, such as the *Adagio* chorales at letter C, two bars before letters E$_2$ and M. (Ex. 8.4)

Music Example 8.4: Frank Corcoran, Symphony no. 2, II, Letter C*ff*.

The degree of timbral integration though makes these events stand out as singular moments of reflection rather like the wide-spanning Stravinskian oboe solo that appears twice, both times emerging from the imprecision of *diversi tempi*. The macro-counterpuntal passages appear ten times throughout the movement, each time bringing both order and apparent chaos in an accumulation of momentum. The passage at the beginning of the movement illustrates the technique involved. (Ex. 8.5)

The first violins lead with a tortuous chromatic line in triplets; this is answered canonically by the second violins at a crotchet's distance, the violas follows at the bar followed by the cellos again at a crotchet's distance. The canon is virtually complete apart from octave transpositions, and rest insertions, always within the canon. There is only one point of departure in the canonic device at A, where the 5/4 bar offsets the violas and cellos entries by a crotchet. Corcoran himself describes these events as a bending of canonic technique to timbral intentions. Here the combination

Music Example 8.5: Frank Corcoran, Symphony no. 2, II, Opening

of metric, ordered flow combined with timbral colour generates the structure and creates the formal imperative. Again the use of percussion is structural as in the *diversi tempi* at letter C_1, which, like letter R in the first movement, underpins the imprecision and sense of 'smeared' time. This, along with the highly measured timpani and percussion at letters E_1, E_2 and O, demonstrates the controlling nature of the percussion and its fundamental relationship with the other timbral groups.

The structuring and ordering of material from the first movement in the 'Tutti' movement manages to cohere the two disparate ends of the dialectic by using the same primordial substances but presented in a social organisation, highly metred and sophisticated. The first re-ordered presentation of material from the first movement occurs at letter B_1. Here one bar of letter A from the first movement is written out in notation and metre but it is not an exact representation and it is not until letter N_1 that an extended and intact structured presentation of material from the first movement (letters D and W) is found. (Exs 8.6 + 8.7)[8]

8 There is one important discrepancy in the material used. The final treble clef B♭s, three time periods after D and two time periods after W in the first movement, are not to be found in the N_1 statement but seem to be transplanted into the coda of the symphony, a point that shall be discussed later.

Music Example 8.6: Frank Corcoran, Symphony no. 2, II, Letter N, *ff*., 'written out'

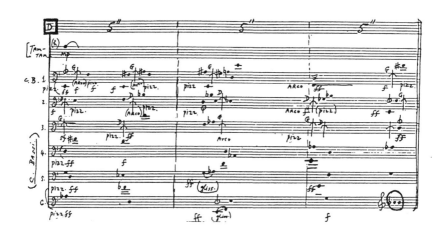

Music Example 8.7: Frank Corcoran, Symphony no. 2, I, Letter D*ff*.,
'primordial substance'

Here the opening basses are not in any sense tamed, but the violence is now structured, and accordingly more accentuated. At the climax of the movement (letters P – Q) material from the first movement (letters G, O and P) is presented in close proximity, temporally tying together differentiated units of the first movement in a telescoping of time periods whilst organising the imprecise material into a complex rhythmic structure. The final re-ordering of the 'Soli' primeval substance appears towards the end of the symphony (18 bars from the end), where the very opening is presented in the most complex of inter-movement orderings condensed from 27 one-second time periods to five bars of 4/4.

The coda of the symphony seems to reflect upon the rarefied residue that remains from the ordering process of the second movement. (Ex. 8.8)

Music Example 8.8 Frank Corcoran, Symphony no. 2, II, Coda

As previously noted, the missing B♭s in the basses (see example 8.6 + 8.7) appear six bars from the end in the third and fourth basses. It is controlled in mood, but still volatile. The significance of the low E in the basses in the first movement is again alluded to as a continuous pedal through the entire coda. Various fleeting intervallic fragments appear, such as F to B♭ and the whole-tones G# to A# and E to F#. The most obvious relationship, however, is the semitonal E–F that appears so many times throughout the work. Here the notes are presented in a purely primal subterranean state in isolation. The last bars separate the two notes by two and then three octaves with a final percussive touch on the high tam-tam. All that remains is a bass high E left to exist alone from the rarefied residue that makes up the coda. The E♭ at the very bottom of the texture creates a smeared whole-tone dissonance with the neighbouring F of the kind that is heard throughout the symphony (specifically at the beginning of the second movement in third and fourth horns (see Ex. 8.5) and the recurring trumpet trio in the middle of the first movement at letter K₁). (Ex. 8.9)

Music Example 8.9: Frank Corcoran, Symphony no. 2, I, Letter K*ff*.

The dynamic markings of the coda differentiate the function of the bass parts (see music Ex. 8.8, final four bars). The dramatisation of parts is made manifest in the dynamic interplay of the three parts. It is clear that the first and second basses remain an independent foundation, reiterating the note E with varying dynamics and articulative shadings. The other parts interact with each other in a more splintered manner, and provide echoes and references of previous material, such as the missing B♭s from letter N₁. In the final bars the function of the first and second bass is realised as it registerally rises above the other parts in a reversal of dynamics growing from *p* to *mf* and remaining long after the other parts have faded out *ppp*.

The symphony is a validation of order over chaos as Corcoran himself has stated: 'at the end of my symphony there is a real gain in order, in the composed control of the material', but the residual primitive substance that undergoes transformation in the second movement is still a potent foundation, an undercurrent that is heard once more in the coda. The final E does not belong to the control of the second movement; it is primal in nature and, in a sense, can be traced to before the beginning of the symphony itself. This is Corcoran's attempt to deal with the past. It is the undeterred obsession with time and our past that has created this post-war symphony. It is the foundation of individual 'Soli' events in an imprecise temporal structure and the manipulation and ordering of this material into a controlled social 'Tutti' space that lies at the heart of this work. The first movement is undoubtedly a form of model for the second but it also holds the vital primal information and substance from pre-history to allow Corcoran to reinvent the post-war present in a dialogue with the past, and to create potential order in chaos through a symphonic dialectic.

9

Passion, painting, poetry, pessimism: extra-musical themes in the string quartets of Ian Wilson

ROBIN ELLIOTT

Ian Wilson has accomplished by the age of thirty-six what many composers would consider a lifetime's work: the first DPhil in composition from the University of Ulster (1990); frequent commissions, performances, broadcasts, and recordings of his music by first-rate professional organisations; a publishing agreement with the prestigious Universal Edition company (1996); numerous scholarships, fellowships, and residency appointments; and election to Aosdána (1998), to name just a few highlights.[1] He has even received the perhaps somewhat dubious distinction of attaining canonic status, as his piano trio *The Seven Last Words* was set for the Northern Ireland A-level music syllabus in 1998.

The five works under consideration in this article were written between 1992 and 2000, and mark an important contribution to the string quartet repertoire.[2] Each of the quartets betrays a significant extra-musical association, variously from religion, art, and literature. Wilson's productivity is impressive: the five quartets are just part of an already large chamber music output that also includes significant works for piano trio and other mixed ensembles, and the chamber music oeuvre in turn is matched by a significant body of vocal and orchestral music. By 2000, Wilson's catalogue numbered over 50 works in total. In March 2000 Wilson began a three-year research fellowship at his alma mater, the University of Ulster, which will allow him to write a chamber opera (to be premiered in Germany in 2003), and thus complete his survey of all the major musical genres.

This enterprise and accomplishment is motivated by a profound love of music, but is also guided by Wilson's committed Christian beliefs. Wilson has stated on numerous occasions that his Christian faith is central to his work as

1 Aosdána is 'an affiliation of artists engaged in literature, music and visual arts. It was established by the Arts Council [of Ireland] in 1983 to honour those artists whose work has made an outstanding contribution to the arts in Ireland'; membership is limited to 200 at any time. Information taken from the Aosdána web site (www.artscouncil.ie/aosdana/).

a composer. The entry on Wilson in *Irish Composers* begins with his words: 'Faith and life are, for me, the principal subjects of music.'³ The score of every piece by Wilson ends with 'D.G.' or 'Deo gratias' ('Thanks be to God'). One thinks immediately of Bach, who wrote 'JJ' ('Jesu juva', meaning 'Jesus, help me') near the start of a score, and 'SDG' ('Soli Deo Gloria' or 'Sit Deo Gloria', meaning 'To God [alone] be the glory') at the end. Although this humble dedication of one's work to God may be thought more characteristic of the eighteenth century than later periods, it lived on into the nineteenth – one thinks of Bruckner, for instance, who dedicated his Ninth Symphony 'An den lieben Gott'. Charles Gounod, for another, viewed 'the communication of artistic vision as a fundamentally Christian act, one in which the artist is rendered "richer by giving than receiving ... He who knows this understands life, faith, and love!"'⁴ The quotation could apply equally well to Ian Wilson.

Such sentiments were more rarely expressed by the major composers of the twentieth century. Stravinsky's *Symphony of Psalms*, according to the title page, was 'composée à la gloire de DIEU' but is dedicated to the Boston Symphony Orchestra. Olivier Messiaen also springs to mind in this connection, but then his highly perfumed Catholic mysticism is of quite a different order from the more traditional Christian beliefs of a Bach or a Bruckner – or indeed of Ian Wilson.

Wilson's faith is expressed not only, indeed not even principally, in settings of religious texts. Instead, it is present in all of his music, an underpinning as solid as his finely crafted musical technique. He explains how this facet of his work as a composer developed:

There eventually came a point when I felt that ... I had gained enough experience to move beyond the actual physicality of drawing notes on paper and to start to examine the why of composing.

At that time, around 1992, the obvious reason for me – someone whose faith was personally important – to write music, was as an act of worship; not music for worship, you must understand, but the actual engagement of my concentration with this ability, the sitting down and writing whatever piece I was working on became for me an expression of faith. This did not mean that every piece was religious in content or inspiration. In fact, even

2 Wilson's sixth quartet, titled *In fretta, in vento*, was completed in December 2001, too late for consideration here. It is in a single movement and quotes from a Bach chorale near the end. The work is dedicated to the memory of the composer's grandmother, who died just after the quartet was completed. (Ian Wilson, personal communication, 19 January 2002)   3 Eve O'Kelly, ed.: *Irish Composers*, fifth edition (Dublin: Contemporary Music Centre, 1997), not paginated. An updated version of the Wilson entry is available on the CMC's web site at www.cmc.ie/composers/ wilsoni.html.   4 Steven Huebner, *The Operas of Charles Gounod* (Oxford: Clarendon Press, 1990), 79. In this passage, Huebner quotes from Comtesse d'Alcantara, *Marcello: Sa vie, son œuvre, sa pensée, et ses amis* (Geneva, 1961), 197.

in the small number that were, I consciously broadened out their themes so that they were universal in their content, written to speak to as broad an audience as possible, no matter what their beliefs. The point is I felt I was honouring this thing I had by exploring it and trying to achieve its potential, and by doing so I was honouring God.[5]

Winter's Edge, the first of the five string quartets, is one of the earliest instrumental works to give evidence of this facet of Wilson's work as a composer.[6] Wilson has written that he regards this work as his 'first complete piece, as not only does it have a secure sense of structure and technique supporting it, but it also has a philosophical reason for coming into being'.[7]

Winter's Edge remains one of Wilson's finest compositions, a compact and beautifully structured work that combines a dense but cogent harmonic language with a wonderfully relaxed, uplifting lyricism. The Vanbrugh String Quartet commissioned the work with funds from the Arts Council of Northern Ireland, and premiered it in Omagh on 10 March 1993. Within a year the ensemble had taken the work on tour to festivals in Zagreb, Malvern, and Dublin, and had recorded it for the Chandos label, bringing Wilson to widespread attention. The Endellion String Quartet of London played the work on tour in Ireland in 1999, the Callino String Quartet played it on tour in the Netherlands and Ireland in 2000, and the Vanbrugh String Quartet has kept the work in its repertoire. On the basis of its performance record, it can be considered Wilson's most successful string quartet to date.

For the Chandos recording, the composer provided the following note:

> Toward the end of his second letter to Timothy, the apostle Paul asks his young disciples to try to visit him before winter.[8] Reflection on this request sowed the seeds of my quartet, and the more I thought about Paul's life, aspects of it such as conflict, transformation, solitude and destiny all gave rise to musical ideas which I was then able to mould into a comprehensible single-movement work. The emotional dichotomy between the death Paul knew awaited him (hence the urgency in his request to Timothy), and the hope for what lay beyond that, is reflected in the musical material – at times violent, at times contemplative, but ultimately seeking to reach higher. In the end, this work

---

5 Ian Wilson, 'The Composer as Prophet?', *Journal of Music in Ireland* i/1 (November–December 2000), 28.   6 *Winter's Edge* was completed in Graymount, Belfast on 24 July 1992 and was published by Universal Edition in 1996 (UE 14082). The quartet has been recorded twice by the Vanbrugh String Quartet: on *Ceathrar*, Chandos CD CHAN 9295 (recorded in 1993, released in 1994) and on *towards the far country*, Black Box CD BBM 1031 (recorded in 1999, released in 2000).   7 Ian Wilson: liner notes to Black Box CD recording BBM 1031 (2000), [3].   8 The scriptural passage to which Wilson refers is II Tim., iv, 21 which reads, in the King James Version of the New Testament, 'Do thy diligence to come before winter'.

is not a depiction of, or even a reflection on, the apostle's life, but that is where the music has its roots.[9]

A great deal of modern Biblical scholarship has not been overly kind to Paul. Born in Tarsus about 10 AD, he was educated in Jerusalem, and as a Jew and Pharisee he zealously persecuted Christians. On the road to Damascus in Syria, he witnessed a mystical vision of Christ. He then embarked upon an evangelical mission to promote his belief in salvation through faith in the Risen Christ, in the process transforming Christianity from a fringe movement to a vibrant faith that would alter the course of Western history. But his uncompromising views on homosexuality and the role of women in the church have been the source of much heated debate in recent times.

The points that Wilson isolates – conflict, transformation, solitude, destiny – go to the heart of our understanding of Paul, whether as a historical figure or a religious leader. Wilson then proceeds to resolve these complex issues into a single dichotomy, which is then capable of being transformed into compelling musical ideas. By the time this process of musical translation has been effected, however, nothing remains which could point unequivocally to the theological inspiration of the quartet. Any number of other scenarios could be imposed after the fact onto the music; indeed, in the absence of Wilson's programme note, it is unlikely that even the most perceptive listener would make a connection between the quartet and the life of Paul. Then again, as Wilson has taken pains to point out, the quartet is not a programmatic depiction of Paul's life; the Pauline inspiration was purely a personal matter for the composer, and each listener is now free to make of it what he or she wishes.

Winter's Edge is in one movement, 229 bars long and 13 to 14 minutes in duration. It opens with a *fortissimo* chord which presents all of the notes of a diatonic C major scale simultaneously, bounded by the octave from f to f'. The expressive indication is 'violent'; the chord decrescendos, is reattacked *sff tremolo sul ponticello*, and dies away again while gradually thinning out to an ethereal four-part chord in high harmonics. It is an arresting gesture, and Wilson notes that he carried this idea around in his head for weeks before actually beginning to write the quartet.[10] The idea returns at bars 82 and 147, more gentle the first time (*p non vib*), more anguished the second (the ethereal harmonics, instead of dying away, get louder and break off suddenly *sff*). These three framing gestures divide the quartet into three sections, the first and last almost equal in length (in terms of bar numbers), the middle one somewhat shorter.

The first section of the quartet is itself in two main parts. The first begins with a fine viola solo, marked *quasi recitative*, that presents two thematic ideas

9 Ian Wilson, quoted in the liner notes to Chandos CD recording CHAN 9295 (1994), 4.   10 Ian Wilson (as n. 7), [3].

that are developed later: a floating, peaceful melody, each phrase of which is set off by rests, and some rather anxious sounding semiquaver scale passages. The peaceful melody is soon transformed into a much more expansive version (violin 1, bar 17) that Wilson has referred to as 'something akin to a fate motif'.[11] The semiquaver passages, based now on an octatonic scale and presented in octaves in the two violins, brings about the first climax of the quartet (bars 30–38). The second part of the first section features a Stravinskian rhythmic ostinato, *pp sempre staccato*, to be played 'as if on tiptoe'. The ostinato gets progressively louder and is interrupted by unpredictable dissonant piercing outbursts. This section comes to a climax with all four instruments playing a short chromatically descending figure in close canon at unison.

A brief cello solo leads into the second section, which features two main ideas: two extended versions of the 'fate' motif in the first violin (bars 87, 117), and canonic ascending and descending scale passages (bars 100, 129). The chord from bar 1 returns *sul ponticello* at bar 142, but transposed up a semitone, initiating a brief transition to the third section. The third section consists of further developments and restatements of material presented earlier: frenzied semiquaver passages (bars 152 *ff* and 183 *ff*) alternate with calm presentations of the 'fate' motif (second violin, bars 169 *ff*; first violin, bars 203 *ff*). The ending of the quartet is breathtaking, as the 'fate' motif soars into the highest register of the first violin over a delicately syncopated figure in the two middle instruments and a slow moving bass line in the upper reaches of the cello. It is music of an intensely spiritual quality, delicate, magical, refined, otherworldly: a glimpse of what may lie beyond this earthly life.

Music Example 9.1: Ian Wilson, *Winter's Edge*, ending (bars 225–229).
Reproduced by kind permission of Universal Edition (London) Ltd.

11 Ibid.

The final chord consists of two superimposed perfect fifths a semitone apart, but the register, dynamics, and tempo are such that the sense is not of dissonant unease, but rather of perfect calm and peacefulness. Rarely has a composer captured so perfectly an atmosphere of inner quietude and restful contemplation.

For the second quartet, *The Capsizing Man and Other Stories*, Wilson turned for inspiration to the sculptures of the Swiss artist Alberto Giacometti (1901–66). Wilson has explained the performance history of the work as follows:

> [T]he work was written 'for my own interest'. The Brindisi Quartet played through the first movement just after it was written in early 1994, at a workshop in UUJ [the University of Ulster at Jordanstown], and they expressed interest in performing the piece once it was complete, which gave me the impetus to finish it. In the end it was the Emperor Quartet, through the Society for Promotion of New Music, who premiered the piece at Maastricht Conservatoire in 1995, and then shortly after that performed it at the Cheltenham Festival. That performance was heard by the woman who was ultimately responsible for my being signed by the publishers Universal Edition, so it's an important piece to me in that respect.[12]

For *The Capsizing Man and Other Stories*, Wilson chose five sculptures by Giacometti that inspired in him a musical gesture that became the kernel idea for each of the five movements in the work. The five sculptures evidently suggested not only a salient musical idea, but also some kind of narrative discourse, hence the use of the word 'stories' in the title rather than 'sculptures'. This in turn leads to two further questions: to what extent does this narrative thrust determine the form and content of each of the five movements, and how does Wilson make the five movements form a coherent larger structure, rather than five unrelated character pieces?

Let us start, as Wilson himself did, with the Giacometti sculptures. The five movements each borrow their title from the sculpture chosen as inspirational starting point:[13]

---

12 Ian Wilson, personal communication, 16 June 2001. *The Capsizing Man* was completed in Greenisland, Co. Antrim, Northern Ireland in July 1994; the premiere performance in the Netherlands took place on 11 May 1995. The work was published by Universal Edition in 1996 (UE 21021) and was recorded by the Vanbrugh String Quartet on *towards the far country* (as n. 5). Wilson arranged *The Capsizing Man* for string orchestra in 1997; this version was premiered by the Irish Chamber Orchestra under Bruno Giuranna in Limerick on 9 March 2000. 13 Pictures of all these Giacometti sculptures are in Yves Bonnefoy (transl. Jean Stewart): *Alberto Giacometti: A Biography of His Work* (Paris: Flammarion, 1991) as follows: *The Capsizing Man*, plate 300; *The Forest*, plate 324; *The Chariot*, plate 335; *The Seated Woman*, plate 266; *The Cat*, plate 342.

Movement	Quartet movement title	Giacometti sculpture (date)
i	The Capsizing Man	L'homme qui chavire (1950)
ii	The Forest	La forêt (1950)
iii	The Chariot	Le chariot (1950)
iv	Seated Woman	Femme assise (1946)
v	The Cat	Le chat (1951)

Plate One: Alberto Giacometti, *L'homme qui chavire / The Capsizing Man* (1950)
Location: Kunsthaus Zürich Photographer: Ernst Scheidegger

Giacometti was born in Stampa in the Italian-speaking part of Switzerland in 1901. He occupies a curious position between the conservative and avant-garde tendencies in modern art. He was closely associated with Jean-Paul Sartre and the existential movement, yet at the same time Edward Lucie-Smith has observed that 'Part of his art-historical importance springs from his defence of figuration at a time when the advantage was with abstract art'.[14] Giacometti worked industriously in his grimy, cramped studio in Paris from the 1920s until the end of his life, except for the war years, which he spent in Geneva. The five sculptures under consideration here all date from the immediate post-war years and are in the style most closely associated with Giacometti: slender, stick-like figures, with highly agitated surfaces. It has been noted that these emaciated figures call to mind the victims of the Nazi concentration camps, but in fact Giacometti was tending towards this style even before the war years.

It is worth dwelling at some length on Giacometti's sculpture *The Capsizing Man*, as it not only inspired Wilson's first movement, but also was chosen as the title for the quartet, and thus presumably in some way unites the work, or at least provides the governing mood of it. Wilson notes that the tragic nature of Giacometti's falling man 'is reflected in the music [of the first movement] where I tried to imagine the terrible frustration of that destiny'.[15] The sorrowful mood of this movement does indeed cast its shadow over the entire quartet, or at least so we are to understand when Wilson notes further that 'In writing this quartet I wanted to broaden my musical language to include a darker vocabulary'.[16]

L'homme qui chavire has variously been translated as 'Staggering man', 'Man falling', or 'Capsizing man'. The verb *chavire* means to overturn or tip over; it is used to describe a boat going upside down, hence the English word 'capsize', which Wilson uses. Giacometti's vision of a man in a perpetual state of tripping is the quintessential visual image of the existential movement. The statue is thought to have been inspired, at least in part, by an accident in 1938 in which Giacometti was knocked down by a car. Giacometti himself attached great significance to this accident, which left him with a slight limp. Jean-Paul Sartre theorized that Giacometti's accident unleashed in the sculptor a nihilistic awareness of the futility of life:

> More than twenty years ago, one evening as he was crossing the Place d'Italie, Giacometti was knocked down by a car. Injured, his leg twisted, he was at first aware, in the lucid faint into which he fell, of a kind of joy: 'At last something's happening to me!' I appreciate his radical attitude: he expected the worst; this life which he loved to the point of never wanting

14 Edward Lucie-Smith, *Lives of the Great 20th-Century Artists* (London: Thames and Hudson, 1999): 269.   15 Ian Wilson (as n. 7), [2].   16 Ibid.

any other had been upset, perhaps smashed by the stupid violence of chance: 'So,' he thought, 'I wasn't born to be a sculptor or even to live; I was born for nothing.'[17]

Giacometti, however, felt that Sartre had twisted his words and imposed a false interpretation upon this event.[18] Yves Bonnefoy proposes an explanation diametrically opposed to Sartre's, namely that Giacometti felt great joy at the accident because 'the knowledge of one's finiteness, which shatters the ego, is the very experience through which love exists ... [t]hat car, when it "dashed" at him, has delivered him from that way of "seeing" from the outside which was merely his fear of death ... Death has freed him from the obsession with nothingness. Death, in that respect, being life itself ... In short, Giacometti emerged from his accident more real.'[19]

Whatever the artist's reaction to this fateful accident and its impact on his life may have been, in translating the experience into a work of art, he made a pessimistic statement about the human condition. Bonnefoy observes that a likely inspiration for *The Capsizing Man* was Rodin's sculpture *Falling Man* of 1883, which depicts a male sinner on the point of tumbling back into Hell.[20] Wilson obviously sees the statue as a bleak image, writing as he does of this 'tragic figure' and the 'terrible frustration of that destiny'. Let us turn now to the music of this movement and see how Wilson has portrayed this tragic capsizing man.

The principal, indeed virtually the only, melodic idea in the first movement of *The Capsizing Man and Other Stories* is a chromatically descending line with a range of an augmented fourth; the range is sometimes expanded, sometimes contracted. This idea is usually presented in syncopation against another chromatically descending line. This chromatic ostinato appears in all but six of the 95 bars in the movement; it makes a very striking musical correlative to the perpetually falling state of the Giacometti statue. The ideas superimposed on these falling chromatic lines are utterly bleak: savage descending octatonic scales (violins, bars 20–22), harshly dissonant chords (violins, double stopped, bars 46 *ff*), and low moaning wails (viola and cello, bars 25–26 and 42–43; the sound is created by bowing slowly on a single note with excessive pressure). The harsh chords and the octatonic scales are loud and violent, while the rest of the movement is in a hushed, subdued dynamic level, like an injured man moaning quietly in pain. In the last eight bars of the move-

---

17 Jean-Paul Sartre (transl. Irene Clephane), *Words* (London: Penguin Books, 1967), 144.   18 Yves Bonnefoy (as n. 13), 494, notes that 'When Alberto ... saw how Sartre had misunderstood his words, he was deeply surprised and indignant, and broke off relations for a while with the man'.   19 Yves Bonnefoy (as n. 13), 268. Giacometti often came up with surprising statements about his own misfortunes. To give another instance, when operated on in 1963 for stomach cancer, he said 'The strange thing is – as a sickness, I always wanted to have this one.' (Lucie-Smith [as n. 14], 272).   20 Yves Bonnefoy (as n. 13), 335.

ment, the chromatic ostinato appears in the upper register of the violins at ever-quieter dynamic levels, as though the music is receding into the distance. Just as Giacometti captures a sense of motion in sculpture with *The Capsizing Man*, so too Wilson manages to create a sense of motion in music by means of this diminuendo.

The Forest, the sculpture that inspired the second movement of the quartet, is subtitled 'Square, seven figures and a head'. Giacometti wrote that the sculpture was inspired by 'a corner of a forest seen over many years (in my childhood) where the trees ... with their bare, upward-thrusting trunks ... always seemed like people standing still and talking to each other'.[21] Wilson's movement is an exercise in Bartókian night music, rather in the manner of the third movement of that composer's String Quartet No. 4. Wilson's movement is dominated by still, quiet, long drawn out chords (*non vibrato*, as in the Bartók movement cited), with eruptions of various sorts: pizzicati, tremolo, some heterophonic scale passages, and towards the end (bars 40–45), a few bird calls in the manner of Messiaen. It is a skilful exercise of its sort, if a little lacking in originality.

The Chariot is among the most striking of all Giacometti's sculptures. It features one of his characteristically elongated woman figures, on top of a small chariot dominated by two large, four-spoked wheels which is said to be modelled on an Egyptian battle chariot.[22] Giacometti himself has said that this sculpture also was inspired by his 1938 accident, specifically an experience in the hospital where he was recovering. He wrote that *The Chariot* derived from 'the tinkling pharmacy wagon of the Bichat hospital which was wheeled in the rooms and which astounded me in 1938'.[23] This was obviously not the only inspiration for the work, as the Egyptian provenance of the chariot shows. But it is another example of the centrality of this near-death experience to much of Giacometti's subsequent artistic development.

The third movement of Wilson's quartet is the most immediately evocative of the five. It is an exhilarating *moto perpetuo* study in demi-semiquavers, with a carefully calculated dynamic arch form. The movement portrays what might happen if the Giacometti sculpture were to come to life: a bizarre figure on a chariot races towards the listener from afar, careens crazily by, and then recedes into the distance. The chariot is heard approaching, but is unseen, in the opening 35 bars; it looms into view at bar 36, totters unsteadily by at bars 50–61, disappears from view at bar 62, and becomes inaudible at the end of the movements (bars 83–85: *diminuendo ... niente*). It is a nicely calculated

21 Giacometti, letter to Pierre Matisse in 1950, quoted in Toni Stooss and Patrick Elliott, *Alberto Giacometti 1901–1966* (Edinburgh: National Galleries of Scotland, 1996), 165. **22** Reinhold Hohl, *Alberto Giacometti: Sculpture, Painting, Drawing* (London 1972), 295, cited in Stooss and Elliott (as n. 21), 166. **23** Giacometti (as n. 21), 166.

effect, and incorporates (at bars 60–61) a brief reference to one of the central pieces from the contemporary string quartet repertoire: Lutoslawski's String Quartet of 1964.

The reference to Lutoslawski may have been unintentional, as was the allusion to a famous American composer in the fourth movement. As Wilson notes, '*Seated Woman* was composed last of all, and is subtitled *Interlude* – four movements felt unbalanced to me and this ephemeral piece, a subconscious homage to Feldman, was the vital missing ingredient'.[24] This brief movement, just 28 bars long, is not only an evocative tribute to Morton Feldman, but also conveys the essence of Giacometti's aesthetic of artistic creation during the war years. The delicate textures, whispy melodic fragments, and hushed dynamics create a reduction in scale of musical materials that corresponds exactly to the reduction in scale of physical dimensions that Giacometti experimented with during the early 1940s. According to legend, the artist returned to Paris from Geneva in 1945 with all of his wartime sculptures fitted into six matchboxes.[25] Here is Giacometti's description of this process of miniaturization:

> To my terror the sculptures became smaller and smaller. Only when small were they like[able], and all the same these dimensions revolted me, and tirelessly I began again, only to end up, a few months later, at the same point. A big figure seemed to me to be false and a small one just as intolerable, and then they became so minuscule that often with a final stroke of the knife they disappeared into dust.[26]

On another occasion, Giacometti states that 'The sense of depth begets silence, drowns objects in silence'.[27] This quotation appears in Bonnefoy's biography of Giacometti directly opposite a full-page colour photo of the statue *The Seated Woman*. The Giacometti sculptures under consideration here were not miniatures: *The Chariot* is 167 cm (66 inches) tall, and the other statues are between 60 and 80 cm (24 and 32 inches) in their longest dimension. But they all share the Swiss artist's distinctive elongated, emaciated style, that paring down to bare essentials that corresponds to the Feldman-influenced reduction of musical materials in Wilson's fourth movement.

The Giacomettian existential angst lifts in the final movement of Wilson's quartet, *The Cat*. This sculpture, along with its companion piece *The Dog*

---

24 Ian Wilson (as n. 7), [2].   **25** The six matchboxes are cited frequently in the Giacometti literature. Yves Bonnefoy (as n. 13), 559 states that it was either a big matchbox (according to Albert Skira) or else (perhaps more plausibly) a small cardboard suitcase (according to Georges Sadoul).   **26** Alberto Giacometti, as quoted by David Sylvester, catalogue of *Alberto Giacometti, Sculpture, Paintings, Drawings*, an exhibition at the Tate Gallery, London 1965. The quotation is reproduced in Edward Lucie Smith, *Late Modern: The Visual Arts since 1945*, 2nd edition (New York: Praeger Publishers, 1976), 193–94.   **27** Alberto Giacometti, quoted in Yves Bonnefoy (as n. 13), 290.

from the same year, is exceptional in Giacometti's output, which otherwise concentrates on human figures – striding, active men and standing, passive women. With *The Cat* another side to Giacometti's character is revealed: his compassion and strong fellow feeling for nature's helpless creatures. Giacometti's reply, when asked once what he would rescue if his studio were to catch fire, was 'the cat' – meaning not the statue, but rather a scrawny feline visitor that would push its way into his studio through a half-open door.[28] Similarly, referring to *The Dog*, his portrayal of a starving, stray mongrel, Giacometti once told Jean Genet, 'The dog is myself. One day I saw it like that in the street. I was that dog.'[29] In part this is a statement like Flaubert's famous 'Madame Bovary, c'est moi', namely that all artistic creation is, in some sense, autobiographical. But at the same time, Giacometti was underlining the essential loneliness at the heart of human existence, at least from the existentialist viewpoint.

Wilson chooses not to view things that way. Instead, he portrays the comic side of Giacometti's cat, its impish, impudent nature. As the composer writes, '*The Cat* was deliberately meant to be somewhat lighter in tone, episodic and possibly reflecting various events in the day of Alberto's cat'.[30] The opening gesture – a high glissando harmonic portraying the cat's miaow followed by pizzicato semiquavers representing the cat prancing around – returns to introduce each episode. One might hazard a guess as to the events portrayed: a pouncing attack on a hapless mouse (bar 14 *ff*), stretching out lazily following this exertion (bar 34 *ff*), purring and preening contentedly while being petted (bar 58 *ff*), slowly drifting off for a cat nap (bar 78 *ff*), and then dashing back off outside after prowling around the studio for a bit (bar 96 to end). The comic touches in the movement are many and well executed. Particularly effective is the wailing quality of the chromatic melody beginning at bar 58, achieved by having the two violins play in unison using one finger only. The movement is an unexpected but welcome change of mood from the rest of the quartet, adding another dimension to Wilson's musical language and to his interpretation of Giacometti's world.

For his third string quartet, Wilson turns once again to a Swiss artist for inspiration and bases his *Towards the Far Country* on paintings by Paul Klee (1879–1940). Unlike Giacometti, whose work has not often been associated with music, Klee has been something of a guiding spirit to many twentieth-century composers, from Schoenberg and Berg through Boulez and R. Murray Schafer to Tan Dun and Ian Wilson. Klee, a talented violinist himself, was the son of a music teacher and in 1906 married the pianist Lily Stumpf. He attended operas and concerts often and practised the violin daily. His art and also his influential theoretical writings are pervaded by musical motifs. Klee

28 Yves Bonnefoy (as n. 13), 51.   **29** Yves Bonnefoy (as n. 13), 50.   **30** Ian Wilson (as n. 7), [2].

compares colour to music, as both have an effect on the senses that is beyond the realm of rational comprehension. The rhythmic effects of subtle gradations of colour animate such Klee paintings as *Fugue in Red* (1921) and *Ancient Sound* (1925). In works such as *Ad Parnassum* (1932) he superimposes different layers to form a complexly textured surface comparable to polyphony in music.

Like *Winter's Edge*, *Towards the Far Country* is in one movement, but at 476 bars and 28 minutes in duration, it is just over twice the length of the first quartet.[31] It was written for the Vanbrugh String Quartet, who premiered it at the Spitalfields Festival in London in June 1997 and played it a month later at the quartet's West Cork Chamber Music Festival in Bantry, Co. Cork.[32] Seven Klee paintings are cited in the score and divide the quartet into sections, though not separate movements. The titles of the paintings, in the order in which they appear in the score (along with the date of the painting and the bar number where it is first cited in the score) are as follows: *Heroic strokes of the bow* (1938, bar 1); *Pastoral rhythms* (1927, bar 55); *Hammamet with mosque* (1914, bar 179); *The legend of the Nile* (1937; bar 254); *Ad marginem* (1930, bar 333); *Death and fire* (1940, bar 376); *Captive* (1940, bar 450).[33] The title of Wilson's third quartet refers not to any of these Klee paintings, however, but rather to a second extra-musical impulse, as the composer explains:

> This quartet takes its impetus from two sources – the first is the work of artist Paul Klee, in whose paintings I saw the sparks for many musical ideas; the second is the idea of a journey, one which begins as a physical negotiation of various terrains and cultures but which actually ends up as a spiritual travel through life and death ... I decided to construct a narrative, both musical and philosophical, which would enable me to incorporate the various musical ideas inspired by the Klee works into a single overall concept.[34]

The quartet's title is perhaps an allusion to Shakespeare's 'undiscovered country from whose bourn no traveller returns' (*Hamlet*), for what begins as a physical journey to Africa (Hammamet in Tunisia and the Nile river) becomes a journey towards death.

31 *Towards the Far Country* was commissioned by the Vanbrugh String Quartet with funds from the Arts Council of Ireland. It was completed in Whitehead, Co. Antrim, Northern Ireland in December 1996, was published by Universal Edition in 1997 (UE 17352) and was recorded by the Vanbrugh String Quartet on *towards the far country* (as n. 6).   **32** Judith Weir was the artistic director of the Spitalfields Festival in 1997; like Wilson, she wrote a work inspired by Klee's *Heroic Strokes of the Bow* (an orchestral piece, written in 1992). The Bantry performance of Wilson's third quartet was broadcast live on RTÉ.   **33** In the literature on Paul Klee, *Heroic strokes of the bow* (original title: *Heroische Bogenstriche*) is sometimes translated as *Heroic Fiddling*; *Pastoral rhythms* is often given as *Pastoral* or as *Pastoral (Rhythms)*; and *Hammamet with mosque* is also known as *Hammamet with its mosque*.   **34** Ian Wilson (as n. 7), [4].

Paul Klee's own journey of discovery took him to North Africa in 1914; the two weeks he spent in Tunisia were a breakthrough in his career. The scenery and lighting conditions he discovered there led him to produce a number of watercolours, including *Hammamet with mosque*, that were an important turning point in his career and left their imprint on all of his subsequent work. After being hounded out of Nazi Germany in 1933 when his art was branded as 'entartete Kunst', Klee found refuge in his native Switzerland, only to be forced to embark on another, even more difficult journey. In 1935 he developed scleroderma, a painful and incurable skin disease that took his life five years later. Many of the late paintings, including *Death and fire* and *Captive*, disclose an artist coming to terms with his own imminent mortality. Wilson, then, has chosen a sequence of Klee paintings that warrant interpreting *Towards the Far Country* as a portrayal of Klee's life and death, but the work transcends this biographical dimension to take on universal significance.

The translations from art to music are much less direct in Wilson's third quartet than they were in the second quartet with the Giacometti sculptures. Klee himself did not try to map musical sounds directly onto corresponding visual images. As Boulez has written,

> Paul Klee does not try to establish a strict parallelism, which would have strong limitations, between the world of sounds and that of sight. The lesson to be learned from him is that the two worlds have their specificity and that the relation between them can only be structural. No transcription could be literal without being absurd.[35]

Instead of pictorial or programmatic musical gestures, Wilson draws upon the physical or spiritual symbolism of each Klee painting, and integrates the musical ideas that flow from this essential concept into his imaginary journey. In this way he manages to create a remarkably logical and nicely structured unfolding of musical ideas.

The opening of the quartet, a series of stridently dissonant, fully scored, loud chords representing *Heroic Strokes of the Bow*, recurs in altered form three times later, at bars 164, 233, and 318.[36] Although this is reminiscent of Musorgsky's use of the promenade theme in *Pictures at an Exhibition*, Wilson notes that these recurrences show that 'the protagonists in this drama, represented by the players, are undergoing certain metamorphoses as their journey progresses'.[37] The first recurrence, at bar 164, is a literal repeat of the opening 14 bars,

35 Pierre Boulez, *Le pays fertile: Paul Klee* (Paris: Éditions Gallimard, 1989), cited on the web page Andante (www.andante.com/aboutus/boulez.cfm).   **36** The first page of the score is reproduced as part of the composer's Universal Edition web pages (www.universaledition.com/truman/en_templates/view.php3?f_id=352).   **37** Ian Wilson (as n. 7), [4].

and acts as a conclusion to *Pastoral rhythms* and an introduction to *Hammamet with mosque*. The second recurrence (bars 233–253) is longer, slower, and quieter, and acts as an interlude between *Hammamet with mosque* and *The legend of the Nile*. The traveller has evidently been transformed by the experience of another cultural landscape. The final return (bars 318–332) is also performed quietly, but pizzicato with unexpected *sforzando* offbeat accents. It serves as a transition to *Ad marginem*, which in turn mediates between the exotic orientalisms of the three previous sections and the menacing approach and peaceful acceptance of death in the final two sections of the quartet.

In the final section of the quartet, *Captive*, Wilson again creates an atmosphere of transcendent beauty. The gently undulating semiquaver perfect fifths pedal in the viola refers to a figure that occurs many times in the cello in *Hammamet with mosque*, thus uniting the physical with the spiritual journey in a masterful summing up. The fear of death, portrayed by fearsome stabbing dissonances in *Death and fire* at bars 388 *ff*, has been overcome; in its place is calm acceptance. The melodic gestures are reduced to gentle one or two-note figures in the other three instruments. All is calm and ordered, and at the end the music simply plays itself out naturally and quietly. The ending is certainly true to Klee's own experience, for he understood death as the start of a journey into the deepest reality; as he said, 'the objective world surrounding us is not the only possible one; there are others, latent'.[38]

Wilson's fourth string quartet, *oil and temper*, was written for the Fourth International Edvard Grieg Memorial Competition for Composers, sponsored by the Oslo Grieg Society. The competition rules specified that the work must be submitted by 1 March 2000, be between 12 and 18 minutes long, and consist of a musical interpretation of three paintings by Edvard Munch: *The Scream* (1893), *Melancholy* (1892), and *The Dance of Life* (1900). The competition provided the external stimulus for writing the quartet, but Wilson undertook the composition because of his interest in the visual arts. The title *oil and temper* is a play on words: 'At least two of the paintings, if not all three, were painted using oil and tempera, and so the title is ... a little wordplay on that, combining the fundamentals of painting and composition – "oil", and "temper", or one's essential disposition'.[39] The quartet is in three movements with the titles taken from the Munch paintings in the order cited above. Wilson was not happy with the outcome of the work, however, and it has been withdrawn, to be revised at a later date.[40]

---

38 Paul Klee, quoted in the Paris WebMuseum web site (www.oir.ucf.edu/wm/paint/auth/klee/). **39** Ian Wilson (as n. 12). **40** The fourth quartet was revised late in 2001, after this article was completed. Wilson changed the title to *Veer*, an allusion to 'veering' off in a new direction and to the German word *vier* ('four' – for the fourth quartet, and also the number of players involved). Of the original three movements, only the first two were retained, making the total playing time just under ten minutes. (Ian Wilson, personal communication, 19 January 2002)

Wilson's fifth string quartet resulted from his appointment in February 2000 to a five-month term as composer-in-residence in County Leitrim. The string quartet was commissioned by Leitrim County Council for the Vogler Quartet from Berlin, who had been appointed to a residency in neighbouring County Sligo in 1999. The quartet was completed in April 2000, and was premiered on 17 August 2000 by the Vogler Quartet in Carrick-on-Shannon, County Leitrim.[41] The title, *...wander, darkling*, is taken from Byron's poem *Darkness*, which begins as follows:

> I had a dream, which was not all a dream.
> The bright sun was extinguish'd, and the stars
> Did wander darkling in the eternal space,
> Rayless, and pathless, and the icy earth
> Swung blind and blackening in the moonless air.

Byron's apocalyptic vision, written in July 1816, was indeed 'not all a dream', for in April 1815 the greatest volcanic explosion known to history occurred in Indonesia. Tambora Volcano expelled so much ash and dust that the sun was dimmed, triggering climactic changes around the world; indeed, 1816 was known as 'the year without a summer'. This resulted in widespread crop failures, and up to 100,000 people died from starvation in the ensuing year, triggering massive social unrest.

Although it derives its title from Byron's poem, Wilson's quartet was inspired by more personal events, which are related to a line later on in the poem: 'War, which for a moment was no more, / Did glut himself again'. The fifth quartet is one of several large scale works, including the violin concerto *Messenger* (1998–9) and *History is vanity* (1999) for solo organ, to result from Wilson's life experiences in Belgrade. He had settled there in 1998 with his Serbian partner, the musicologist Danijela Kulezic. In October of that year the two came back to Belfast for the birth of their son Adam, but they returned to Belgrade in January 1999. At the end of March 1999, after three days of NATO bombing, they were forced to leave Belgrade:

> I never felt that my life was out of my hands so much as when we were there [in Belgrade]. Just a feeling of total helplessness. In my own naïvety I remember thinking 'Well, they'll never bomb a European city'. Just completely naïve in the ways of the world, really. We had to leave behind what we couldn't carry.[42]

---

41 The premiere performance and a subsequent performance by the Vogler Quartet at the Sligo Contemporary Music Festival on 24 November 2000 are available for listening at the Contemporary Music Centre (Ireland) – Sound Archive CD 33 and Sound Archive CD 01/10 respectively. 42 Ian Wilson, as

Wilson and his family spent a few months in Northern Ireland, and then found safe harbour in a home in the countryside near Carrick-on-Shannon in August 1999. Wilson evidently found the surroundings congenial to his work: in quick succession he completed *an angel serves a small breakfast* (his second violin concerto), *Spilliaert's Beach* for alto flute and piano, and the fourth and fifth string quartets.

What is immediately evident in the fifth quartet is the increased use of new playing techniques. Unusual timbral ideas had been used but rarely in the earlier quartets, and were largely confined to traditional methods such as *glissando*, *non vibrato*, and *sul ponticello*. In ... *wander, darkling* devices of a more contemporary nature are employed, including quarter-tones, the use of metal mutes, bowing on top of and behind the bridge, and playing on the body of the instrument. These new sounds 'were employed structurally, as part of the overall emotional fabric of the work, and not just as colourful patches'.[43]

Quarter-tones are used expressively in at least three different ways. Firstly, they are used to give richly nuanced colouring to melodic lines, whether in a single instrument (e.g., bars 52–54 and 120 *ff*), or two or three instruments playing in octaves (e.g., bars 27 *ff*, 70 *ff*, and 83 *ff*). Secondly, they also provide vertically nuanced colouring to melodic lines, when two or more instruments play together in 'mistuned' octaves (e.g., bars 99–100 and 145–149). Finally, quarter-tones are used to create ultra-dissonant harmonic clusters, as at bars 107–114, where the interval of a fourth is filled in by seven adjacent quarter-tones. In each case, the quarter-tones provide a vivid intensification of the expressionist melodic and harmonic vocabulary of the quartet.

Wilson has written about the programmatic content of the fifth quartet as follows: 'The main idea was of the wind – as if we were being blown around the globe by it ("winds of fate", etc.) – and so the opening idea in the piece relates to that, and is itself motivic rather than purely atmospheric'.[44] As is to be expected from Wilson, the quartet features a carefully thought out formal structure, with manifold recurrences and cross-relations between different sections. The opening 'wind' motif, created by having the quartet play alternately on the bridge (*super pont.*) and on the side of their instruments, is an eerie effect that makes for a very striking opening to the work. The first four bars return at bars 61–64 to close the first section of the quartet, and shorter fragments recur many times in the rest of the work. The section in which the players bow on the side of their instrument (bars 5–6) is an unpitched rhythmical canon; it recurs at bars 13, 25, 42, 114 and 125. A closely related idea is a pitched rhythmical canon with each entry a semiquaver apart; this occurs at bars 33, 116, and 201, thus knitting together the beginning, middle, and end of the work.

quoted in Michael Dungan, 'A Richer Life in Leitrim', Contemporary Music Centre Ireland *New Music News* (February 2000), 10.   **43** Ian Wilson (as n. 12).   **44** Ibid.

There are only a few passages in the quartet that are to be played in a traditional manner – it is the musical equivalent of a world turned upside down. The fifth quartet is intense, dark, harrowing and tortured, from beginning to end. Even a passage played 'normally', such as the one beginning in bar 173, is reminiscent of the most desolate moment in a work by Shostakovich. The rest of the quartet, where the extraordinary wails and howls of non-traditional playing resources dominate, is almost too pained and explicit an outcry to bear. It is hard to imagine ... *wander, darkling* sitting comfortably in a concert programme with works from the traditional quartet repertoire; it has much more in common with Ligeti's String Quartet No. 2 (1968) than with a quartet by Beethoven or even Britten. Wilson's goal was evidently to make us feel the agony of a world gone mad, and in this he has succeeded admirably.

Do Wilson's string quartets, then, amount to a cohesive and personal contribution to the rich repertoire for this medium? Yes, decidedly so. The influences on Wilson's style are many and varied – Stravinsky, Messiaen, Bartók, Feldman, and Lutoslawski have been identified as guiding spirits here; Richard Whitehouse has noted traces of Schnittke, Sibelius, and Robert Simpson[45] and no doubt others could easily be added to the list. As to aesthetic stance, Wilson is clearly opposed to the formalist viewpoint of Stravinsky, who famously stated that 'music is, by its very nature, essentially powerless to *express* anything at all'.[46] Each of Wilson's quartets draws upon a rich and stimulating source of extra-musical inspiration, but transmutes this into music that stands on its own two feet as a pure formal structure. Wilson's musical language is a rich mixture of tonal and non-tonal idioms, diatonic, chromatic, and octatonic pitch collections, static and active gestures, tragic and comic moods. But from this mix, something decided original emerges; Wilson is a composer with important things to say, the technical ability to express his ideas well, and a fertile creative imagination.

45 Richard Whitehouse, Review of Vanbrugh String Quartet performance of Ian Wilson's first three string quartets on Black Box CD recording BBM 1031 (2000), *Gramophone Magazine* lxxviii/937 (February 2001), 72.   **46** Igor Stravinsky, *An Autobiography* (New York: W.W. Norton, 1962), 53. Stephen Walsh, *Stravinsky: A Creative Spring. Russia and France, 1882–1934* (London: Jonathan Cape, 1999), 514 points out that the autobiography was likely ghostwritten by Valechka Nouvel. For a recent discussion and rejection of Stravinsky's formalist aesthetic see Richard Taruskin, 'Stravinsky and the Subhuman', *Defining Russia Musically* (Princeton: Princeton University Press, 1997), 364ff.

10

Roots and directions in twentieth-century Irish art music

AXEL KLEIN

As we leave the twentieth century behind us, we are in the advantageous position of being able to survey the complete period, unlike many earlier publications on the history of twentieth-century music, which could obviously only review it in part. But just as when one comes to the end of a long novel, we find that more recent events remain much more distinct in our minds than do earlier ones. In order to achieve a broad perspective it is therefore necessary to go right back to the beginnings around 1900. Of course, even with a small country like Ireland it is impossible to consider the full picture of twentieth-century music. This last century has surpassed all others in the pace of its developments; never before has life changed so rapidly. Today's Ireland is a very different country from that of a hundred years ago: two world wars, civil wars, global economic changes, increasing urbanisation, and the development of the mass media and electronic communication have all contributed to shaping Western culture in such a profound and irreversible way that we are prone to forget our roots. Irish society especially was transformed from an underdeveloped rural culture to a modern and connected urban society within a shorter period than most other European countries.

In spite of this, our knowledge of history generally was never greater and never before was there so much specialized research. Irish art music is well positioned therefore for investigation as there can be few areas of the humanities which cry out so much for intensive study. Why is it then that so many Irish composers of the past three decades often sensed that they were working in a vacuum and claimed that there was no tradition of classical music in Ireland? Was the evidence of more than a thousand years of art music in Ireland, from medieval monastic culture to the Irish harpers in the Tudor courts, of international and indigenous composers in Dublin over a period of 400 years, of Dublin's musical life being second only to London in the British Isles of the eighteenth century (and many other examples) not enough? Apparently not. More evidence must be gathered, documented and assessed in order to prove that, although there have indeed been ups and downs in Irish musical history, there has never actually been a vacuum.

Surveys of Irish musical history still arouse the perception of a borrowed culture dependent on England, and in so far as that is true, it is equally certain that a similar evaluation can apply to many other countries on the European periphery, from Portugal to Finland and from Ireland to the Balkans. The large continental centres in Germany, France and Italy dominated art music everywhere else for a considerable time. But that does not imply that a borrowed music was 'un-Irish'. Likewise, the fact that Anglo-Irish art music in the past was not the music of the population's majority is also no serious criterion. Classical music has rarely been the music of the people. For centuries, appreciating art music required access to higher education and this has changed only, if at all, during the twentieth century. In much the same way, Bach or Beethoven are as remote to the average German as are Roseingrave or Geary to the average Irishman or woman, yet they still constitute a vital component of a people's cultural heritage. The prevalent perception of a 'borrowed' culture tends to diminish both our appreciation and the level of interest we are willing to grant to music in Ireland. It perpetuates a feeling of inferiority throughout Irish history which is inappropriate in an assessment of a musical endeavour which is proven to have occured.

I

The story of twentieth-century Irish music opens with romantic images not yet shattered by violence and doubt. Harmony and pathos, pride of place, and confidence in the future innocently developed and generated the hope that with 'a generous measure of Home Rule, there is every reason to believe that in the new social order music will develop on right lines, and we may hope for a national school of music such as the world has never seen.'[1] Thus wrote William Henry Grattan Flood, the tireless activist for the Irish cause in music after 1900. His hope has not yet been realised, since the world may still be waiting for the Irish 'national school of music', if indeed it waits at all. In 1955, the literary critic Denis Donoghue, writing about Irish music of the preceding twenty years, suggested that 'there is in Ireland to-day no composer whose works an intelligent European musician *must* know'.[2] Reading this one is tempted to think that Flood's heroic dream was shattered so badly that, thirty years later, there was no Irish composer worth listening to. But thirty-six years later in 1991, John Kinsella was to suggest that 'art music has such

---

1 W. H. Grattan Flood, *Introductory Sketch of Irish Musical History* (London n.d. [1922]), 99.   **2** Denis Donoghue, 'The Future of Irish Music', *Studies* 44 (Spring 1955), 110.

a fragile foothold here that we must be considered as an emerging Fourth World nation in this respect'.[3] So was it all in vain? The failure of Irish music to make any real impact at all internationally constitutes a sober fact for which numerous reasons may be found. The most serious and ironic one is that Irish music also failed to make any impact in the very land from which it came. The question of why music played such a minor role in the 'land of song' has been trenchantly discussed by Harry White in *The Keeper's Recital*.[4] However, the neglect of music in the history of ideas in Ireland should not lead to the assumption that there have been no active Irish composers this century or none worth knowing. But it does explain why some composers felt that they were working in a vacuum.

Information is vital, education a prerequisite, and appreciation a necessity to form opinions and to evaluate contemporary developments. Enlightened thinking is easily overshadowed, however, by nationalist sentiments. Flood's nationalistic enthusiasm must have led him to actually believe what he wrote, but he could just as well have been aware that the actual chances of a 'national school of music' were rarely as grim as at the time of his own study quoted above. Since the beginning of the First World War Irish music was at a low ebb and did not recover until the late 1920s. Denis Donoghue, writing in the 1950s, eventually comes to the conclusion that there *is* indeed a composer in Ireland with great potential [Brian Boydell], but in his analysis of the other 28 composers listed in Fleischmann's *Music in Ireland*[5] he overlooks much of the œuvres of, for example, Ina Boyle, Rhoda Coghill, Norman Hay and, even Aloys Fleischmann, which he would surely have taken into account had he known this music. And Kinsella speaks from the perspective of the interested party, the neglected composer, and this high degree of frustration among composers has often formed a sad subplot to the story of Irish music.

Irish composers have often been prophets in their own country. And just as prophets occasionally retreat into reclusion, some composers also withdrew so far into their studios that the public became completely unaware of their existence. Some of the most outstanding pieces of Irish music in the twentieth century lay hidden from audiences for decades. The 32 settings of poems by James Joyce which Geoffrey Molyneux Palmer (1882–1957) composed between 1907 and 1949 are among the most advanced Irish song compositions of their time, but were not discovered and premiered until 1982. The first large-scale Irish work which was influenced by contemporary European developments was not in fact Frederick May's String Quartet in c minor, but

---

3 In a letter to the author dated 19 April 1991 and documented in my study *Die Musik Irlands im 20. Jahrhundert* (Hildesheim: George Olms Verlag, 1996), 130.   4 Harry White, *The Keeper's Recital: Music and Cultural History in Ireland, 1770–1970* (Cork: Cork University Press, 1998).   5 Aloys Fleischmann (ed.), *Music in Ireland: A Symposium* (Cork: Cork University Press, 1952).

the cantata *Out of the Cradle Endlessly Rocking* for tenor, chorus and orchestra by Rhoda Coghill (1903–2000), written in 1923 and first performed in 1990. The May quartet of 1936 has had the greater impact, but even this piece was not performed until 1949.

How is it also that the work of one of the most talented Irish composers of the early decades of this century, Ina Boyle (1889–1967), remains unknown, unperformed, and unrecorded? She composed such orchestral works as *The Magic Harp* (1919), the symphony *Glencree* (1927), *The Dream of the Rood* (1930), *From the Darkness* (1951), an impressive String Quartet in e minor (1934) and many songs which are also well worth hearing. Her innate modesty and secluded abode in the Wicklow Mountains meant that she sadly never achieved recognition in her own lifetime. Here is excellent material for postgraduate study. Another composer who remains neglected is Mary Dickenson-Auner (1880–1965), an Irish emigré to Romania and Austria. She performed with Bartók and Schönberg in Vienna and composed six symphonies (including an 'Irish' symphony dating from 1941), four operas, two oratorios and much chamber music, including two 'Irish' string quartets. As her biographer states, 'touching on Schönberg's twelve-note compositions Mary Dickenson-Auner developed a 'polyphone' musical concept … exploring a new tonality by enriching traditional diatonic material with the use of sonorities of four, five, six and seven notes'.[6]

Of note is also a third woman composer, Adela Maddison (1866–1929), born in Ealing into an Irish family, the composer of an orchestral *Irische Ballade* (1909) and the ballet *The Children of Lir* (1920).[7] And finally, I could add Alicia Adelaide Needham (1863–1945), born in Downpatrick, certainly a popular ballad composer, but one all too forgotten.

One therefore can hardly continue to allege an artistic poverty in Irish music as such discoveries clearly do not indicate a past musical void in this country; they say more about *our* failure to recognise, appreciate and promote what music there actually is. There are still countless discoveries to be made in Irish music, even in the work-lists of composers who might be considered better-known. As yet, much of the œuvres of such prolific and eclectic composers as Gerard Victory (1921–95) and James Wilson (b. 1922) are too recent

---

6 Margarete Engelhardt-Krajanek, 'Mary Dickenson-Auner, Violinistin – Pädagogin – Komponistin. Leben und Werk' (PhD diss. University of Wuppertal, 1995) and Engelhardt-Krajanek, 'Mary Dickenson-Auner (1880–1965)', in: Kay Dreyfuss, Margarete Engelhardt-Krajanek, Barbara Kühnen, *Die Geige war ihr Leben – Drei Frauen im Portrait* (Strasshof: Vier-Viertel Verlag, 2000), 99–231. A CD recording of her *Irish Symphony* is available: Thorofon CTH 2259 (1994). The above quote is from her entry on the composer in Ludwig Finscher (ed.), *Die Musik in Geschichte und Gegenwart*, new edition, biographical part, vol. 5, (Kassel and Stuttgart: Bärenreiter, 2001), 983–4, my translation. 7 See Sophie Fuller, *The Pandora Guide to Women Composers: Britain and the United States, 1629–Present* (London: Pandora, 1994), 203–6.

to attempt a retrospective appraisal and only time will tell which pieces will actually survive in the repertoire. But it still requires the efforts of musicologists to study the scores and listen to the recordings in order to initially distinguish the good from the dross. This has rarely been undertaken, with the possible exception of Charles V. Stanford (1852–1924), who stylistically belongs to the nineteenth century[8], and Seán Ó Riada (1931–71), whose original art music is so scarce that such a survey was not particularly onerous.[9] The editors of this volume are publishing a monograph on the life and work of Brian Boydell (1917–2000),[10] but such rarities only serve to highlight the fact that much research still awaits future scholars.

II

Although an attempt to group Irish composers together into stylistic categories necessarily excludes some, it can nevertheless still serve as a useful step towards gaining an overview of the development of Irish music during the twentieth century. Western art music outside the Austro-Germanic countries around the turn of the century was largely dominated by either nationally-influenced folklorism in the smaller countries and by impressionism in the larger ones, with possible combinations of the two such as can be found in the work of Manuel de Falla, to name only one prominent example. Although there is no clear-cut definition of musical impressionism it has become an accepted term for music which expands traditional harmonic progression by modal or chromatic means and which conveys moods rather than presenting tightly-structured musical forms. It is therefore a pity that a Celtic impressionist such as Arnold Bax (1883–1953) could not claim Irish heritage, although his cycle of orchestral tone poems called *Éire*, comprising the works *Into the Twilight* (1908), *In the Faery Hills* (1909) and *Rosc-Catha* (1910), were written during the years when Bax lived in Ireland for most of the time and owned a house in Rathgar, Dublin (1905–14). He used his Irish pseudonym, Dermot O'Byrne, for his literary activities only and, under this guise, communicated frequently with the most famous writers of the Celtic Twilight period. His music might well have served as a good starting point to discuss

---

8 Apart from the 1936 biography by Harry Plunket Greene, there are two new studies in preparation, one by Jeremy Dibble and one by Paul J. Rodmell (see the bibliography in this volume).   **9** See Seóirse Bodley, *The Original Compositions*, in: Bernard Harris & Gerard Freyer, *Integrating Tradition: The Achievement of Seán Ó Riada* (Ballina, Irish Humanities Centre & Keohanes, 1981), 28–40 and Gearóid Mac an Bhua [Gerard Victory], *Seán Ó Riada: A shaothar sa traidisiún Eorpach*, in: Tomás Ó Canainn & Gearóid Mac an Bhua, *Seán Ó Riada: A Shaol agus a Shaothar* (Blackrock: Gartan, 1993), 140–283.   **10** Gareth Cox, Axel Klein, Michael Taylor (eds.), *The Life and Music of Brian Boydell* (Dublin: Irish Academic Press, forthcoming).

twentieth-century music in Ireland within a European context, but I do not intend to pursue this as Bax can not be considered an Irish composer as such.[11]

There are, however, examples of impressionist music written by Irish-born composers, if one considers some late-comers. It has rarely been generally recognised, for instance, that the arrangements of Irish traditional songs by Herbert Hughes (1882–1937) have a decidedly impressionist quality about them which raise them above the status of mere arrangements. Hughes' musical language is quite advanced and, in the preface to his first collection of *Irish Country Songs* (1909), he refers to Claude Debussy: 'Musical art is gradually releasing itself from the tyranny of the tempered scale ... and if we examine the work of the modern French school, notably that of M. Claude Debussy, it will be seen that the tendency is to break the bonds of this old slave-driver and return to the freedom of primitive scales.'[12] Hughes followed Bax in achieving a 'Celtic' type of impressionism using melodic contours derived from traditional music. In Hughes' case, although writing simpler accompaniments, his music does show that folk song and sophisticated art music can be successfully blended. Joan Trimble (1915–2000) continued in these footsteps writing attractive and well-structured songs, piano duets and chamber music between 1937 and 1949. Although this music post-dates European developments, it should be considered in a British context.

The most original contribution to Irish musical impressionism is the cantata *Out of the Cradle Endlessly Rocking* (1923) by Rhoda Coghill to a text by Walt Whitman. Whitman's poem is ametric, and Coghill's musical adaptation is a rhapsody which eschews conventional melodies, frequently employs wholetone scales, allows the solo tenor a remarkable freedom and a high degree of independence from the instrumental and choral parts. The piece is all the more astonishing since it is the work of a twenty-year old student, who, thus far, had never heard a real orchestra (she grew up during World War I and the Irish Civil war) and who gained her knowledge of orchestration from the study of printed scores of Stravinsky and Debussy. Apart from the later orchestration of a piano piece, this was to remain the only large-scale work by her. Coghill ceased composing in the late 1940s, due perhaps (besides private reasons) to the fact that in an contemporaneous Irish culture dominated by literature, she was to gain more public recognition through her collections of poems. It appears that Ireland may well have lost another potentially great composer who might have developed her talent had she been living in a different country.

A more assiduous approach to Irish impressionist music can be seen in the efforts of Ina Boyle and Norman Hay. Boyle often painted in dark colours,

11 The attention which has sometimes been given to Bax in an Irish musical context surely exceeds his real importance by far. **12** Herbert Hughes, *Irish Country Songs: Preface to Vol. 1* (London: Boosey, 1909), iv.

such as in *The Magic Harp* (1919) for orchestra, *Still Falls the Rain* (1948) for alto voice and string quartet, or *From the Darkness* (1951), a symphony for alto voice and orchestra. 'Dark' does not imply depressive here though, but rather refers to a penchant for low registers. Boyle's music is intimate, in Elizabeth Maconchy's words 'predominantly quiet and serious, never brilliant, though it has its moments of wit and passion'.[13]

Norman Hay (1889–1943) appears all but forgotten today; his name has virtually disappeared from concert programmes despite the reputation he enjoyed during his lifetime. Although none of his compositions before 1918 have survived, it is recorded that he received Feis Ceoil prizes for some of them; a Fantasy for String Quartet on Irish folk songs was awarded the Cobbett-Prize in 1917 and a year later he received the Carnegie Trust Award for his String Quartet in A major, a difficult piece which remains neglected. This is a pity as it is a very worthwhile score, full of colour and refined rhythmic structures. His symphonic poem *Dunluce* (1921) was performed at the 1925 London Promenade Concert Series. More intricate and complex are his later works such as the two cantatas *To Wonder* (1924) and *Paean* (1930), works combining aspects of Irish traditional music with a chromatic-harmonic approach, which still convince in appeal today. Adding Boyle and Hay to the Irish concert repertoire would surely enrich musical life in Ireland.

III

One of the most important debates in Irish musical culture has centred around the issue of folk music, a discussion which has also reverberated throughout the British Isles and possibly beyond. It was an Irish composer, Charles V. Stanford (1852–1924), who triggered a symphonic folk music movement on the British Isles with his *Irish Symphony* (1887), one of the earliest and most influential examples. Though clearly possessing the potential to assume the mantle of a 'national composer' in Ireland, the fact that he lived in England and was a staunch unionist at a time of political change made him rather suspect. His own romantic perception of Ireland was an unreal one. It is interesting to speculate as to what might have happened had he been born thirty years earlier (thus avoiding the thorny conservative issue as well as any reservations about his Germanic influences) and had remained in Ireland, two facts which would compel us to consider him in national terms. As it happened, he fell between all stools, accepted by no one group: too English for the Irish, too Irish for the English,[14] and too much of both for the Germans.

13 Elizabeth Maconchy, *Ina Boyle: An Appreciation with a Select List of her Music* (Dublin: Dolmen Press, 1974).   14 '… Stanford wrote for an English audience indifferent or hostile to the cultural (und ultimately

In terms of musical development, his aesthetic successor Hamilton Harty (1879–1941) pursued much the same artistic approach. Both Stanford and Harty disqualified themselves from serious consideration within modernism.[15] Yet both enjoyed a certain popularity in early twentieth-century Irish music circles after being hailed as models by the Feis Ceoil organizers[16] and, beginning with John F. Larchet (1884–1967), a number of Irish composers were, consciously or not, to follow in their footsteps.

In addition, such approaches to nationalism in Irish music[17] were often criticised because of the very simplicity and formal perfection of a traditional melody which deemed it unsuitable for treatment by a classically trained composer.[18] This discussion again highlighted the dilemma of many composers who tried to write nationally discernible music (and with it gain cultural identification) only to find themselves condemned as being 'West-British'. Historically, this is in contrast to evidence from other Western cultures where the use of traditional melodies or folk dance rhythms in opera, orchestral, chamber or vocal music have produced an impressive corpus of nationally identifiable compositions. Notwithstanding the actual motivation of using a folk tune (which differs from Stanford to Larchet right up to the present day) the employment of ethnic elements in art music from the point of view of a work's construction does not present any inherent compositional problem. Problems only arise when an ethnic repertoire is exclusively identified with a particular cultural group (in the case of Ireland, the Gaelic/Catholic majority) and their interpretation of authenticity.

But folklorism has many facets in twentieth-century music quite apart from non-musical associations with nationalism. A new function of folklorism[19] as

political) implications of a pervasively Irish art'. see Harry White (as n. 4), 109. **15** By virtue of their own public statements, e.g. Charles Villiers Stanford, 'On Some Recent Tendencies in Composition', in: Stanford, *Interludes: Records and Reflections* (London: John Murray, 1922), 89–101, and Hamilton Harty, 'Modern Composers and Modern Composition', *Musical Times* 65 (1924), 328–32, and 'No New Music That Will Live!' Sir Hamilton Harty Recommends Hissing of 'Pretentious Nonsense' in Modern Works', *The Musical Mirror* 5 (1925) 10, 190. **16** See the many writings by Annie Patterson in the *Weekly Irish Times*, for examples. Both Stanford and Harty also adjudicated at different periods at the Feis Ceoil. **17** It is important to refer here to the writings of Joseph J. Ryan, notably 'Nationalism and Music in Ireland' (PhD diss., National University of Ireland, 1991) and *Nationalism and Irish Music*, in Gerard Gillen and Harry White (eds.), *Music and Irish Cultural History (Irish Musical Studies 3)*, (Dublin: Irish Academic Press, 1995), 101–15. **18** Examples abound in literature, more recent ones are Seóirse Bodley, '... the essentially linear quality of traditional Irish music is not easily integrated into music that is essentially harmonic.' Bodley, *Ireland, I. Art music*, in: Stanley Sadie (ed.), *The New Grove Dictionary of Music and Musicians* (London: Macmillan, 1980), 316, and Harry White, '... Stanford's music does exemplify a crucial miscalculation ... that it is the assumption that the traditional airs themselves (or edited versions thereof) could be absorbed into art music as the basis of an authentic *Irish* style.', White (as n. 4), 106. Ryan criticizes Stanford's and Harty's Irishness as not being innate and as 'approaching Irish music from the outside', Ryan, 1995 (as n. 17), 112. **19** See Hermann Danuser, *Die Musik des 20. Jahrhunderts (Neues Handbuch der Musikwissenschaft vol. 7)*, (Laaber: Laaber Verlag, 1984), chapter: *Funktionswandel des*

a possible solution to the emerging and ubiquitous dissolution of tonality in the early decades of this century was espoused by May and Fleischmann as well as being evident in the œuvres of the two 'Anglo-Irish' composers Moeran and Maconchy. The link to the European mainland and to the source of this new stylistic approach was strongest in Elizabeth Maconchy (1907–94). Born in England, raised in Ireland, educated in England and married to an Irishman, she was able to straddle both worlds equally. Her studies in Prague and her friendship with Kodály embued her music with the most 'continental tone' among British composers. Since she lived in England and was not a part of musical life in Ireland, she cannot really be considered an Irish composer. Nevertheless, some compositions were written and/or performed in Ireland but the only actual commissions from Ireland were to write two pieces for the Cork Choral Festival, *Nocturnal* (1965) and *Prayer before Birth* (1972). Her orchestral music to the ballet *Puck Fair* (1940) was written in Ireland as was her String Quartet No. 5 (1948).

Ernest John Moeran (1894–1950) is often considered together with Arnold Bax, not because of any musical parallels, but because of the fact that they were both fairly well-known English-born composers who both died in Ireland within a few years of each other. Moeran, however, was half-Irish (his father was from Dublin) and from about 1934 spent more time in Ireland than in England. Important orchestral pieces either received their premiere in Ireland or were mainly written here such as his Symphony in g minor (1937). The new function of folklorism (as referred to above) can be sensed in many of his orchestral pieces, in much of his chamber music and some of his piano pieces. Best known in this regard are the concertos for violin (1942) and violoncello (1945), important contributions to Irish musical culture, so much so that after his death Fleischmann described him as 'one of the few major composers who have lived and worked here, with any real understanding of the people and of their traditional music'.[20]

Much of Aloys Fleischmann's (1910–92) music from between the mid-1930s to the late 1940s conveys a similar understanding, a fact which is perhaps surprising considering his outspoken criticism of folkloristic elements in art music. In the now well-known debate[21] in the short-lived periodical *Ireland To-day* in 1936 he argued strongly against any atavistic use of traditional melodies or scales, which were so ubiquitous until well into the 1950s (and, in some cases, beyond). This debate represented a watershed in Irish music and marks, on the one hand, the beginning of modernism in Ireland, and on

Folklorismus, 48–62.   **20** Aloys Fleischmann, 'The Music of E.J. Moeran', *Envoy* 4 (1951), 16 (March), 60.   **21** See Klein (as n. 3), White (as n. 4), and Philip Graydon, 'Modernism in Ireland and its Cultural Context in the Music and Writings of Frederick May, Brian Boydell and Aloys Fleischmann' (MA thesis, NUI Maynooth, 1999). See the abridged version in this volume.

the other, an extreme conservativism. The œuvres of Éamonn Ó Gallchobháir (1906–82), Redmond Friel (1907–79), Thomas C. Kelly (1917–85), Daniel McNulty (1920–96), and a host of others, comprised a prolific body of orchestral suites and variations, choral music, piano and chamber pieces which wedded traditional melodies and rhythms to classical forms and instruments. Though sometimes attractive in their own right, this music (rooted in the educational and artistic efforts of Carl Gilbert Hardebeck, 1869–1945) was so detached from contemporary international developments and owed so much to 19th-century aesthetics, that it can not be taken very seriously in a twentieth-century art music context. It is interesting to note that these composers and arrangers were succeeded by an even younger generation including Shaun Davey (b. 1948) and Bill Whelan (b. 1950) – a phenomenon that remains peculiar to Ireland.[22] Nowhere else would this music have achieved such a high level of general acceptance as twentieth-century art music. If one were to seek parallels in other arts, the atavism of this approach might be found in naïve paintings or historical novels.

On the other side of the spectrum, Philip Graydon has shown[23] that the respective œuvres of May, Fleischmann and Boydell abound with examples of a subtle, sometimes subconscious Irishness, which undoubtedly has its roots in traditional music. These three composers justly comprise the 'grandfathers' of contemporary Irish music and all three were outspoken opponents of narrow-minded musical nationalism. Before 1960, the work of this 'triumvirate' (Graydon) contains the most advanced and international Irish music and yet it could arguably not have been written anywhere else. It is a development of the 'new folklorism' concept concealing that very folklorism so deeply that often the composers themselves did not notice it at the time of writing. As Brian Boydell remarked: 'One absorbs certain turns of phrase which are in the national music which go into one's bones and come out the other way. There is one particular little figure which keeps cropping up in my music, and I notice it keeps on cropping up in Irish folk music. It's completely unconscious, but it just happens.'[24]

I have argued elsewhere that Frederick May's music is as international as it is suffused with a pastoral folklorism derived from his studies with Vaughan Williams[25] and that a similar eclecticism may be found in Fleischmann.[26] Whereas Fleischmann chose this idiom consciously 'to demonstrate the possibility of diatonic modal writing at a time when serialism was beginning to

---

22 See the contribution of Harry White in this volume. **23** Graydon (as n. 21). **24** Charles Acton, 'Interview with Brian Boydell', *Éire-Ireland* 5 (1970) 4, 105. **25** Klein, 'The Composer in the Academy (2), 1940–1990', in: Richard Pine & Charles Acton (eds.), *To Talent Alone – The Royal Irish Academy of Music, 1848–1998* (Dublin, Gill and Macmillan, 1998), 421f. **26** In Klein, 1996 (as n. 3), 400 and Klein, 'Aloys Fleischmann: An Inspiration', in: Ruth Fleischmann (ed.), *Aloys Fleischmann (1910–1992) – A Life for Music in Ireland Remembered by his Contemporaries* (Cork: Mercier, 2000), 309–13.

take over'[27] and abstained from it from the mid-1940s, it is hard to ascertain exactly how conscious the subtle use of small ethnic musical elements was with May. As for Boydell, who openly eschewed any attempt at Irishness, it is clear that we have a case of an influence through the natural and musical environment, which the composer did not disavow.

It has rarely been pointed out that later generations, too, were interested in such subtle representations of Irishness in their music. For instance, in the case of John Buckley (b.1951) this derives from embellishments typically found in traditional melody. Since this is neither embedded in modal harmony nor conventional melody it is difficult to discern, but when alerted to it, the composer gives a similar reply as Boydell above: 'The only Irishness I can perceive is a highly ornamented style of melodic writing, such as one finds in sean-nós singing. I have not consciously developed this link and it is only recently that it has been pointed out to me.'[28] Buckley's otherwise freely atonal music used to have stronger Irish qualities in his early work, such as in his orchestral scores *Taller than Roman Spears* (1976) and *Fornocht do chonac thú* (1980), the programmes of which earned him the epithet of a modern celticist.[29] The more recent works of Jane O'Leary (b.1946) present a similar case insofar as many of her works after *c*.1983 employ passages of modal harmony or folksong-like melody which she ascribes to unconscious influences during the compositional process.[30]

The most coherent and challenging use of traditional music in a modern context, however, has been the music of Seóirse Bodley (b. 1933), especially during a period from *c*.1972 to 1980. Beginning with the two-piano piece *The Narrow Road to the Deep North* (1972) and arguably culminating in his piece for small orchestra A *Small White Cloud Drifts Over Ireland* (1975) and the extended song cycle *A Girl* (1980), he no longer sought to fuse the traditional with the sophisticated, but openly confronted the different musical materials, traditional melodies clashing with modern discords, triads with clusters. It has been the most challenging encounter of the two Irish musical traditions so far and did not meet with general acceptance or approval. Bernard Harris writing about a performance of Bodley's Chamber Symphony No. 2 (1982) stated that '[I] really can't make up my mind about Seóirse Bodley's music ... his use of ... "Irish-style melodic fragments" I find increasingly hard to accept ... what I do find worth questioning is the assumption that music that is authentically Irish need sound like music in a folk idiom that also lives in our island.'[31]

27 Anthony Quigley, sleeve notes for *Charles Lynch / Piano Vol. 1*, New Irish Recording Company (1971), which features Fleischmann's *Suite for Piano* (1933). **28** Buckley in a letter dated 18 February 1991 and quoted in Klein, 1996 (as n. 3), 306. **29** P.M. Hamel, 'Zwischen Keltentum und Avantgarde – Der irische Komponist John Buckley', *MusikTexte* no. 20 (1987), 19–21. **30** O'Leary in a letter dated 18 June 1991.
31 Bernard Harris, 'Celtic Dream', *Soundpost*, August/September 1982.

On a more provocative note, fellow composer Raymond Deane criticised Bodley's 'attempts to wed traditional Irish music to an 'avant-garde' idiom (that) can only lead to a kind of Bord Fáilte aesthetic' and concludes: 'Such music as Bodley's does a grave disservice to the tradition to which it purports to pay homage.'[32]

Such sharp criticism illustrates the ongoing conflict of musical traditions and respective individual perceptions thereof. Harris, in his review, disregarded the cultural conflict that Bodley presented and, although Deane is entitled to his opinion, it was not a homage to tradition that Bodley intended. As much as Bodley sought out the musical conflict, he also drew inspiration from structural parameters of traditional music such as irregular metres and ornaments and employed them in a manner never before attempted. Charles Acton caught Bodley's aesthetic more appropriately in a review of the first performance of *A Small White Cloud* ... at the Dublin Festival of Twentieth-Century Music in January 1976: 'In its quarter of an hour I felt that here may be a synthesis that I have been desiring for 30 years, the thing that Ó Riada ought to have reached from 'Hercules' and the Ceoltóirí, but did not; the creation of an Irish music that was far from those foreign-sounding and derivative Irish rhapsodies of decades ago.'[33] In a long history of exchanges between traditionally inherited and imported composed music in Ireland, this extended period in the work of Bodley represents the only instance of a cultural encounter of the two musical traditions in which both remained uncompromisingly intact,[34] a unique achievement which, in my opinion, is not sufficiently appreciated today.

A rarely explored path to achieve a unique Irish voice in modern music is by the use of traditional ethnic instruments in an art music context – a pattern generally more often pursued by contemporary East Asian composers than by European ones. When applied, however, this leads to surprisingly fresh and novel sounds as in Roger Doyle's (b. 1949) *Ceól Sidhe* (1973) for uilleann pipes, Irish harp and tin whistle, or in his more recent *Under the Green Time* (1995) for uilleann pipes and electronics and *Tradarr* (1999) for sean-nós singer, uilleann pipes, woodwinds, double bass and electronics. A similar effect, even more unfamiliar perhaps, was achieved in *Macehead* (1992) by Michael Holohan (b. 1956), a piece for bronze age horns, uilleann pipes and percussion with an extremely archaic sound alluding to prehistoric times.

Finally, Frank Corcoran (b. 1944) is able to explore these sonic possibilities and references to pre-colonial Irish culture without indigenous instru-

---

32 Raymond Deane in *Soundpost*, first part of the quote from issue April/May 1983 in the column 'Tailpiece', the second from issue June/July from a review of a concert on 26 April 1983 at Trinity College Dublin.   33 Charles Acton, '20th Century Festival starts', *Irish Times*, 6 January 1976.   34 With the possible exception that Bodley did not use traditional instruments.

ments, as in *Music for the Book of Kells* (1990) for five percussionists and piano or in his series of (partly) electronic pieces about the ancient tale of Sweeney, the mad king. So from Boydell's *Megalithic Ritual Dances* (1956), via Buckley's *Taller than Roman Spears* (1976), to Corcoran's *Mad Sweeney* (1998) and beyond, there is an aesthetically remarkable attempt in Irish music to embrace an indigenous culture long gone, a culture in which Irishness was not defined by its degree of popularity but by mythical art forms which required education and therefore a deeper understanding of music, and so parallels much of today's 'classical' music.

IV

In many respects the musical development in twentieth-century Ireland lagged behind that of other countries – it still does in some respects, in terms of second level education and with regard to the general acceptance of an Irish classical tradition for example. Some compositional 'schools' which were prevalent in other countries for a while never quite gained a foothold in Ireland, such as dodecaphony. The first Irish composition using a twelve-note row was A.J. Potter's (1918–80) *Variations on a Popular Tune* (1955), but the lively, entertaining character of this piece contrasts sharply with the aesthetics of the Second Viennese School. Even in more serious compositions with twelve-note rows such as his *Sinfonia de Profundis* (1969) Potter's brand of serialism is of a much more accessible kind. Although more sophisticated, the same remains true of Seán Ó Riada's *Nomos No. 1: Hercules Dux Ferrariae* (1957), a work often falsely lauded for its integration of traditional Irish elements and twelve note procedures.[35]

Likewise, individual developments of dodecaphony in the 1960s rarely resulted in consistently serial Irish compositions, although serialism undoubtedly influenced many composers to varying degrees (e.g. Ó Riada, Bodley, Victory, James Wilson, John Kinsella (b. 1934), Jerome de Bromhead (b. 1947), Eric Sweeney (b. 1948) etc.). But as in Kinsella's String Quartet no. 3 (1977), or Victory's *Five Mantras* (1965) for string orchestra and *Kriegslieder* (1967) for tenor, mixed chamber choir and small ensemble,[36] Irish serialism seems to have become 'absorbed in the eclectic palettes of a generation of composers who were writing within an essentially pluralist tradition.'[37]

Electroacoustic music arrived in Ireland in the 1970s with the work of Roger Doyle (b. 1949), who, with Michael Alcorn (b. 1962), is one of the most prominent Irish exponents of electroacoustic music. Doyle considers the

---

35 See Seóirse Bodley (as n. 9).   36 See my analyses in Klein (as n. 3), 248–56.   37 Gareth Cox, 'Webern Reception in Ireland', *Sprachen und Kultur* 15 (1998), 29–32.

computer to be *the* musical instrument of the twentieth century and his views on the medium are well-documented.[38] The presence of a number of Irish composers working in this medium[39] and the establishment of studios and educational programmes in many Irish universities demonstrate that Irish composers are actively exploring contemporary developments in the electro-acoustic area.

The fourth quarter of the century shows that Ireland has been comparable with compositional developments in other parts of the world, lagging behind no more, but instead, providing some leaders in new aesthetic currents. The examples of Gerald Barry (b. 1952) and Kevin Volans (b. 1949) illustrated the latter, when their music was an integral part of the New Simplicity debate in Germany of the mid to late 1970s. It is therefore no surprise to see their work published (a rare phenomenon in Irish music) when one considers the commercial needs of publishers to find representatives of styles regarded as 'trendy' rather than considering quality as the sole factor in publishing decisions. For those composers not profiting from publication of scores, it is gratifying that at last two record companies (Marco Polo and Black Box Music) with the help of the Irish Arts Council have begun publishing whole series of CDs with music by living Irish composers and that these recordings[40] are not confined to published scores. They also include music written in diverse styles from ultra-modern to 'post-neo-classicism', an area with some Irish leaders too; the more recent works by Bodley and Kinsella (despite their obvious dissimilarities) fall into that category, as do some works by Jane O'Leary (b. 1946), Philip Martin (b. 1947) or John Gibson (b. 1950).

In considering roots and directions in twentieth century Irish music, a path based on compositional schools and currents, I could only sketch some of the many individual perspectives which are prevalent in Ireland today. The younger generation of Michael McGlynn (b. 1964), Ian Wilson (b. 1964), Benjamin Dwyer (b. 1965), Gráinne Mulvey (b. 1966), Elaine Agnew (b. 1967), Deirdre Gribbin (b. 1967), Donnacha Dennehy (b. (1970), Rob Canning (b. 1974), Ailís Ní Riain (b. 1974), Jennifer Walshe (b. 1974), David Fennessy (b. 1976) and Andrew Hamilton (b. 1977) will surely make their mark in the twenty-first century and will do this nationally and internationally in a cultural environment much different from the one described here.

When Irish concert promoters, organisers, ensembles, the universities and the music schools begin to uncover and revive Irish works from the eighteenth

---

38 See his articles 'A Composer's Story', *Crane Bag* 6 (1982) 1, 55–58 and 'Death of a Medium', *Journal of Music in Ireland* 1 (2000), 5–9. **39** Such as Seóirse Bodley, Frank Corcoran, Fergus Johnston (b. 1959) Donnacha Dennehy (b. 1970), Donal Hurley (b. 1950) Michael Alcorn. See Paschall de Paor's article in this volume. **40** For complete listings, including earlier Irish music, see Klein, *Irish Classical Recordings: A Discography of Irish Art Music* (Westport, Conn.: Greenwood, 2001).

and nineteenth centuries, perform the early twentieth-century operas by Butler, O'Dwyer, Esposito or Harvey Pélissier, the orchestral scores by Boyle and Hay, the songs by Palmer, Coghill or May, the chamber music by Dickenson-Auner and other composers mentioned – when innovative Irish concert programming thus embraces music from the early eighteenth to the early twenty-first century, only then will a healthy state of Irish musical culture have been attained.

11

A twentieth-century Irish music bibliography

COMPILED BY AXEL KLEIN

This bibliography of Irish art music in the twentieth century is divided into two sections: a general one devoted to surveys, trends and backgrounds and a biographical section listing additional sources for individual composers. It lists published material in the form of books, articles in periodicals, entries in dictionaries and encyclopedias, many substantial newspaper articles and also includes unpublished postgraduate theses.

I have not included aural and visual sources despite their excellent documentary value because of the sheer difficulty of tracing them all and the impossibility of any attempt at comprehensiveness. For the same reason I have also omitted manuscript sources (with a few notable exceptions) and government documents. For information on recorded musical sources I refer readers to my *Irish Classical Recordings: A Discography of Irish Art Music* (Greenwood Press: Westport CT 2001), which lists music by Irish composers past and present published on LPs, MCs and CDs beginning at the mono long-playing era.

This bibliography therefore reflects the current status of printed sources of scholarship and criticism on Irish music. In the absence of any sustained or successful effort to establish a musicological periodical in Ireland, it reveals how musical topics have long been accommodated in interdisciplinary journals. The dearth of monographs devoted specifically to Irish art music for so long can be noted (perhaps due to the literary domination of Irish culture and the problems with the very definition of 'Irish music'), but this has been rectified somewhat in the last decade.

Abbreviations for standard encyclopedias

KdG: *Komponisten der Gegenwart (KdG)*, edited by Walter-Wolfgang
Sparrer and Hans-Werner Heister (Munich: edition text + kritik, 1992ff). [loose-leaflet
    dictionary with two to three supplements a year, five vols., 2002]

MGG1: *Die Musik in Geschichte und Gegenwart (MGG)*, first edition, edited by Friedrich Blume (Kassel: Bärenreiter 1949–68) with two supplement vols. (1973, 1979) and an index volume (1986).

MGG2 *Die Musik in Geschichte und Gegenwart (MGG)*, second revised edition, edited by Ludwig Finscher (Kassel: Bärenreiter & Stuttgart: Metzler, subject part in 10 vols. (1994–99) and biographical part in 17 volumes (1999–2007).

New Grove 1 *The New Grove Dictionary of Music and Musicians*, 20 vols., edited by Stanley Sadie (London: Macmillan, 1980).

New Grove 2 *The New Grove Dictionary of Music and Musicians*, revised version, 24 vols., edited by Stanley Sadie (London: Macmillan, 2001).

I. GENERAL

Acton, Charles. 'Towards an Irish Music', *Envoy*, no. 3 (September 1950), 75–8.

——. 'Music in Ireland', *Musical Opinion and Music Trade Review*, lxxx (1957) 953, 279.

——. 'Irish Music for Export', *Éire-Ireland*, ii (1967) 3, 34–41.

——. *Irish Music and Musicians* (Dublin: Eason & Son, 1978).

——. 'Irish Pianists', *GPA Irish Arts Review* (1988), 116–24.

Aprahamian, Felix. 'Irish Piano Music: Charles Lynch', *Gramophone*, l (1972) 594 (November), 935.

An Chomhairle Ealaíon/The Arts Council. *Annual Reports* 1951 ff., (Dublin: The Arts Council, 1952 ff.).

Arts Council of Ireland, The (eds.). *Living and Working Conditions of Artists: A Summary of the Main Results of a Survey of Irish Artists* (Dublin: The Arts Council, 1980).

Barry, Gerald. 'The Association of Young Irish Composers', *Counterpoint*, iv (1972) December, 12–14.

Bax, Arnold. 'Foreword', in: Aloys Fleischmann (ed.), *Music in Ireland: A Symposium*, iii–iv (Cork: Cork University Press, 1952).

Bodkin, Thomas. *Report on the Arts in Ireland* (Dublin: An Gúm, 1949).

Bodley, Seóirse. 'A Composer's View', *Trinity News: Music Supplement*, 3 December 1964, 10.

——. 'Ireland § 1: Art Music' New Grove 1.

Bowles, Michael. 'A Commentary on Irish Musical History', *The Capuchin Annual*, xx (1950–1), 329–50.

——. 'A Musical Aspiration of National Unity', *Irish Times* (early 1970s).

Boydell, Barra. *Music and Paintings in the National Gallery of Ireland* (Dublin: National Gallery of Ireland, 1985).

——. 'Impressions of Dublin: 1934' *Dublin Historical Record*, xxxviii (1983–4), 88–104.

Boydell, Brian. 'Music in Ireland', *The Bell*, xiv (1947) 1, 16–20; with replies by Aloys Fleischmann (ibid.), 20–4, and Michael Bowles (ibid.), 24–5.

——. 'Culture and Chauvinism', *Envoy*, no. 2 (May 1950), 75–9.

——. 'The Future of Music in Ireland', *The Bell*, xvi (1951) 4, 21–9; with replies by Aloys Fleischmann (vol. xvi, no. 5, 5–10), P.J. Malone (ibid., 10–13) and Joseph O'Neill (ibid., 13–18).

—— (ed.). *Four Centuries of Music in Ireland* (London: BBC, 1979).

——. 'Half a Century of Music in Dublin', *Dublin Historical Record*, xxxvii (1984) 3 & 4, 117–121.

——. *The Roaring Forties and Thereabouts* (unpublished autobiography), 1994.

Bracefield, Hilary. 'Stagnant Backwater?', *Soundpost*, i (1981), 18–19.

——. 'The Northern Composer: Irish or European?' in: Patrick F. Devine and Harry White (eds.), *The Maynooth International Musicological Conference: Selected Proceedings, Part One (Irish Musical Studies 4)* (Dublin: Four Courts Press, 1996), 255–62.

Brown, Terence. *Ireland: A Social and Cultural History, 1922–1985* (London: Fontana, 1985).

Classical Ireland (Dublin: Lacethorn Publishing, 1999–2000 [4 issues]).

Cooke, Jim. *College of Music: A Musical Journey 1890–1993* (Dublin: College of Music, 1994).

Corcoran, Frank. 'New Irish Music', *Interface: Journal of New Music Research*, xii (1983) 1–2, 41–4.

Cork Review, The. Music in Cork (Cork: Triskel Arts Centre, 1992).

Cox, Gareth. 'The Development of Twentieth-Century Irish Art Music' *Musik als Text – Bericht über den Internationalen Kongress der Gesellschaft für Musikforschung Freiburg 1993*, Kassel 1999, 560–2.

—— (ed.). *Acton's Music: Reviews of Dublin Musical Life, 1955–1985* (Bray Co. Wicklow: Kilbride Books, 1996).

——. 'Webern Reception in Ireland' *Sprachen und Kultur*, 15 (1998), 29–32.

——. 'German Influences on Twentieth-Century Irish Art-Music', in: Joachim Fischer et al. (eds.), *Deutsch-Irische Verbindungen/Irish-German Connections (Schriftenreihe Literaturwissenschaft 42)*, (Trier: Wissenschaftlicher Verlag, 1998), 107–114.

Creely, Marion et al. *European Music Year 1985: Yearbook for Ireland*, (Dublin: Irish Committee for the European Music Year, 1985). With contributions by Marion Creely, Brendan Breathnach, Aloys Fleischmann, Martin Adams, Brian Boydell, Hans Waldemar Rosen and Michael Taylor.

Cull, Gráinne. Piano Music for Children by Irish Composers (MA thesis, University of Limerick, 1999).

Daly, Kieran Anthony. *Catholic Church Music in Ireland, 1878–1903*, (Dublin: Four Courts Press, 1995).

Deale, Edgar M. (ed.). *A Catalogue of Contemporary Irish Composers* (Dublin: Music Association of Ireland, 1968,²1973).

Deane, Raymond. 'Diabolus in natura: The "Nature" of New Music', *Maynooth Review* (December 1978), 22–30.

——. 'Caterer and Comforter? The Composer in Modern Ireland', *Irish Review*, xv (1990) Spring, 1–4.

——. 'The Honour of Non-Existence: Classical Composers in Irish Society', *Irish Musical Studies*, 3 (1995), 199–211.

——. 'In Praise of Begrudgery', in: Niall Doyle (ed.), *The Boydell Papers: Essays on Music and Music Policy in Ireland* (Dublin: Music Network, 1997), 26–32.

——. 'A Different Music', *Irish Times*, 28 December 1999.

Delany, Patrick. 'A Concert Hall for Dublin?', *The Bell*, xvii (1952) 10, 5–10; with replies by: Edgar M. Deale (vol. xvii, no. 11, 16–19); James Chapman (ibid., 19–21); Walter Beckett (ibid., 21); Aloys Fleischmann (ibid., 21–23).

Dervan, Michael. 'Charles Acton Reflects', *Music Ireland*, i (1986) 3, 8–12.

——. 'Contemporary Music: People Do Listen', *Irish Times* (weekend supplement), 8 July 1989.

——. 'Now you see them, now you don't', *Music Ireland*, v (1990) 8, 12.

Devane, James. 'Is an Irish Culture Possible?', *Ireland To-day*, i (1936) 1, 21–32.

Dibble, Jeremy. 'The Composer in the Academy (1) 1850–1940', in: Richard Pine and Charles Acton (eds.), *To Talent Alone: The Royal Irish Academy of Music 1848–1998* (Dublin: Gill & Macmillan, 1998), 400–18.

Directory of Musicians in Ireland (Dublin: Music Network, 1998).

Donlon, Louise. *Catalogue of Works from the Composers' Commission Scheme, 1980–90* (Dublin: Arts Council, 1992).

Donoghue, Denis. 'The Future of Irish Music', *Studies*, 44 (1955) Spring, 109–14.

Doyle, Niall (ed.). 'Towards a National Music Policy', *The Boydell Papers: Essays on Music and Music Policy in Ireland* (Dublin: Music Network, 1997) in: N. Doyle (ed.), 19–25.

Drury, Martin. 'Tacit Approval', in: Niall Doyle (ed.), *The Boydell Papers: Essays on Music and Music Policy in Ireland* (Dublin: Music Network, 1997), 11–18.

Dungan, Michael. 'Money for Music', *New Music News*, February 1999, 9–12.

——. 'Driven, Determined and Busy', *New Music News*, February 2001, 9–11.

Dwyer [O'Dwyer], Robert. 'Imitations of Palestrina', *New Ireland Review*, xv (1900), 155–60.

Fadlu-Deen, Kitty. 'Contemporary Music in Ireland', MA thesis, (University College Dublin, 1968).

Fallon, Brian. 'Musical Life and Lives', in: Brian Fallon, *An Age of Innocence: Irish Culture, 1930–1960* (Dublin: Gill & Macmillan, 1999), 247–56.

Farrell, Hazel. Aspects of Pitch Structure and Pitch Selection in Post-War Irish Composition: An Analytical Study of Tonal and Post-tonal Referential Collections in Selected Works by Irish Composers (Ph.D Diss. University of Limerick, 2002).

Fleischmann , Aloys. 'The Outlook of Music in Ireland', *Studies*, xxiv (1935) March, 121–30.

——. 'Ars Nova: Irish Music in the Shaping', *Ireland To-day*, i (1936) 2, 41–8.

——. 'Composition and the Folk Idiom', *Ireland To-day*, i (1936) 6, 37–44.

——. 'Music in U.C.C.', *U.C.C. Record* (1945), 4 (Summer), 38–42.

——. 'Music and its Public', *U.C.C. Record* (1946), 7 (Summer), 28ff.

—— (ed.). *Music in Ireland: A Symposium* (Cork: Cork University Press and Oxford: B.H. Blackwell, 1952).

——. 'Dublin', *Grove's Dictionary of Music and Musicians* (London: Macmillan, 1954).

——. 'Cork', New Grove 1.

——. 'Music and Society 1850–1921', in: W. E. Vaughan (ed.), *A New History of Ireland*, vol. 6 (Oxford: Oxford University Press, 1996).

Forbes, Anne-Marie H. 'Celticism in British Opera 1878–1938', *Music Review*, 47 (1987), 176–83.

Fox, Ian. 'An Island Full of Noises', *Counterpoint*, i (1969) July.

—— (ed.). *100 Nights at the Opera: An Anthology to Celebrate the 40th Anniversary of the Wexford Festival Opera* (Dublin: Town House, 1991).

——. 'An Isle Full of Noise? Recent Developments and Current Status of Music in Ireland', *Studies*, lxxxi (1992) Spring, 34–40.

[Gillen, Gerard and White, Harry (eds). *Irish Musical Studies* (Dublin 1990 ff.) see under title].

Gorham, Maurice. *Forty Years of Irish Broadcasting* (Dublin 1967).

Grindle, William Henry. *Irish Cathedral Music: A History of Music at the Cathedrals of the Church of Ireland* (Belfast: The Institute of Irish Studies/Queen's University, 1989).

Groocock, Joseph. *A General Survey of Music in the Republic of Ireland* (Dublin 1961).

Harris, Bernard. 'Contemporary Irish Music', *Anglo-Irish and Irish Literature: Aspects of Language and Culture*, vol. I, 207–12 (Uppsala: Uppsala University Press, 1988).

Harrison, Bernard. *Catalogue of Contemporary Irish Music* (Dublin: Irish Composers' Centre, 1982).

Harty, Hamilton. 'Modern Composers and Modern Composition', *Musical Times*, lxv (1924), 328–32.

——. '"No New Music That Will Live": Sir Hamilton Harty Suggests an Antidote to the "Accursed Jazz", "Private Hells" for "Disgusting Music"', *Musical Mirror*, v (1925) 10, 197.

Heneghan, Frank. *The Founding of the Feis Ceoil and its Influence on Music Education in Ireland* (Dublin: City of Dublin Vocational Education Committee, 1988).

Herron, Donald. *Deaf Ears: A Report on the Provision of Music Education in Irish Schools* (Dublin: The Arts Council, 1985).

Hollfelder, Peter. *Geschichte der Klaviermusik*, 2 vols. (Wilhelmshaven: Florian Noetzel, 1989), chapter 'Irland' in vol. 2, 1108–15. Expanded edition, 1999.

Hufstader, Jonathan. 'Thomas Kinsella and Irish Music', *Canadian Journal of Irish Studies*, 21 (1995) 2, 19–31.

Hughes, Anthony. 'Music in Ireland: The Future', in: Brian Boydell (ed.), *Four Centuries of Music in Ireland* (London: BBC, 1979), 60–3.

——. 'The Society and Music', in: J. Meenan and D. Clarke (eds.), *The Royal Dublin Society, 1731–1981* (Dublin: 1981), 265–77.

Ireland's Music World. Dublin 1973 (7 monthly issues).

Irish Composer, The. Essays on Contemporary Music ed. by the Association of Irish Composers, vol. i, November 1988.

Irish Music Guide. Published in seven parts by the magazine *Music Ireland* and the Contemporary Music Centre, Dublin 1987. (1) *Administration, Education, Libraries, Museums and Galleries*; (2) *Cultural and Professional Organisations, Musical Clubs and Societies, Arts Centres, Musical Instrument Makers & Repairers*; (3) *The Trade: Retail and Wholesale, The Recording Industry*; (4) *Survey of 1986, Events 1987*; (5) *Composers and Performers*; (6) *The Media and Publishers*; (7) *Venues*.

Irish Music Handbook. Dublin: Music Network, 1996.

Irish Musical Monthly, The: A Journal devoted to the Interests of Music in Church and School, vol. i, Heinrich Bewerunge (ed.), (Dublin, Cork, Belfast: Browne and Nolan, March 1902 – February 1903).

Irish Musical Studies, ed. by Gerard Gillen and Harry White (vols. i–iii), Patrick F. Devine and Harry White (vols. iv–v), Gerard Gillen and Anthony Johnstone (vol. vi).

– vol. i: *Musicology in Ireland* (Dublin: Irish Academic Press, 1990).

– vol. ii: *Music and the Church* (Dublin: Irish Academic Press, 1993).

– vol. iii: *Music and Irish Cultural History* (Dublin: Irish Academic Press, 1995).

– vol. iv: *The Maynooth International Musicological Conference 1995. Selected Proceedings Part One* (Dublin: Four Courts Press, 1996).

– vol. v: *The Maynooth International Musicological Conference 1995. Selected Proceedings Part Two* (Dublin: Four Courts Press, 1996).

– vol. vi: *An Anthology of Irish Church Music* (Dublin: Four Courts Press, 2001).

Irish Performing Arts Yearbook (London: Rhinegold, 1992 ff.).

Irish Times, (anonymous articles):

——. 'The Irish Musical Festival', 18 May 1897 (about the first Feis Ceoil).

——. 'Only Capital in Europe without a Concert Hall', 11 April 1956.

——. 'Music Makers Portrait Gallery', 2 July 1960.

——. Debate on 'Contemporary Music' in Letters to the Editor, July–August 1989: 14 July: Raymond Deane; 18 July: Philip G. Gormley; 21 July: Frank Corcoran; 26 July: Gerald Barry and Fergus Johnston; 27 July: Brendan Dunne and R.M. Conroy; 2 August: Raymond Deane.

Jones, Percy. 'A Survey of the Music of Ireland', *Irish Ecclesiastical Record*, 87 (1957), I: 170–8, II: 252–9, III: 355–61.

Journal of Music in Ireland. November 2000 ff. (bi-monthly).

Keary, Reamonn. Survey of Irish Piano Music from 1970 to 1995 (MA thesis, Maynooth: National University of Ireland, 1995)

Kelly, Noel. Music in Irish Primary Education (MA thesis, University College Cork, 1978).

Kennedy, Brian P. *Dreams and Responsibilities: The State and the Arts in Independent Ireland* (Dublin: The Arts Council, undated [1990],²1998).

——. 'Paying the Piper, Calling the Tune', in: Niall Doyle (ed.), *The Boydell Papers: Essays on Music and Music Policy in Ireland* (Dublin: Music Network, 1997), 5–10.

Klein, Axel: '"... bis auf den heutigen Tag unfähig"? Gitarrenmusik aus Irland', *Gitarre & Laute*, xii (1990) 3, 55–65 (incl. 1st movt. of John Buckley's *Sonata for Guitar*).

——. 'Kein Land am Rand? Dublin 1991: Die Musikszene in der "Europäischen Kulturhauptstadt"', *Neue Zeitschrift für Musik*, clii (1991) April, 14–17.

——. 'Großbritannien/Irland: Länder ohne Musik?', *Neue Zeitschrift für Musik*, clii, October, 1991, 11–16.

——. 'New Guitar Music From Ireland: A Survey', *Classical Guitar*, 10 (1992) I: April, 20–22, II: May, 39–42.

——. 'Fließende Grenzen: Die irische Musikszene', *Neue Zeitschrift für Musik*, cliv (1993) 3, 22–4.

——. *Die Musik Irlands im 20. Jahrhundert* (Hildesheim, Zürich, New York: Georg Olms Verlag, 1996).

——. 'Irland', MGG2.

——. 'Irish Composers and Foreign Education: A Study of Influences', in: Patrick F. Devine and Harry White (eds.), *The Maynooth International Musicological Conference: Selected Proceedings, Part One, (Irish Musical Studies 4)*, (Dublin: Four Courts Press 1996), 271–84.

——. 'Musik ohne Publikum: Die zwanziger Jahre in Irland', in Werner Keil (ed.), *Musik der zwanziger Jahre* (Hildesheim: Georg Olms Verlag, 1996), 166–85.

——. 'An "old eminence among musical nations": Nationalism and the Case for a Musical History in Ireland', in: Tomi Mäkelä (ed.), *Music and Nationalism in 20th-Century Great Britain and Finland* (Hamburg: von Bockel Verlag, 1997), 233–43.

——. 'The Composer in the Academy (2) 1940–1990' in: Richard Pine and Charles Acton, *To Talent Alone: The Royal Irish Academy of Music 1848–1998* (Dublin: Gill & Macmillan, 1998), 419–28.

——. *Irish Classical Recordings: A Discography of Irish Art Music* (Westport, Connecticut: Greenwood Press, 2001).

Larchet, John F. 'A Plea for Music', in: W.G. Fitzgerald (ed.), *The Voice of Ireland: A Memorial of Freedom's Day* (Dublin: Virtue & Co., 1926), reprinted in T. Maher, *The Harp's a Wonder* (Mullingar: Uisneach Press, 1991), 121–6.

Larchet-Cuthbert, Sheila. *The Irish Harp Book* (Cork and Dublin: The Mercier Press, 1975,³1993).

Loveland, Kenneth. 'Dublin's Modern Festival', *Music and Musicians*, xvii March, 1969, 36.

——. 'Composers in Search for a National Identity' *Counterpoint*, iv, October, 1972.

Lyons, F.S.L. *Culture and Anarchy in Ireland, 1890–1939* (Oxford: Oxford University Press, 1982).

McCaffery, Michael. 'Ever Decreasing Circles ... ?', *Music Ireland*, iii (1988) May, 16–17.

McCarthy, Marie. 'The Transmission of Music and the Formation of National Identity in Early Twentieth-Century Ireland', in: Patrick F. Devine and Harry White (eds.), *The Maynooth International Musicological Conference: Selected Proceedings, Part Two, (Irish Musical Studies 5)*, (Dublin: Four Courts Press 1996), 146–59.

——. 'Music Education in the Emergent Nation State', in: Richard Pine (ed.), *Music in Ireland 1848–1998* (Cork: Mercier Press and Boulder/Colorado: Irish American Book Company, 1998), 65–75.

——. *Passing It On: The Transmission of Music in Irish Culture* (Cork: Cork University Press, 1999).

McCormack, W.J. (ed.). *The Blackwell Companion to Modern Irish Culture* (Oxford: Blackwell, 1999).

McGinley, Rachel. A survey of Irish Cello Works from 1939 to 1997 (MA thesis, Maynooth: National University of Ireland, 1997).

McHugh, Barbara. 'Music in St Patrick's Cathedral, Dublin, 1865–1915', (MA thesis, University College Dublin, 1980).

McLachlan, John. 'The Composer in Society', *Journal of Music in Ireland*, i (2001) 5 (July/August), 5–10.

McRedmond, Louis (ed.). *Written on the Wind: Personal Memories of Irish Radio 1926–1976* (Dublin: Radio Telefís Éireann with Gill and Macmillan, 1976).

Martyn, Edward. 'The Gaelic League and Irish Music', *Irish Review*, i (1911), 449ff.

May, Frederick. 'Music and the Nation', *Dublin Magazine*, xi (1936) July– September, 50–6.

——. 'The Composer in Ireland', *The Bell*, xiii (1947) 4 (January), 30–6.

——. 'The Composer in Ireland', in: Aloys Fleischmann (ed.), *Music in Ireland: A Symposium* (Cork: Cork University Press, 1952), 164–77.

——. 'The Composer and Society', *The Bell*, xix (1954), July.

Molloy, Dinah. *Find your Music in Ireland* (Dublin: The Arts Council, 1979).

Murphy, Anne M. 'The Requiem and Contemporary Irish Music: A Study of the Musical and Religious Significance of the Requiem in the Repertoire of Contemporary Irish Composers' (PhD diss., St Patrick's College, Maynooth, 1994).

Music Association of Ireland. *Annual Report*, Dublin: M.A.I. 1948 ff.

Music Ireland. Dublin: Amadeus Publications, 1986–91 (ten issues per year).

Music Network (editors). *Directory of Musicians in Ireland* (Dublin: Music Network, 1998).

Music World. Dublin, 1951–2 (five issues, bi-monthly).

Neeson, Seán. 'When Gaelic Tunes are Whistled in the Streets', *Irish Press*, 12 April 1935.

New Music News. Dublin: The Contemporary Music Centre, 1990 ff. (three issues per year).

Ní Ógáin, Úna & Ó Duibhir, Riobard [O'Dwyer, Richard]. *Dánta Dé: Idir senn agus nuadh* (Dublin: Óifig an tSoláthair, 1928).

O'Broin, Eimear: 'Music and Broadcasting', in: Richard Pine (ed.), *Music in Ireland, 1848–1998* (Cork: Mercier Press and Boulder/Colorado: Irish American Book Company, 1998), 109–120.

O'Byrne, Robert. 'Everybody's Friends', *Music Ireland*, iii (1987–8) December– January, 8–13.

——. 'Competing for Cash 1988', *Music Ireland*, iii (1988) March, 15.

——. 'Contemporary Music: Why Will No One Listen', *Irish Times*, 5 July 1989.

Ó Gallchobháir, Éamonn. 'Music – Atavism', *Ireland To-day*, i (1936) 1, 56–8.

O'Keefe, Patrick. A Survey of Contemporary Irish Music for Clarinet and Piano (MA thesis, Maynooth: National University of Ireland, 1997).

O'Kelly, Eve (ed.). *Irish Composers* (Dublin: Contemporary Music Centre, 1993 ff.).

——. 'Finding Our Voice: Music in Ireland Today', *Brio*, xxxii (1995) 2, 94–102.

O'Kelly, Pat. *The National Symphony Orchestra of Ireland 1948–1998: A Selected History* (Dublin: RTÉ, 1998).

O'Leary, Jane. 'Dublin Festival of Twentieth Century Music', *Perspectives of New Music*, xvii (1979) 2, 260–7.

——. 'Contemporary Music in Ireland: Developments in the Past Twenty Years', in: Patrick F. Devine and Harry White (eds.), *The Maynooth International Musicological Conference: Selected Proceedings, Part One, (Irish Musical Studies 4)*, (Dublin: Four Courts Press 1996), 285–95.

——. 'Women Composers in Ireland: A Changing Profile' *IAWM Journal*, October 1996, 16–17 [IAWM = International Alliance for Women in Music].

——. 'Creating an Audience for Contemporary Music', in: Richard Pine (ed.), *Music in Ireland 1848–1998* (Cork: Mercier Press and Boulder/Colorado: Irish American Book Company, 1998), 121–9.

——. '25 Years of Concorde', *Journal of Music in Ireland*, i (2001) 6 (November/December), 5–9.

Ó Súilleabháin, Mícheál. 'Irish Music Defined', *Crane Bag*, v (1981) 2, 83–87.

——. 'The Art of Listening', *Crane Bag*, vi (1982) 1, 59–61.

Patterson, Annie. *The Story of Oratorio* (London: Walter Scott and New York: Charles Scribner's Sons, 1898,[2] 1902).

——. 'The Interpretation of Irish Music', *Journal of the Ivernian Society*, ii (1909), 31–42.

——. 'The Folk-Music of Ireland: Its Past, Present, and Future Aspects', *Musical Quarterly*, vi (1920), 455–67.

——. [many contributions to *The Weekly Irish Times*, *c*.1900 to 1920]

Phelan, Helen. '"Roma locuta, causa finita?": The Perception, Interpretation and Implementation of Conciliar and Post-Conciliar Directives regarding Liturgical Music in the Republic of Ireland, 1962–92', in: Patrick F. Devine and Harry White (eds.), *The Maynooth International Musicological Conference: Selected Proceedings, Part One, (Irish Musical Studies 4)*, (Dublin: Four Courts Press 1996), 119–26.

Pine, Richard (ed.). *Music in Ireland 1848–1998* (Cork: Mercier Press and Boulder/Colorado: Irish American Book Company, 1998); therein by the ed.: 'Preface', 11–16; 'Music in Ireland 1848–1998: An Overview', 17–26.

– and Acton, Charles (eds). *To Talent Alone: The Royal Irish Academy of Music 1848–1998* (Dublin: Gill & Macmillan, 1998).

Prendergast, Mark. *Irish Rock* (Dublin: O'Brien Press, 1987).

Reilly, Seamus. 'James Joyce and Dublin Opera 1888–1904', in: Sebastian D.G. Knowles (ed.), *Bronze by Gold: The Music of Joyce* (New York and London: Garland Publishing, 1999), 3–31.

Rogers, Brendan. 'An Irish School of Music', *New Ireland Review*, xiii (1900), 149–59.

Royal Irish Academy of Music 1856–1956, Centenary Souvenir (Dublin: Corrigan & Wilson, 1956).

Ryan, Joseph J. 'Nationalism and Music in Ireland', PhD diss. Maynooth: National University of Ireland, 1991).

——. 'Assertions of Distinction: The Modal Debate in Irish Music', in: Gerard Gillen and Harry White (eds.), *Music and the Church (Irish Musical Studies 2)*, (Dublin: Irish Academic Press, 1993), 62–77.

——. 'Nationalism and Irish Music', in: Gerard Gillen and Harry White (eds.), *Music and Irish Cultural History (Irish Musical Studies 3)*, (Dublin: Irish Academic Press, 1995), 101–15.

——. 'Music and the Institutions', in: Richard Pine (ed.), *Music in Ireland, 1848–1998* (Cork: Mercier Press and Boulder/Colorado: Irish American Book Company, 1998), 98–108.

——. 'The Tone of Defiance', in: Harry White and Michael Murphy (eds.), *Musical Constructions of Nationalism* (Cork: Cork University Press, 2001), 197–211.

Saorstát Éireann Official Handbook. Bulmer Hobson (ed.), (Dublin: An Gúm, 1932).

Schaarwächter, Jürgen. *Die britische Sinfonie, 1914–1945* (Köln: Dohr, 1995).

Smith, Gus. *Love and Music: The Glorious History of the Dublin Grand Opera Society, 1941–1998* (Dublin and London: Atlantic Publishers, 1998).

Travers Smith, H. 'A Musical League for Dublin', *Irish Statesman*, I [old series], 26 July 1919, 119; II [old series], 27 March 1920, 300.

Trimble, Joan. *Notes on Dublin, 1912–1930*, unpublished manuscript (17 pp.), 1987.
University of Dublin. *Bicentenary of the Founding of the Chair of Music 1764–1964: A Trinity News Supplement*, vol. xii, no. 5, 3 December 1964.
Walsh, Caroline. 'The Saturday Profile: Michael Bowles', *Irish Times* (c. 1975).
——. 'Concert Hall Opens in Fanfare of Glory', *Irish Times*, 10 September 1981.
White, Harold R. 'The Feis Ceoil', *Irish Life*, 28 July 1916, 21–25.
——. 'The Feis Ceoil', *Irish Life*, 18 May 1917, 173–176.
White, Harry. 'Musicology in Ireland', *Acta Musicologica*, lx (1988) 3, 290–305.
——. 'Frank Llewellyn Harrison and the Development of Post-War Musicological Thought', *Hermathena*, cxlvi (1989) Summer, 39–47.
——. 'A Canadian Model for Music in Ireland', *Canadian Journal of Irish Studies*, Summer 1990, 1–7.
——. 'Brian Friel, Thomas Murphy and the Use of Music in Contemporary Irish Drama', *Modern Drama*, xxxiii (1990) 553–563.
——. 'Music and the Perception of Music in Ireland', *Studies*, lxxix (1990), 38–45
(——. editor with Gerald Gillen: *Irish Musical Studies* [Dublin 1990 ff.], see under title)
——. *The Keeper's Recital: Music and Cultural History in Ireland, 1770–1970* (Cork: Cork University Press, 1998).
——. 'Ireland. I. Art Music', *New Grove 2*.
——. 'Nationalism, Colonialism and the Cultural Stasis of Music in Ireland', in: Harry White and Michael Murphy (eds.), *Musical Constructions of Nationalism* (Cork: Cork University Press, 2001), 257–271.
Wilson, James. 'The Composer in Ireland Today', *Soundpost*, 1 (1981) April–May, 30.

II. INDIVIDUAL COMPOSERS

Agnew, Elaine
Collins, Tom. 'Elaine Agnew', *New Music News*, September 1993, 9–11.

Alcorn, Michael
Russ, Michael. *New Grove 2*.

Barry, Gerald
Barry, Gerald. 'The Intelligence Park', *Contemporary Music Review*, v (1989), 229–37.
Bye, Antony. 'Gay Days Spent in Gladness', *Musical Times*, cxxxiv (1993) September, 496–500
Clarke, Jocelyn. 'Pleasantly Alienating and Strangely Seductive', *New Music News*, February 1995, 9–11.
Clements, Andrew. 'A Short Journey Around "The Intelligence Park"', *Opera*, xli (1990) 7, 804–7.
Cox, Gareth. 'The Music of Gerald Barry as an Introduction to Contemporary Irish Art-Music: Twentieth-Century Music in the New Leaving Certificate Syllabus (1999–2001)', in: Liam Irwin (ed.), *Centenary Essays, Mary Immaculate College* (Dublin: Colour Books, 1998), 61–72.
——. *MGG2*.
——. *New Grove 2*.

Deane, Vincent. 'The Music of Gerald Barry', *Soundpost*, 1 (1981) June–July, 14–17.

Dervan, Michael. 'Bowers of Bliss, of Blood.', *An Droichead*, Summer 1986, 4–6.

——. 'The Gerald Barry Experience', *Irish Times*, 27 June 2000.

Dungan, Michael. 'A Messenger with Fresh News', *New Music News*, May 2000, 9–11.

Jack, Adrian. 'Introducing Gerald Barry', *Musical Times*, cxxix (1988) August, 389–93.

——. 'Unspeakable Practices', *Music Ireland*, v (1990) 7, 7–9.

Volans, Kevin. *Summer Gardeners: Conversations with Composers* (Durban: Newer Music Edition, 1985) [with chapter about Gerald Barry].

—— with Bracefield, Hilary. 'A Constant State of Surprise: Gerald Barry and "The Intelligence Park"', *Contact* no. 31 (1987) Autumn, 9–19.

Bax, Arnold[1]

Andrews, Dennis (editor). *Cuchulan among the Guns: Sir Arnold Bax's Letters to Christopher Whelen from 1949 to 1953* (Cumnor: Dennis Andrews, 1998).

Bax, Arnold. *Farewell, My Youth* (London, New York, Toronto: Longmans, Green, 1943).

Fleischmann, Aloys. 'Arnold Bax', *Recorded Sound*, iii (1968) 29/30, 273–76.

——. 'The Arnold Bax Memorial', *UCC Record*, xxxi (1956), 25–30.

Foreman, Lewis. *Bax: A Composer and his Times* (London and Berkeley: Scolar Press, 1983, ²1988).

——. *New Grove 2*.

H., C. 'Mr Arnold Bax in a Celtic Fog', *The Spectator*, no. 4926 (1922), 764–5.

Hull, Robert H. *A Handbook on Arnold Bax's Symphonies* (London, 1932).

Klein, D.L. *Structural Principles of the Sixth Symphony by Arnold Bax* (London, 1983).

Parlett, Graham. *Arnold Bax: A Catalogue of His Music* (London, 1972).

——. *A Catalogue of the Works of Sir Arnold Bax* (Oxford, 1999).

Puffet, Derrick. 'In the Garden of Fand: Arnold Bax and the "Celtic Twilight"', in: Jürg Stenzl (ed.), *Art Nouveau, Jugendstil und Musik*, (Zürich 1980), 193–210.

Scott, D.B. *The Symphonies of Arnold Bax* (Hull, 1978).

Walker, Arthur Dennis. *MGG2*.

Wilson, D.J. *The Orchestral Development of Arnold Bax* (Bangor, 1975).

Beckett, Walter

Burn, Sarah M. 'Walter Beckett', *New Music News*, May 1996, 5.

Ryan, Joseph J. *New Grove 2*.

Bewerunge, Heinrich

Daly, Kieran Anthony. *Catholic Church Music in Ireland, 1878–1903: The Cecilian Reform Movement* (Dublin: Four Courts Press, 1995).

Klein, Axel and Lickleder, Christoph. *MGG2*.

White, Harry. 'Heinrich Bewerunge (1862–1923). Ein Beitrag zur Geschichte des Caecilianismus in Irland. Mit einem Werkverzeichnis von Frank Lawrence', *Kirchenmusikalisches Jahrbuch*, lxxiv (1990), 41–66.

——. (translated as) 'Towards a History of the Cecilian Movement in Ireland', in: Gerard Gillen and Harry White (eds.), *Music and the Church (Irish Musical Studies 2)*, (Dublin: Irish Academic Press, 1993), 78–107.

---

1 The listing on Bax is confined to the most important publications.

——. 'Heinrich Bewerunge and the Cecilian Movement in Ireland, in: Harry White, *The Keeper's Recital: Music and Cultural History in Ireland, 1770–1970* (Cork: Cork University Press, 1998), 74–93.

——. *New Grove 2.*

Bodley, Seóirse

Acton, Charles. 'Interview with Seóirse Bodley', *Éire-Ireland*, v (1970) 3, 117–33.

Barry, Malcolm. 'Examining the Great Divide', *Soundpost*, iii (1983) October–November, 15–20.

Bodley, Seóirse. 'A Composer's View', *Trinity News: Music Supplement*, 3 December 1964, 10.

Dungan, Michael. 'Seóirse Bodley', *New Music News*, September 1996, 9–11.

Feehan, Fanny. 'The Importance of Being Seóirse', *Hibernia*, xliii, 4 January 1979.

Klein, Axel. *KdG.*

——. 'Aber was ist heute schon abenteuerlich?' Ein Porträt des irischen Komponisten Seóirse Bodley', *MusikTexte*, no. 52, January 1994, 21–25.

——. *MGG2.*

——. *New Grove 2.*

Murphy, Daniel et al. (eds). *Education and the Arts*, XXIII: Seóirse Bodley (Dublin: Trinity College, 1987), 230–8.

O'Connor, Honor. 'Sounds and Voices: Aspects of Contemporary Irish Music and Poetry', in: *Anglo-Irish and Irish Literature: Aspects of Language and Culture*, vol. II, (Uppsala: Uppsala University Press, 1988), 211–217.

Ó Cuinneagáin, Pádhraic. 'The Piano Music of Seóirse Bodley' (MA thesis, Maynooth: National University of Ireland, 1992).

Bowles, Michael

Walsh, Caroline. 'The Saturday Profile: Michael Bowles', *Irish Times* (*c.*1975).

Ryan, Joseph J. *New Grove 2.*

Boydell, Brian

Acton, Charles. 'Interview with Brian Boydell', *Éire-Ireland*, v (1970) 4, 97–111.

——. 'Brian Patrick Boydell', *Irish Arts Review*, 4 (1987) 4, 66–7.

Battersby, Eileen. 'Brian's double forte', *Irish Times*, 6 November 1997.

Cox, Gareth. 'Octatonicism in the String Quartets of Brian Boydell', in: Patrick F. Devine and Harry White (eds.), *The Maynooth International Musicological Conference: Selected Proceedings, Part One, (Irish Musical Studies 4)*, (Dublin: Four Courts Press 1996), 263–70.

——. *New Grove 2.*

—— with Klein, Axel and Taylor, Michael (editors), *The Life and Music of Brian Boydell* (Dublin: Irish Academic Press [forthcoming])

Dungan, Michael. 'Everything except Team Games and Horse Racing', *New Music News*, February 1997, 9–11.

Farrell, Hazel. The String Quartets of Brian Boydell (MA thesis, Waterford Institute of Technology, 1996)

Fleischmann, Aloys. 'Brian Boydell', *Hibernia*, xxxii (1968) 9.

——. 'Boydell, Brian (Patrick)', in: Brian Morton and Pamela Collins (eds.), *Contemporary Composers* (Chicago and London: St. James Press, 1992), 110–113.

Graydon, Philip. 'Modernism in Ireland and its Cultural Context in the Music and Writings of Frederick May, Brian Boydell and Aloys Fleischmann' (MA thesis, Maynooth: National University of Ireland, 1999).

Klein, Axel. *KdG.*

——. *MGG2.*

Murphy, Daniel et al. (eds.). *Education and the Arts*, XXII: Brian Boydell (Dublin, 1987), 219–229.

O'Kelly, Eve. 'An On-going Tradition', *New Music News*, May 1992, 7–9 + 18.

Boyle, Ina

Burn, Sarah M. *New Grove 2.*

Doctor, Jennifer. '"Working for her Own Salvation": Vaughan Williams as Teacher of Elizabeth Maconchy, Grace Williams and Ina Boyle', in: Lewis Foreman (ed.), *Vaughan Williams in Perspective* (London, 1998), 181–201.

Fuller, Sophie. *The Pandora Guide to Women Composers, Britain and the United States, 1629 – Present* (London: Pandora 1994), 67–8.

Klein, Axel. *MGG2.*

Maconchy, Elizabeth. *Ina Boyle: An Appreciation with a Select List of her Music* (Dublin: Dolmen Press, 1974).

Powerscourt, Sheila. 'Powerscourt and Ina Boyle', in: Sheila Powerscourt, *Sun Too Fast* (Dublin, 1974), 201–15.

Buckley, John

Brophy, David 'The Piano Compositions of John Buckley' (MA thesis, University of Dublin, Trinity College, 1995).

Cox, Gareth. *MGG2.*

Dervan, Michael. 'Taking the Strain ...', *An Droichead*, Winter 1986, 18–20.

Grimes, Jonathan. 'Music and Sculpture', *New Music News*, May 1999, 7–8.

Hamel, Peter Michael. 'Zwischen Keltentum und Avantgarde: Der irische Komponist John Buckley', *MusikTexte*, no. 20 (1987), 19–21.

O'Flynn, Mary 'Towards a Philosophy of Music Education: An Encounter with John Buckley' (MA thesis, University of Dublin, Trinity College, 1990).

O'Leary, Martin. *New Grove 2.*

Scallan, Eithne. 'The Life and Times of an Irish Composer', *In-Choir* iii (1987) 3, 6–8.

Wright, David C.F. 'John Buckley', www.musicweb.uk.net/buckley/index.htm (1992).

Butler, Thomas O'Brien

'Irish Opera at the Theatre Royal', *Irish Times*, 5 December 1903.

Byers, David

Doherty, Dónal. The Organ Music of David Byers (MA thesis, Maynooth: National University of Ireland, 1991)

Clarke, Rhona

Dervan, Michael. 'Insatiable Curiosity', *Music Ireland*, iii (1988) 10, 16.

Wright, David C.F. 'Rhona Clarke', www.musicweb.uk.net/rclarke/index.htm (2000).

Corcoran, Frank

Corcoran, Frank. '"I'm a Composer" – "You're a What?"', *Crane Bag*, vi (1982) 1, 52–54.

———. 'My Music is a Four-Letter-Word ("Ceol")', *Journal of Music in Ireland*, i (2001) 3 (March/April), 18–19.

Cox, Gareth. *New Grove 2*.

Dervan, Michael. 'A Very Worried Man', *Irish Times*, 22 September 1995.

Feehan, Fanny. 'Music for Review', *Sunday Independent*, 22 November 1981.

Klein, Axel. *MGG2*.

Kreutziger-Herr, Annette. *KdG*.

Davey, Shaun

Murphy, Michael. *New Grove 2*.

O'Connor, Honor. 'Sounds and Voices: Aspects of Contemporary Irish Music and Poetry', in: *Anglo-Irish and Irish Literature: Aspects of Language and Culture*, vol. II. (Uppsala: Uppsala University Press, 1988), 211–217.

Deale, Edgar M.

Dungan, Michael. 'Man of the Century', *New Music News*, May 1997, 9–11.

O'Kelly, Eve. 'Edgar Deale', *New Music News*, February 2000, 12.

———. *New Grove 2*.

Wright, David C.F. 'Edgar Deale', www.musicweb.uk.net/deale/index.htm (1994, rev. 2000).

Deane, Raymond

Battersby, Eileen. 'Haunted by an Old Chinese Story', *Irish Times*, 9 October 1999.

Dungan, Michael. 'A Very ad hoc Person', *New Music News*, May 1998, 9–11.

———. 'The Wall of Cloud', *New Music News*, September 1999, 7.

Healy, Jonathan. The Piano Music of Raymond Deane (MA thesis, Maynooth: National University of Ireland, 1996).

Klein, Axel. *MGG2*.

White, Harry. *New Grove 2*.

de Barra, Séamas

Spratt, Geoffrey. 'A Preliminary Study and Catalogue of the Works of Seámas de Barra', 1989 (unpubl.).

Dickenson-Auner, Mary

Engelhard-Krajanek, Margarete, 'Mary Dickenson-Auner, Violinistin – Pädagogin – Komponistin, Leben und Werk' (PhD diss., University of Wuppertal, 1996).

———. 'Mary Dickenson-Auner 1880–1965', in: Kay Dreyfus, Margarethe Engelhardt-Krajanek, Barbara Kühnen (eds.), *Die Geige war ihr Leben – Drei Frauen im Portrait* (Strasshoff: Vier-Viertel-Verlag, 2000), 99–231.

———. *MGG2*.

Doyle, Roger

Cunningham, Michael. 'Work in Process: Babel Bitmap: A Collaboration', *Circa*, no. 69, Autumn 1994, 35–42 (with CD).

Doyle, Roger. 'A Composer's Story', *Crane Bag*, vi (1982) 1, 55–58.

———. 'Death of a Medium', *Journal of Music in Ireland*, i (2000) 1 (November/December), 5–9.

Dungan, Michael. 'Just Discovering', *New Music News*, September 1999, 9–11.

Klein, Axel. *MGG2*.
——. *New Grove 2*.
Prendergast, Mark. *Irish Rock: Roots, Personalities, Directions*, (Dublin: O'Brien Press, 1987), 223–6.

Duff, Arthur
Ryan, Joseph J. *New Grove 2*.

Esposito, Michele
Aiello, G.L. [= Mario Esposito]. *Al musicista Michele Esposito* (Castellamare di Stabia, 1956).
Bowyer Bell, J. 'Waiting for Mario: The Espositos, Joyce and Beckett', *Éire-Ireland*, xxx (1995) 2, 7–26.
Dibble, Jeremy. *MGG2*.
Horner, Keith. *New Grove 2*.
Jachino, Carlo. *MGG1*.
[*Musical Times*]. 'Michele Esposito', vol. xliv (1903) November, 705–707.
O'Sullivan, Mary. 'The Legacy of Michele Esposito to Pianistic Life in Dublin' (M.A. thesis, Maynooth: St Patrick's College, 1991).
van Hoek, Kees. 'Michele Esposito: Maestro of Dublin', *Irish Monthly*, June 1943, 223–30.
Watton, L. 'Michele Esposito, a Neapolitan Musician in Dublin 1882–1928' (MA thesis, Belfast: Queen's University, 1987).

Farrell, Eibhlis
Cox, Gareth. *New Grove 2*.
Fuller, Sophie. *The Pandora Guide to Women Composers, Britain and the United States, 1629 – Present* (London: Pandora, 1994), 116–17.

Ferguson, Howard
(anonymous). 'In memoriam Howard Ferguson', *Musical Times*, cxl (1999), Winter, 7–8.
Cobbe, Hugh. 'Howard Ferguson at 80', *Musical Times*, cxxix (1988) October, 507–510.
Ferguson, Howard and Hurd, Michael (eds.). *Letters of Gerald Finzi and Howard Ferguson* (Woodbridge: Boydell, 2001).
Hurd, Michael. *New Grove 2*.
Ridout, Alan (ed.). *The Music of Howard Ferguson* (London: Thames, 1989).

Fleischmann, Aloys
Beausang, Ita and de Barra, Séamas. 'Aloys Fleischmann', *New Music News*, September 1992, 5–7.
Dawney, Michael. 'Aloys Fleischmann in Conversation', *Composer*, no. 56 (1975), 29–31 and no. 57 (1976), 37–8.
De Barra, Séamas. *New Grove 2*.
Dervan, Michael. 'Unflaggening Energy', *Music Ireland*, v (1990) 5, 7–8.
——. 'Dr Aloys Fleischmann: An Appreciation', *Irish Times*, 23 July 1992.
Fleischmann, Ruth (editor): *Joan Denise Moriarty: Founder of Irish National Ballet* (Cork: Mercier Press and Boulder, Colorado: Irish American Book Company, 1998).

Includes: Séamas de Barra. 'Aloys Fleischmann's Ballet Music', 104–113.

——. (ed.): *Aloys Fleischmann, 1910–1992: A Life for Music in Ireland Remembered by Contemporaries* (Cork: Mercier Press, 2000).

Graydon, Philip. 'Modernism in Ireland and its Cultural Context in the Music and Writings of Frederick May, Brian Boydell and Aloys Fleischmann' (MA thesis, Maynooth: National University of Ireland, 1999).

Klein, Axel. *KdG*.

——. *MGG2*.

Murphy, Daniel et al. (eds.). *Education and the Arts*, 'XX: Aloys Fleischmann', (Dublin: Trinity College, 1987), 198–206.

O'Byrne, Robert. 'Cork's Tightrope', *Music Ireland*, ii (1987) May, 8–11.

French, Percy

Healy, J.N. *Percy French and his Songs* (Cork, 1966).

Lamb, Andrew. *New Grove 2*.

O'Dowda, Brendan. *The World of Percy French* (Belfast: Blackstaff Press, 1981, ²1982, expanded edition, 1991).

Tongue, Alan. *A Picture of Percy French* (Belfast: Greystone, 1990, ²1991).

Vousden, Val. 'Percy French: An Appreciation', *Capuchin Annual*, xvi (1945–6), 317–326.

Guilfoyle, Ronan

Dungan, Michael. 'Getting his Ideas Across', *New Music News*, September 2001, 9–11.

Hammond, Philip

Russ, Michael. *New Grove 2*.

Hardebeck, Carl Gilbert

Allen, Gregory. 'The Blind Bard of Belfast: Carl Gilbert Hardebeck', *History Ireland*, vi (1998) Autumn, 38–43.

Bowles, Michael. 'Carl Hardebeck did much for music in Ireland', *Irish Times* (early 1970s).

'Hardebeck', by Germaine Stockley, Michael Bowles, James Campbell, Aloys Fleischmann, John F. Larchet, Frederick May, Seán Neeson, Seán O'Boyle, Vincent O'Brien, Cathal O'Byrne, J.J. O'Connor, Fr Senan, *Capuchin Annual*, xiv (1943), 222–38, prefixed by autobiographical article 'Fifty Years at Work' by Carl Hardebeck, 220–1.

Klein, Axel. *MGG2*

O'Boyle (O Baoill), Seán. 'Carl Hardebeck', *Capuchin Annual* xix (1948), 80–7.

Ryan, Joseph J. *New Grove 2*.

Harty, Hamilton

C.. 'Hamilton Harty', *Musical Times*, lxi (1920) April, 227–30.

Greer, David (ed.). *Hamilton Harty: His Life and Music* (Belfast: Blackstaff Press, 1978).

—— (ed.). *Hamilton Harty: Early Memories* (Belfast: Queen's University, 1979).

——. 'Hamilton Harty Manuscripts', *Music Review*, xlvii (1987), 238–52.

——. 'The Composition of The Children of Lir', in: Gerad Gillen and Harry White (eds.), *Musicology in Ireland (Irish Musical Studies 1)*, (Dublin: Irish Academic Press, 1990), 74–98.

——. *Hamilton Harty's Swansong* (Belfast: Queen's University, 1994).

Hammond, Philip. 'A Harty Revival', *Soundpost*, ii (1982) June–July, 20–2.

Howes, Frank. 'A Note on Harty's Irish Symphony', *Musical Times*, lxvi (1925), 223–4.

Kennedy, Michael. *New Grove 2*.

Klein, Axel. *MGG2*

McNaught, William Gray. 'Hamilton Harty's Irish Symphony', *Musical Times*, lxvi (1925) 255.

Russell, John F. 'Hamilton Harty', *Music and Letters*, xxii (1941), 216–224.

W.B.R. 'Hamilton Harty's Irish Symphony', *Irish Statesman* II [new series], 31 January 1925, 660.

Hay, Norman

Burgess, Barry. *New Grove 2*.

Byers, David. 'Norman Hay: Odds on Favourite?', *Soundpost*, ii (1982) February–March, 15–17.

Klein, Axel. *MGG2*

Hughes, Herbert

Byers, David. 'Herbert Hughes: A Centenary Note', *Soundpost*, ii (1982) February–March, 26.

Hughes, Herbert. *Irish Country Songs* vol. 1 ('Preface'), (London: Boosey & Co., 1909).

Ryan, Joseph J. *New Grove 2*.

Ingoldsby, Marian

Metrustry, Deborah. 'An Interview with Marian Ingoldsby', *New Music News*, January 1991, 8–9.

Kelly, T.C.

Ryan, Joseph J. *New Grove 2*.

Kinsella, John

Dervan, Michael. 'A Fresh Approach at RTÉ', *Soundpost*, iii (1983) 5, 13–15.

Dungan, Michael. 'A Significant Contribution', *New Music News*, February 1996, 9–11.

Klein, Axel. *New Grove 2*.

Larchet, John F.

White, Harry. *New Grove 2*.

Wright, David C.F. 'John Larchet', www.musicweb.uk.net/larchet/index.htm (1995).

Maconchy, Elizabeth

Cole, Hugo and Doctor, Jennifer. *New Grove 2*.

Fuller, Sophie. *The Pandora Guide to Women Composers, Britain and the United States, 1629 – Present* (London: Pandora, 1994), 198–202.

Howes, Frank. 'Elizabeth Maconchy', *The Monthly Musical Record*, lxix (1939) July–August, 165–8.

Johnson, Stephen. 'Cherished Memories', *Gramophone*, lxvii (1988) November, 825.

Macnaghten, Anne. 'Elizabeth Maconchy', *Musical Times*, xcvi (1955) June, 298– 302.

Maconchy, Elizabeth. 'A Composer Speaks', *Composer*, xlii (1971–2), 24–8.

Matthew–Walker, Robert. 'Maconchy, (Dame) Elizabeth', in: Brian Morton and Pamela Collins (eds.), *Contemporary Composers* (Chicago and London: St James Press, 1992), 599–602.

Wright, David C.F. 'Elizabeth Maconchy', www.musicweb.uk.net/machonchy/index. htm (1996, rev. 2000).

Maddison, Adela
Fuller, Sophie. *The Pandora Guide to Women Composers, Britain and the United States, 1629 – Present* (London: Pandora, 1994), 203–206.
——. *New Grove 2*.

Martin, Philip
Cummings, Robert D. 'The Jig is up! A Great Irish Composer', *Classics Cosmik*, April 1998.

May, Frederick
Acton, Charles. 'Frederick May: An Appreciation', *Irish Times*, 10 September 1985.
Feehan, Fanny. 'The Fiery Soul', *Hibernia*, xxxix, 10 January 1975.
——. 'Frederick May: The Forgotten Genius', *Sunday Tribune* (early 1980s).
Graydon, Philip. 'Modernism in Ireland and its Cultural Context in the Music and Writings of Frederick May, Brian Boydell and Aloys Fleischmann' (MA thesis, Maynooth: National University of Ireland, 1999).
Kent, Kay. 'Frederick May', *Irish Times*, 12 December 1974.
Klein, Axel. *KdG*.
Ryan, Joseph J. *New Grove 2*.
T.O.S. [Tomás Ó Súilleabháin?]. 'Spring Nocturne: A Profile of Frederick May', *Counterpoint*, ii (1970) November, 14–18.
Wright, David C.F. 'Frederick May', www.musicweb.uk.net/may/index.htm (1993, rev. 1999).

Moeran, Ernest John
Bax, Arnold. 'E.J. Moeran: 1894–1950', *Music and Letters*, xxxii (1951) 1, 125–7.
Evans, Edwin. 'Moeran's Symphony in G minor', *Musical Times*, lxxix (1938), 94–9.
——. 'Moeran's Violin Concerto', *Musical Times*, lxxxiv (1943) August, 233–4.
Fleischmann, Aloys. 'The Music of E.J. Moeran', *Envoy*, iv (1951), March, 60–6.
Foss, Hubert. *Compositions of E.J. Moeran* (London: Novello, 1948).
——. 'Ernest John Moeran (1894–1950)', *Musical Times*, xcii (1951) January, 20–2.
Heseltine, Philip. 'E J Moeran', *Music Bulletin*, June 1924.
Hill, Lionel. *Lonely Waters: The Diary of a Friendship with E.J. Moeran* (London: Thames, 1985).
Hull, Robert. 'Moeran's Symphony in G minor', *Monthly Musical Record*, lxviii (1938) 793, 15–17.
Hurd, Michael. *MGG1*.
Klein, Axel. *KdG*.
McNeill, Roderick. 'Moeran's Unfinished Symphony', *Musical Times*, cxxi (1980), 771–7.
——. 'A Critical Study of the Life and Works of E.J. Moeran' (PhD diss., University of Melbourne, 1982).
Ottaway, D. Hugh. 'The Music of E.J. Moeran', *Disc*, v (1951) 17, 6–11.
Payne, Anthony. *New Grove 2*.
Self, Geoffrey Robert. *The Music of E.J. Moeran* (London: Toccata Press, 1986).

——. 'E.J. Moeran: Unpublished Letters and Songs', *British Music*, xvi (1994), 33–43 (with a postscript in vol. xvii, p. 63).

Statham, Heathcote. 'Moeran's Symphony in G Minor', *Music Review*, i (1940), 245–54.

Westrup, J.A.. 'E.J. Moeran', in: A.L. Bacharach (ed.), *British Music of Our Time* (London: Pelican Books, 1946), 175–84.

Wild, Stephen. *E.J. Moeran* (London: Triad Press, 1973).

Murphy, Gerard

O'Dea, Tom. 'An Irishman's Diary', *The Irish Times*, 27 June 2000.

Nelson, Havelock

Nelson, Havelock. *A Bank of Violets: The Musical Memoirs of Havelock Nelson* (Belfast: Greystone, 1993).

O'Brien, Vincent

'For Vincent O'Brien', by Fr Senan, Germaine Stockley, P.J. Little, Patrick Donohue, 'E.G.', Carl Hardebeck, Thomas J. Kiernan, John McCormack, Mons. Lorenzo Perosi, Thomas MacGreevy, Leo Maguire, Fr John Moloney, Thomas O'Donnell, Joseph S. Sheehy, *Capuchin Annual*, xvi (1945–6), 229–47.

Ó Gallchobháir, Éamonn

Ryan, Joseph J. *New Grove 2*.

O'Leary, Jane

Clarke, Jocelyn. '"I'm just going to start in and see what happens"', *New Music News*, September 1994, 9–11.

Fuller, Sophie. *The Pandora Guide to Women Composers, Britain and the United States, 1629 – Present* (London: Pandora, 1994), 224–6.

Klein, Axel. *New Grove 2*.

Scahill, Adrian. The Piano Music of Jane O'Leary (MA thesis, Maynooth: National University of Ireland, 1995).

Townsend, Declan. Jane O'Leary's Piano Quintet "Apart/Together": Fly on the Wall at Vanbrugh String Quartet Preparation', *Journal of Music in Ireland*, i (2001) 5 (July/August), 28–9.

Ó Riada, Seán

Acton, Charles. 'Seán Ó Riada: The Next Phase', *Éire-Ireland*, ii (1967) 4, 113–25.

——. 'Interview with Seán Ó Riada', *Éire-Ireland*, vi (1971) 1, 106–15.

——. 'Seán Ó Riada dead', *Irish Times*, 4 October 1971.

——. 'I gCuimhne Sheáin Uí Riada', *Éire-Ireland*, vi (1971) 4, 3–5.

Bodley, Seóirse. 'Remembering Seán Ó Riada', *Capuchin Annual*, xliii (1972), 302–4.

Deane, Raymond. 'Ó Riada is Dead: Long Live Ó Riada!', *Journal of Music in Ireland*, i (2001) 2 (January/February), 5–7.

Fleischmann, Aloys. 'Seán Ó Riada's Nomos II', *Éire-Ireland*, 7 (1972) 3, 108–115.

Harris, Bernard and Freyer, Grattan. *Integrating Tradition: The Achievement of Seán Ó Riada* (Ballina: Irish Humanities Centre & Keohanes and Chester Springs, Penn. (USA): Dufour Editions, 1981).

Maillard, Jean Henri O. 'Seán Ó Riada, compositeur irlandais (1931–1971)', *Education Magasin*, xxvii (1972) 189, 337–9.

Major, Brendan. 'The Survival of Irish Traditional Music', *Contact*, no. 19 (1978), 17–20.

Ó Canainn, Tomás & Gearóid Mac an Bhua [Gerard Victory]. *Seán Ó Riada: A Shaol agus a Shaothar* (An Charraig Dhubh, Co. Bhaile Atha Cliath [Blackrock, Co. Dublin]: Gartan, 1993).

O'Connor, Honor. 'Sounds and Voices: Aspects of Contemporary Irish Music and Poetry', in: *Anglo-Irish and Irish Literature: Aspects of Language and Culture*, vol. II (Uppsala: Uppsala University Press, 1988), 211–217.

Ó Gadhra, Nollaig. 'Bínse ag Seinnt Ceoil', *Journal of Music in Ireland*, ii (2001) Nov.Dec., 21–4.

White, Harry. 'Seán Ó Riada and the Crisis of Modernism in Irish Music', in: Harry White, *The Keeper's Recital: Music and Cultural History in Ireland, 1770–1970* (Cork: Cork University Press, 1998), 125–150.

——. *New Grove 2*.

Wright, David C.F. 'Seán Ó Riada', www.musicweb.uk.net/oriada/index.htm (1993, rev. 1997).

Ó Súilleabháin, Mícheál

Carolan, Nicholas. *New Grove 2*.

O'Byrne, Robert. 'Creating A New Hybrid', *Music Ireland*, iv (1989) 6, 10.

Palmer, Geoffrey Molyneux

Klein, Axel. *New Grove 2*.

Russel, Myra (editor). *James Joyce's Chamber Music: The Lost Song Settings* (Bloomington, Indiana: Indiana University Press. 1993) [with accompanying cassette].

Potter, Archibald Joseph

Acton, Charles. 'Interview with A.J. Potter', *Éire-Ireland*, v (1970) 2, 115–41.

——. 'An Appreciation: Dr A.J. Potter', *Irish Times*, 7 July 1980.

Bodley, Seóirse. *New Grove 2*.

Stanford, Charles Villiers

Dibble, Jeremy. *New Grove 2*.

——.*Charles Villiers Stanford: Man and Musician* (Oxford: Oxford University Press) [in preparation].

Greene, Harry Plunket. 'Stanford's Songs', *Music and Letters*, ii (1921) 94–106.

——. *Charles Villiers Stanford* (London: Edward Arnold, 1935).

Hudson, Frederick. *MGG1*.

——. *New Grove 1*.

Murphy, Michael. 'Race, Nation and Empire in the Irish Music of Sir Charles Villiers Stanford', in: Richard Pine (ed.), *Music in Ireland 1848–1998* (Cork: Mercier Press and Boulder, Colorado: Irish American Book Company, 1998), 46–55.

Norris, Gerald. *Stanford, the Cambridge Jubilee, and Tchaikowsky* (Newton Abbot, 1980).

Porte, John F. *Sir Charles V. Stanford* (London: Kegan Paul, Trubner and New York: E.P. Dutton, 1921).

Rodmell, Paul J. *The Life and Works of Charles Villiers Stanford*, (Aldershot: Ashgate) 2002.

Stanford, Charles Villiers. *Studies and Memories* (London: Archibald Constable, 1908).

——. *Pages from an Unwritten Diary* (London, 1914).

——. 'Some Thoughts concerning Folk Song and Nationality', *Musical Quarterly*, i (1915) 2, 232–245.

——. *Interludes: Records and Reflections* (London: John Murray, 1922).

——. *Musical Composition* (London: Macmillan and Stainer & Bell, 1922).

Sweeney, Eric

Cox, Gareth. *New Grove 2*.

Sweeney, Eric. 'A Folio of Original Composition' (DPhil diss. Jordanstown: University of Ulster, 1993).

Trimble, John

Acton, Charles. 'Many Lives a-living', *New Music News*, May 1995, 9–10.

Burn, Sarah M. *New Grove 2*.

Hammond, Philip. 'Woman of Parts', *Soundpost*, v (1984–5) December–January, 24–7.

Victory, Gerard

Dawney, Michael. 'Victory, Gerard', in: Brian Morton and Pamela Collins (eds.), *Contemporary Composers* (Chicago and London: St James Press, 1992), 944–6.

Dervan, Michael. 'Victory for the Contemporary Cause', *Irish Times*, 24 December 1991.

Murphy, Anne M. 'Gerard Victory's "Ultima Rerum"', in: Gerard Gillen and Harry White (eds.), *Music and the Church (Irish Musical Studies 2)*, (Dublin: Irish Academic Press, 1993), 164–89.

——. *New Grove 2*.

Murphy, Daniel et al. (eds.): *Education and the Arts*; 'XXI: Gerard Victory' (Dublin: Trinity College, 1987), 206–19.

O'Kelly, Eve. 'An On–going Tradition', *New Music News*, May 1992, 7–9 + 18.

Wright, David C.F. 'Gerard Victory', www.musicweb.uk.net/victory/index.htm (1989, rev. 1995).

Volans, Kevin

Dungan, Michael. 'Freedom and Rebellion', *New Music News*, September 1997, 9–11.

FitzGerald, Des. 'Kevin Volans: Withdrawn from Chaos', *Classical Ireland*, no. 3, Summer/Autumn 1999, 44–5.

Loppert, M. 'Volans: The Man who Strides the Wind', *Opera*, xliii (1993), 1102–4.

Taylor, Timothy D. 'When We Think about Music and Politics: The Case of Kevin Volans', *Perspectives of New Music*, xxxiii (1995) 1 & 2, 504–36.

——. *New Grove 2*.

Wilson, Ian

Dungan, Michael. 'A Richer Life in Leitrim', *New Music News*, February 2000, 9–11.

Russ, Michael. *New Grove 2*.

Wilson, Ian. 'Rich Harbour', *Choir and Organ*, iv (1996), 24–7

——. 'The Composer as Prophet?', *Journal of Music in Ireland*, i (2000) 1 (November/December), 28–30.

Wilson, James

Klein, Axel and Cox, Gareth. *KdG*

O'Kelly, Eve. 'Wilson at Seventy', *New Music News*, September 1992, 10–12.

——. *New Grove 2*.

Wright, David C.F.. 'James Wilson', www.musicweb.uk.net/wilsonj/index.htm (1991, rev. 1998).

Wood, Charles

Blake, Leonard. 'New Light on Charles Wood', *Hymn Society of Great Britain and Ireland Bulletin*, vii (1972) 10.

Copley, Ian. 'Charles Wood, 1866–1926', *Musical Times*, cvii (1966) June.

——. *The Music of Charles Wood: A Critical Study* (London: Thames, 1978, [2]1994).

Dibble, Jeremy. *New Grove 2*.

Gatty, Nicholas. 'Charles Wood: A Personal Note', *Monthly Musical Record*, lix (1929) 354.

Hull, Robin. 'Charles Wood: Quartet in D', *The Listener*, xvii (1937) 418.

Nosek, M.H. 'Wood: A Personal Memoir', *Musical Times*, cvii (1966), 492–3.

Walker, Ernest. 'Charles Wood's String Quartets', *Monthly Musical Record*, lix (1929) December, 353–4.

Index